UNITED STATES OF AMERICA
THE
DEATH PENALTY

Amnesty International Publications

First published 1987 by Amnesty International Publications
1 Easton Street, London WC1X 8DJ, United Kingdom

Copyright Amnesty International Publications 1987

ISBN 0 86210 114 X
AI Index: AMR 51/01/87
Original Language: English

Printed by Shadowdean Limited, Mitcham, Surrey

Contents

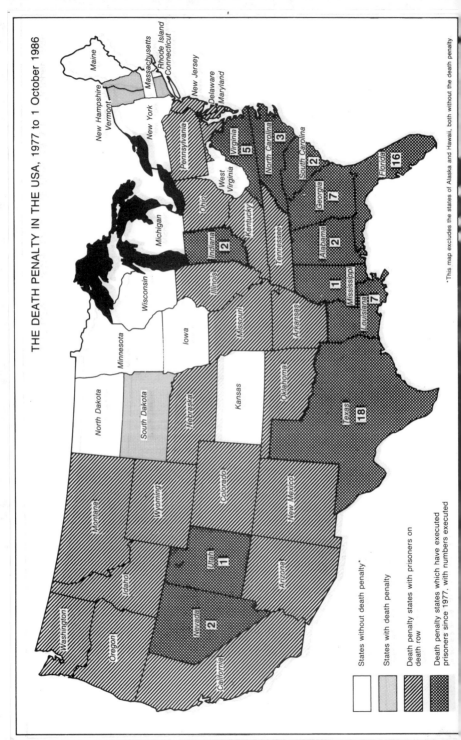

THE DEATH PENALTY IN THE USA, 1977 to 1 October 1986

States without death penalty*

States with death penalty

Death penalty states with prisoners on death row

Death penalty states which have executed prisoners since 1977, with numbers executed

*This map excludes the states of Alaska and Hawaii, both without the death penalty

Preface

The United States of America (USA) is a federal republic of 50 states and the District of Columbia.[1] Each of the 50 states exercises a large measure of internal self-government, having its own constitution, elected government and legislature, laws and court system. The federal government has jurisdiction over matters of national interest, including defence, foreign affairs, internal security, postage and coinage. There is also a national, federal, system of laws and courts, which applies to all United States (US) citizens. The federal penal code covers offences falling within the federal jurisdiction, such as crimes committed against federal agents or on federal property, or crimes against national security, such as treason, espionage or aircraft piracy.

The large majority of criminal offences, including most of those currently carrying the death penalty, are committed in violation of state laws and are therefore prosecuted in the state courts, usually in the particular region of the state where the crime occurred. The penal codes vary from state to state, although the English common law tradition shared by all US states and the federal jurisdiction, has resulted in strong similarities between the various systems.

Although the states have independence in framing legislation, their laws and practice must be compatible with the US Constitution, approved in 1789, which confers basic rights upon all US citizens. The most important fundamental rights and liberties are contained in the Amendments to the US Constitution, particularly the first 10 Amendments which are known as the Bill of Rights. These provide basic guarantees to every US citizen of, among other things, freedom of religion, speech and assembly; the right, upon being charged with a criminal offence, to a speedy trial by an impartial jury and to the

---

1. The District of Columbia (DC) covers the area in which the city of Washington, the seat of the US Government, is situated. It is a separate jurisdiction within the USA, having its own laws, courts and system of internal government. According to a provision in the US Constitution, Congress (the US federal legislature) has exclusive sovereignty over DC and passes all laws applying to this jurisdiction.

assistance of counsel; and freedom from cruel and unusual punishments. The US Supreme Court, which has nine Justices (appointed by the US President to serve for life), is the highest judicial court and acts as the final arbiter, or interpreter, of the US Constitution. If the US Supreme Court finds that any state or federal law is in violation of the US Constitution, it may declare the law to be invalid.

Anyone convicted under a state law has the right to lodge appeals in the federal courts if he or she claims a violation of any of his or her federal constitutional rights. In such cases appeals in the state courts, which may review alleged violations of both state and federal constitutional rights, must first be exhausted.

Introduction

In 1972 the US Supreme Court ruled that the arbitrary manner in which the death penalty was then applied amounted to "cruel and unusual punishment", in violation of the Constitution. The ruling invalidated most existing death penalty statutes. Before this, there had already been a steady decline in the use of the death penalty in the USA, with a moratorium on executions from 1967. However, a further Supreme Court ruling in 1976 permitted individual states to reinstate the death penalty for murder according to guidelines set by the Court. The ruling upheld new laws that had already been enacted in some states after 1972 and led to a resumption of executions. Between January 1977 and May 1986, 58 prisoners were executed, with many more awaiting the outcome of legal appeals. In May 1986 a total of 1,720 prisoners were under sentence of death in 33 states, the highest figure ever recorded in the USA; 37 states had laws authorizing the death penalty at that time.

Only four prisoners were executed between 1976 and 1982, three of whom had dropped their final appeals and demanded to be executed. There has been a steady increase in the rate of executions since then, a trend which is expected to continue as prisoners exhaust their legal appeals.

Amnesty International opposes the death penalty unconditionally, believing it to be the ultimate cruel, inhuman and degrading punishment and a violation of the right to life, as proclaimed in the Universal Declaration of Human Rights and other international human rights instruments. The organization works for the abolition of the death penalty throughout the world and appeals for clemency in all cases where executions are feared to be imminent, regardless of the nature of the crime of which the prisoner has been convicted.

This report examines the death penalty in the USA from this point of view and also raises a number of concerns based on how the death penalty is applied in practice. It includes the findings of an Amnesty International mission to four states in 1985 and information collected during the course of its general work against the death penalty since it was reinstated in the 1970s. The report was written in May 1986 but includes important subsequent Supreme Court rulings on issues related to the death penalty; it has also been possible to update some information and statistics.

In its 1972 ruling, the Supreme Court found that the unlimited discretion given to judges or juries to decide whether or not to impose the death penalty in capital trials had led to random and capricious sentencing. Several of the justices found also that the death penalty — although very rarely imposed at that time — had fallen disproportionately on the poor and on minority groups. The guidelines set by the Court in this and other rulings in the 1970s were intended to ensure that, in future, the death penalty would be fairly and consistently applied, and imposed only for the most serious and unmitigated crimes. The capital punishment laws enacted after 1972 have restricted the types of crime for which the death penalty may be imposed and provide for a separate sentencing hearing, in which juries or judges must weigh aggravating and mitigating circumstances before deciding whether to impose a life or death sentence on convicted capital offenders. Other procedural safeguards include the automatic review of death sentences by state supreme courts.

Despite these measures, there is evidence that in practice the death penalty remains both arbitrary and discriminatory. Although it is now imposed only on people convicted of murder where there are aggravating circumstances (such as an accompanying felony), only a small proportion of offenders accused of such crimes are sentenced to die. The death penalty continues to be unevenly applied, both nationally and within states, and there are wide disparities in the sentencing of similar offenders.

This report examines the circumstances which result in one offender being sentenced to death while another is not, and concludes that race, where the crime was committed, discretionary decisions taken by local prosecutors in their charging and sentencing recommendations, and the competence and resources of defence attorneys may play a greater role in determining who is sentenced to death than the nature of the crime or defendant.

It describes individual cases in which the death penalty has appeared particularly inappropriate or unfair. These include cases where executed prisoners were under 18 years old when the crime was committed, in clear violation of international standards; showed signs of mental illness or retardation or had mitigating circumstances not revealed at the sentencing stage of their trials. In several cases, disparate sentences were imposed on co-defendants against whom there was equal evidence of guilt, with one prisoner being executed while another was sentenced to life imprisonment or less. At least one execution was of a prisoner who did not commit or plan the killing but participated in a contemporaneous offence; in another, an accomplice to a murder was executed while the actual killer received a life sentence. These and other cases suggest that the death penalty has not been applied in the fair and even-handed fashion envisaged by the Supreme Court in its 1976 decision, nor has it necessarily been reserved only for the very worst crimes and the most culpable offenders.

The report looks at the appeals available to capital defendants and finds that they have not served to redress underlying deficiencies in the system. Although a relatively large number of prisoners have had their death sentences overturned on appeal, the courts are limited in their ability to assess broader issues of arbitrariness or discrimination, especially where this occurs at an early stage of the judicial process. Executive clemency, which has rarely been granted in capital cases since 1976, has also failed to safeguard against the imposition of unfair or unduly harsh sentences. Several prisoners have been executed when there appeared to be especially strong grounds for exercising clemency.

Amnesty International believes that no system of capital punishment can ensure that the death penalty is fairly and consistently applied. The US Supreme Court ruled in 1976 that mandatory death sentences, imposed regardless of any mitigating or aggravating circumstances relating to the crime or offender, were unconstitutional. However, the present system of "guided discretion" has also failed to ensure fairness or consistency in sentencing. The aggravating or mitigating circumstances that juries or judges must weigh before deciding whether to impose a life or death sentence on convicted capital offenders may be open to widely differing interpretations. The choice of sentence may depend on the skills of defence attorneys in their presentation of evidence, the vigour with which the prosecutor seeks the death penalty, the defendant's demeanour or relative status in the community, and a host of other extraneous factors. There is wide discretion, too, at other stages of the judicial process. Many crimes for which death is a possible penalty are not tried as capital crimes because prosecutors have decided to bring alternative charges. As shown in this report, factors beyond the circumstances of the crime itself may play a part in these decisions.

The report describes how the death penalty may even distort the judicial process. There is concern, for example, that a practice used by most US states of excluding opponents of the death penalty from serving as jurors in capital trials may produce juries not only more inclined to impose death sentences, but also more likely to convict, or to convict on more serious charges, than those chosen under the normal jury selection procedures. Thus, capital defendants, whose lives are at stake, may be tried before less impartial juries than those sitting in ordinary criminal trials.

Other measures, although intended to provide the maximum safeguards against error, have given rise to further contradictions. The complex and lengthy procedures and the high cost of capital trials, for example, may discourage prosecutors from seeking the death penalty in all but a few cases, increasing the disparities in sentencing among similar offenders. They have also placed heavy burdens on defence attorneys, discouraging many lawyers from taking on capital cases and making it harder for poor defendants to get adequate legal representation. These and other concerns are summarized at the end of this report.

Since 1976, the Supreme Court has continued to rule on death penalty cases; however, its more recent decisions have tended to uphold state procedures, narrowing the ground for future appeals on broad constitutional questions. (Appendix 8 contains a summary of the most important Supreme Court rulings on the death penalty that are referred to in the text.)

At the time of writing one of the few remaining systematic challenges to the death penalty was on the question of race. In October 1985 an appeal was lodged with the Supreme Court in which it was claimed that the Georgia death penalty statute was applied in a manner which discriminated against certain categories of offender on racial grounds. The appeal cited the findings of a detailed research study which showed that killers of whites, especially black killers, were far more likely to be sentenced to death than killers of blacks, after allowing for non-racial factors. The Court granted *certiorari* (agreed to hear the appeal) in the case in July 1986 and this decision was still pending in October 1986.

Amnesty International is aware of the serious problem of violent crime in the USA, where criminal homicides have averaged 20,000 a year from 1979 to 1985. In recent years state governments have given this, and strong public support for the death penalty, as grounds for retaining the death penalty. However, detailed research in the USA and other countries has produced no evidence that this penalty deters crime more effectively than other punishment. There is evidence, moreover, that the death penalty places a disproportionate burden on the criminal justice system and may divert resources from other, more effective, forms of law enforcement.

Although there is strong public support for the death penalty in the USA, several polls indicate that this is not unqualified. Some recent polls suggest that public support for the death penalty might decrease if other penalties were shown to be equally effective.

Certain sectors of the US population have consistently opposed the death penalty, including the leadership of most of the main religious denominations. A number of state governors have also maintained their opposition to the death penalty.

All but one of the prisoners under sentence of death in May 1986 had been convicted under state laws. The death penalty is also authorized for certain offences under federal military law — a soldier convicted of murder under the Uniform Code of Military Justice was under sentence of death at the time of writing (in addition to the 1,720 inmates reported by states to be on death row in May 1986). Several bills to reinstate the death penalty under federal civilian law have been introduced into Congress since 1972 but none has yet been enacted. A further bill was before the US Senate in May 1986.

Amnesty International hopes that this report will encourage the state and federal authorities and the public to re-examine their attitudes towards the death penalty, and to promote its abolition in all jurisdictions in which it still applies.

Amnesty International's mission to the USA

In June 1985 an Amnesty International mission visited the states of Florida, Georgia, Texas and Louisiana, to discuss the organization's concerns on the death penalty.[1] The mission met the aides and counsel to the Governors of Florida and Texas; the Attorney General of Georgia; the Deputy Attorney Generals of Texas and Louisiana; the Boards of Pardons and Paroles in Georgia, Louisiana and Texas; the Chief Justice of the Florida Supreme Court; the Chiefs of Police of Houston (Texas) and Atlanta (Georgia) and other officials. The mission also met lawyers representing capital defendants.

More than two-thirds of all executions carried out between January 1977 and June 1985 were in these four states, when Florida and Texas having the nation's largest death row populations.

The mission's findings are referred to, where applicable, throughout the report, with special attention given to the clemency procedures in the states visited. The report also contains information on other states and the situation on the death penalty in the USA generally.

An Amnesty International mission previously visited Florida in May 1979 to plead with state officials for the commutation of death sentences in the cases of more than 130 prisoners then on death row in the state. In December 1979 another Amnesty International

---

1. The delegates were John Alderson, former Chief Constable of Devon and Cornwall, England; Ezzat Fattah, Professor of Criminology at Simon Fraser University, Vancouver, Canada; and two members of Amnesty International's Research Department.

mission visited California, Ohio, Georgia and Washington DC, for discussions on the death penalty with state and federal officials.

In April 1980 Amnesty International presented a proposal for a presidential commission of inquiry on the death penalty in the USA to President Carter. No response was received.

Recent historical background

The death penalty, 1900 to 1967

Recent research indicates that more than 13,000 people have been legally executed in the USA and the pre-Independence states in the past 300 years.[1] Until the late 19th century, most executions were carried out by local jurisdictions within states, and systematic records were kept only after executions in each state were brought under the control of a centralized penal authority; this had occurred in most states by the end of the 1920s. From 1930 onwards, national records of state-imposed executions were compiled annually by the US Department of Justice. These show that 3,829 people were executed under the state civil authorities from 1930 to 1967.

The number of executions increased considerably in the early 20th century, from 155 in the decade of the 1890s to more than 1,000 during the 1920s. More executions were carried out in the 1930s than in any other period in recent US history, reaching a peak of 199 in 1935 — the highest recorded figure for any single year. Thereafter the number of executions gradually declined, although there were more than 100 a year until 1950. After 1950 there was a more rapid decline in the use of the death penalty and by the mid-1960s executions had become rare. After 1967, executions ceased altogether pending the resolution of various legal challenges to the death penalty.[2] In 1972 the US Supreme Court issued a ruling in a key case (*Furman* v. *Georgia*), invalidating most existing death penalty statutes. The death penalty was reinstated after a second Supreme Court ruling (*Gregg* v. *Georgia*) in 1976, which permitted individual states to reintroduce it

---

1. This estimate is based on research by Watt Espy, Director, Capital Punishment Research Project, Headland, Alabama. By 1982 he had verified some 13,630 executions by cross-checking information from various sources. The list is known to be incomplete. Some researchers have estimated that there were as many as 18,000 to 20,000 executions from 1622 to 1980 (see Hugo Adam Bedau, *The Death Penalty in America*, third edition, Oxford University Press, 1982, p.1, hereafter referred to as Bedau, *The Death Penalty in America*).

2. Appendix 6 gives the annual number of executions since 1930.

in accordance with constitutional guidelines (see below). This decision signalled an end to the *de facto* moratorium on executions from 1967 to 1976.

More than half of all executions between 1900 and 1967 were carried out in the southern states.[3] Executions were also frequently carried out in several other states with large urban populations, notably New York and Pennsylvania in the Northeast, California in the West and Ohio in the North Central region. The overall regional figures from 1930 to 1967 were: Northeast — 608; North Central — 403; West — 511; and South — 2,307. Georgia had the largest number of executions in any one state during this period: 366, from 1930 to 1964. New York had the largest recorded number of executions from 1900 to 1963: 682.

The large majority of executions were carried out for the crime of murder, followed by rape — for which the death penalty was imposed almost exclusively in the southern states.[4] Four hundred and fifty-five people were executed for rape from 1930 to 1964. Death sentences were occasionally imposed in some states also for armed robbery, attempted rape, assault by a prisoner serving a life sentence, kidnapping and espionage. Some 70 people were executed for these crimes after 1930.

By the 1920s, juries or judges in most US jurisdictions had discretion to decide whether an offender convicted of a capital offence should be sentenced to death or life imprisonment.[5]

Racial discrimination and the death penalty, 1900 to 1967

There is strong evidence of racial discrimination in the application of the death penalty up to 1967, especially in the southern states. About two-thirds of offenders executed there from 1930 to 1967 were black,

3. National Prisoner Statistics, Capital Punishment 1979, list states in the southern region as: Delaware, Maryland, Virginia, West Virginia, North Carolina, South Carolina, Georgia, Florida, Kentucky, Tennessee, Alabama, Mississippi, Arkansas, Louisiana, Oklahoma and Texas; the District of Columbia is also included on this list.

4. Rape was a capital offence in 19 (mainly southern) jurisdictions before 1972. Of 560 executions for rape recorded from 1900, only seven took place outside the South, in a number of Mid-Western (southern border) states and the District of Columbia.

5. The death penalty was originally mandatory under English law for defendants found guilty of a capital offence. Tennessee, Alabama and Louisiana were the first states to authorize discretionary death sentences for murder (between 1838 and 1846). Between 1860 and 1900, 20 states and the Federal Government did the same. By 1926 the practice had been adopted in 33 jurisdictions, with seven more states following suit between 1949 and 1963 (data given in Bedau, *The Death Penalty in America*, p.10).

although they constituted a minority of the population. In some individual states, an even higher proportion of those executed were black (see table below). The greatest disparities were in rape cases, in which the death penalty was imposed almost exclusively on blacks, usually in cases involving white victims — 405 (or 89 per cent) of the 455 prisoners executed for rape after 1930 were black.

Although there was a high crime rate among blacks in the South, studies of this period have shown that blacks were executed disproportionately to any differences in the incidence of relevant crimes by blacks and whites. A study of Virginia, for example, showed that blacks alone were executed for rape from 1908 to 1962 but only 55 per cent of those imprisoned for rape were black.[6] A study conducted by the Center for Studies in Criminology and Criminal Law at the University of Pennsylvania examined the outcome of 3,000 rape cases in 11 southern states from 1945 to 1965 and found that blacks (especially in cases with white victims) were far more likely to be sentenced to death than whites convicted of similar crimes.[7]

These and other studies have also shown that executed black offenders had had fewer appeals and had been less likely to have their sentences commuted.[8]

The historical disparity in execution rates between white and black offenders in the South continued until relatively recently. Fifty-four per cent of recorded executions for rape since 1930 took place after 1940, accounting for nearly one in four of all executions in the South during this period.

---

6. Data published in Virginia Law Review, 1972, cited in William J. Bowers, *Legal Homicide: Death as a punishment in America, 1864-1982*, Northeastern University Press, Boston, Massachusetts, 1984 (hereafter referred to as Bowers, *Legal Homicide*).

7. The study was carried out by Professor Marvin E. Wolfgang and Anthony Amsterdam. It found racial disparities after taking into account factors such as offender and victim characteristics, degree of severity of the crime, injuries inflicted and the commission of another contemporaneous felony. The findings, together with those of other research studies into racial discrimination, are summarized in "Race, Judicial Discretion and the Death Penalty" by Marvin E. Wolfgang and Marc Reidel in vol. 407 of *The Annals of the American Academy of Political and Social Science*, 1973, pp. 119-133, extracts reproduced in Bedau, *The Death Penalty in America*, pp. 194-205.

8. Two of the earliest systematic investigations of racial disparities — conducted by Guy B. Johnson in 1941 and Harold Garfinkel in 1949 — traced the treatment of black and white capital offenders in selected southern states through several stages of the judicial process. They found that blacks were disproportionately sentenced to death for all crimes at every stage and that the differences were even more marked when the victims were white.

There was less evidence of racial discrimination in the large, predominantly white, urban and industrial centres of the North, Northeast and West, where the large majority of offenders executed after 1900 were white. However, as the black populations in these industrial areas outside the South grew after 1940, so did the number of blacks executed. Some later studies have suggested that social and economic class was a stronger factor in death sentencing than race in these areas.[9]

When the *Furman* decision invalidated most death penalty statutes in 1972, more than 50 per cent of the 600 prisoners then under sentence of death nationally were blacks, although blacks constituted only 11 per cent of the population. In the South, the ratio remained much higher — in Florida, for example, there were twice as many blacks as whites on death row in 1972.

Executions by race of offenders in selected states, 1900 to 1965

States	Blacks	Whites
Virginia 1908-1962	205	33
Alabama 1927-1965	127	26
Georgia 1924-1964	340	82
North Carolina 1901-1961	286	76
South Carolina 1912-1962	194	47

These figures were compiled from the list of executions by state since 1900 given in Bowers, *Legal Homicide*, Appendix A.

Early moves to abolish the death penalty

There were abolitionist movements in a number of states in the early 19th century.[10] From 1830 onwards legislative committees were established in several of them to consider abolishing the death

9. A 1969 study of first-degree murder convictions in California from 1958 to 1966 suggested a shift from race to social class as a major factor in death sentencing and that "blue-collar" defendants were more likely to be sentenced to death than similar "white-collar" offenders. A 1979 study of an unnamed northern industrial city by Steven Boris found that in 1972 (the period studied) occupational and social class differences between offender and victim were more significant than race in the passing of death sentences. (Both studies cited in Bowers, *Legal Homicide*, pp. 213-4.)

10. The abolitionist movement in America first began with the Quakers in Pennsylvania in the 18th century. They did not achieve the repeal of Pennsylvania's capital statutes but the law was reformed in 1794 to provide for the first common-law formulation of "degrees" of murder, and the elimination of the death penalty for all crimes except murder in the "first degree", that is, "willful, deliberate and premeditated killing" or a killing committed in the course of another felony. (See Bedau, *The Death Penalty in America* p.4 and Sarah Dike, *Capital Punishment in the USA*, National Council on Crime and Delinquency, 1982.)

penalty. In 1847 the Territory of Michigan (later to become a state) became the first English-speaking jurisdiction in the world to abolish the death penalty for all crimes except treason. Wisconsin and Rhode Island abolished the death penalty for all crimes in the 1850s, Maine in 1887 (after an earlier brief period of abolition) and, in the early 1900s, Minnesota and North Dakota (the latter for all but exceptional crimes[11]). All six states remain abolitionist today. Several other states abolished the death penalty in the early 20th century but reinstated it after a few years.

Opposition to the death penalty became more widespread in the 1950s and 1960s, a period during which a number of other countries abolished it. From 1957 to 1969, nine US states either abolished the death penalty for all crimes or (as in New York and Vermont) retained it for a few offences only, such as murder of a law enforcement officer or murder by a prisoner already serving a life sentence. In 1960 Alaska and Hawaii joined the USA as abolitionist jurisdictions.

In the 1960s organizations such as the Legal Defense and Educational Fund Inc. (LDF), founded by the National Association for the Advancement of Colored People (NAACP), sponsored research whose findings showed racial discrimination, jury bias and unevenness in the application of the death penalty.[12] Assisted by lawyers of the LDF and the American Civil Liberties Union (ACLU), a growing number of defendants appealed to the federal courts, challenging the constitutionality of the state capital laws. By 1968 a number of key cases affecting the death penalty statutes of various states were awaiting decisions by the US Supreme Court, and this led to the unofficial moratorium on executions after 1967. (The last two executions of this period took place in Colorado and California in 1967.) In 1972 the Supreme Court issued its decision in what had become the leading case: *Furman* v. *Georgia*.

Furman v. Georgia (1972): Suspension of the death penalty in US law

In *Furman* v. *Georgia*, the Supreme Court ruled by five votes to four that the death penalty, as imposed under then existing laws,

---

11. Treason and first-degree murder by a prisoner serving a life sentence for first-degree murder.

12. The NAACP was founded in 1909 to promote equality and justice for blacks and other minorities. The LDF became a separate independent body in the mid-1950s. Committed to the aims of the NAACP, it litigates in the area of racial equality. The LDF has also represented capital defendants of all races, and has litigated on general aspects of the death penalty, including conditions on death row.

constituted "cruel and unusual punishment" in violation of the Eighth and Fourteenth Amendments to the US Constitution. The Eighth Amendment prohibits the infliction of "cruel and unusual punishments"; according to the Fourteenth Amendment, the state may not deprive a person of "life, liberty or property, without due process of law, nor deny to any person within its jurisdiction the equal protection of the laws".

The ruling was based primarily on what the judges saw as the death penalty's "arbitrary and capricious" application, due to the unlimited discretion afforded to the sentencing authority (juries or judges) in capital trials. Although the decision referred specifically to the *Furman* and two companion cases, it effectively invalidated all existing state death penalty laws, most of which contained provisions similar to the Georgia statute's. The ruling led to the vacation of death sentences in the cases of over 600 prisoners then on death row in states throughout the USA.

Although five of the nine justices reached consensus in finding that the death penalty, as it was then applied, violated the Constitution, each filed a separate opinion. Only Justices Brennan and Marshall found that the death penalty was inherently "cruel and unusual" punishment. The others based their opinions on the uneven manner in which it was applied, together with the infrequency of its imposition at that time.[13] One of the judges said that the death penalty was so rarely and randomly imposed that it was "cruel and unusual" in much the same way as being "struck by lightning".

Several found that the death penalty was also discriminatorily imposed. Justice Douglas stated:

". . . the discretion of judges and juries in imposing the death penalty enables the penalty to be selectively applied, feeding prejudices against the accused if he is poor and despised and lacking political clout, or if he is a member of a suspect or unpopular minority, and saving those who, by social position, may be in a more protected position."

After the *Furman* decision, states began revising their statutes to modify the discretion given to juries or judges in capital trials. Some

---

13. Justice Douglas, for example, said that, whereas in past decisions the Supreme Court had assumed punishment by death was not cruel and unusual unless the manner of execution was inhuman and barbarous, the death penalty should now be construed as "unusual" if it was selectively and irregularly applied, or applied in a manner that discriminated against offenders by race, wealth or class, in violation of the Fourteenth Amendment. Justice White found that it was so infrequently imposed that it served no legitimate state purpose and was therefore "cruel and unusual punishment" in violation of the Eighth and Fourteenth Amendments.

states reintroduced a mandatory death penalty for certain crimes (as had existed originally in both US and English law). Others introduced a form of guided discretion in sentencing. By 1975, 33 states had introduced revised death penalty statutes. However, because the *Furman* decision had not ruled the death penalty as such unconstitutional, and each of the judges had differing views, the situation remained uncertain until the new laws were tested in the Supreme Court.

Supreme Court rulings reinstating the death penalty, 1976 to 1978

Gregg v. Georgia (1976)

The first major test cases involved appeals by prisoners sentenced to death under new laws enacted in Georgia, Texas and Florida, each of which provided for some form of guided discretion in sentencing. The cases were considered together and in 1976 the Supreme Court issued its decision in the lead case: *Gregg* v. *Georgia*.

In this and related cases,[14] the Court ruled by seven votes to two that the death penalty for murder was constitutional, as imposed under the revised statutes in Georgia, Texas and Florida. Each of the three statutes contained the following provisions:

☐ In trials for offences for which the death penalty may be authorized, the determination of guilt or innocence must be decided separately from the sentence.

☐ If a defendant is found guilty of a capital offence, the trial court must then conduct a separate sentencing hearing to determine whether the defendant should be sentenced to death or life imprisonment. In deciding on the appropriate sentence, the court must consider aggravating and mitigating circumstances in relation to both the crime and the offender.

The statutes also provided for automatic review of death sentences by the highest state court of appeal, to ensure that the death penalty was imposed proportionately to the gravity of the offence and/or even-handedly under state law.

The Supreme Court found that the above provisions promised to eliminate the arbitrariness in death sentencing under the old laws. The *Gregg* v. *Georgia* decision thus sanctioned the reintroduction of the death penalty under a system of "guided discretion". It established the principles which governed subsequent capital punish-

---

14. The related cases, upholding the post-*Furman* statutes of Florida and Texas, were *Proffit* v. *Florida* and *Jurek* v. *Texas*.

ment laws, and the statutes upheld in Georgia, Texas and Florida have served as models for other states.

Mandatory sentences

In two other 1976 decisions, *Woodson* v. *North Carolina* and [Stanislaus] *Roberts* v. *Louisiana*, the Supreme Court ruled that mandatory death sentences were unconstitutional. The statutes in both states had provided mandatory death sentences for all first-degree murder convictions. In a further ruling on this question, [Harry] *Roberts* v. *Louisiana*, 1977, the Supreme Court ruled that mandatory sentences were unconstitutional even when imposed for a restricted category of crime (murder of a police officer acting in the course of his or her duty), on the grounds that the sentencing authority must still consider mitigating circumstances relating to the offender in such cases. The rulings invalidated mandatory death sentences provided for in 21 states, and several hundred prisoners consequently had their sentences modified to life imprisonment.

In a footnote to the [Harry] *Roberts* v. *Louisiana* decision, however, the Supreme Court expressly reserved judgment on whether a mandatory death sentence would be unconstitutional if imposed for murder committed by a prisoner serving a life sentence. This question had still not been decided by the Court at the time of writing. Since 1972, at least two prisoners in Alabama have been sentenced to death under such a provision. (Both were pursuing appeals in 1986.)[15] A statute enacted in New York State contained a similar provision until it was ruled unconstitutional by the New York Court of Appeals (the state's highest court) in 1984.[16] No other states are believed to provide for mandatory death sentences in these circumstances.

Further Supreme Court rulings on the death penalty

In *Gregg* v. *Georgia*, the Supreme Court had considered only whether, and under what circumstances, the death penalty was constitutional if imposed for the crime of murder. The statutes in

---

15. The mandatory death sentence provision in Alabama for inmates who commit murder while already serving life terms (for any offence), is contained under an 1862 law, which was not affected by the *Furman* or subsequent rulings.

16. The New York Statute was introduced in 1974 and originally provided mandatory sentences also for the killing of a police or prison officer, until this was invalidated by the *Woodson* and *Roberts* rulings. Until the 1984 ruling by the New York Court of Appeals, it retained the provision for a mandatory death sentence for prisoners serving a prison term of 15 years to life.

Georgia and several other states also retained the death penalty for a number of other crimes.

In *Coker* v. *Georgia* (1977), the Supreme Court ruled that the death penalty was "grossly disproportionate and excessive" for the (non-homicide) rape of an adult woman. Georgia was one of only three states which had reintroduced the death penalty for rape after 1972. The *Coker* decision meant that rape of an adult was no longer a capital offence.

Citing the *Coker* ruling in a summary opinion given in *Eberheart* v. *Georgia* (1977), the Supreme Court also held that a sentence of death imposed for the crime of kidnapping would be "cruel and unusual".

One other important Supreme Court decision in the 1970s developed the standards by which the death penalty could be imposed. In *Lockett* v. *Ohio* (1978), it struck down an Ohio statute which provided that a death sentence must be imposed on an offender convicted of aggravated murder, unless one of only three specifically enumerated mitigating circumstances was present. The Supreme Court held that the Eighth and Fourteenth Amendments to the Constitution required the sentencing authority to consider any circumstances that might be presented in mitigation, before choosing between a life or death sentence.

The defendant whose death sentence was vacated in this ruling was Sandra Lockett, convicted of participating in a murder committed by an accomplice during the robbery of a pawn-shop. Sandra Lockett had stayed outside in a car while the robbery (and murder) took place. That she had not directly participated in the murder and had not known that a killing would occur or planned that one should, was not among the mitigating circumstances listed in the statute and the judge was unable to consider these points in his sentencing decision.[17]

The death penalty was still authorized under several state laws for offences such as armed robbery, rape of a minor and kidnapping committed under certain statutory aggravating circumstances. Although these provisions have not been tested by the Supreme Court, it is thought likely that the Court would, in view of the *Coker* and *Eberheart* decisions, hold the death penalty to be excessive punishment for such crimes if they did not result in loss of life.

Although the Supreme Court continued to rule on appeals in

---

17. The actual killer (whose gun reportedly went off accidentally during a struggle with the victim) accepted a negotiated plea for a life sentence, in return for testifying for the state. Sandra Lockett was convicted of aggravated murder and sentenced to death after refusing two offers by the state of lesser sentences — first it offered to accept a guilty plea to manslaughter in return for her cooperation with the state; then, after the state had prepared its case, it offered to accept a guilty plea to aggravated murder and not to seek the death penalty.

capital cases after 1978, the above decisions provided the main guidelines under which the death penalty is currently authorized. Later rulings by the Court (referred to elsewhere in this report) have tended to uphold state death penalty laws, removing impediments to the penalty and narrowing the grounds for future appeals on constitutional questions.

By the time of writing in May 1986, 37 states had death penalty legislation in force and 33 had prisoners under sentence of death.[18] Death penalty statutes which had been enacted in two other states after 1972 — New York and Massachussetts — were ruled unconstitutional by the state supreme courts in 1984.

A list of states with current death penalty statutes and the number of prisoners under sentence of death in each state at the time of writing is contained in Appendix 1.

---

18. Vermont is listed as one of the states with death penalty legislation at the time of writing. However, the statute (which provides for a penalty of death or life imprisonment for the murder of a correctional (prison) employee or law enforcement officer while in the performance of their duties) is a pre-*Furman* law. As of May 1986 the law had not been amended to provide sentencing guidelines in line with the US Supreme Court's 1976 decision in *Gregg* v. *Georgia*. While, technically, the law remains in force, it has not been tested in the light of the Supreme Court ruling.

Laws and legal procedures

Thirty-seven states now have statutes authorizing the death penalty, each containing different provisions for defining a capital crime designed to remain within the constitutional guidelines set by the Supreme Court.

Crimes carrying the death penalty

In most states, only murder (usually in the first degree) where there are aggravating circumstances is a capital offence. These circumstances are usually listed in the statute, among the most common being:

☐ that the crime was especially heinous, atrocious or cruel;

☐ that it involved multiple victims;

☐ that it was committed during the commission or attempted commission of a number of additional specified felonies, such as robbery, rape or kidnapping;

☐ that it was for pecuniary gain;

☐ that the victim was a police or correctional (prison) officer acting in the course of his duty;

☐ that the offender was a prisoner serving a sentence on conviction of a previous capital crime or an offence involving violence;

☐ that the offender had a prior conviction for a violent crime;

☐ that the offender caused or directed another to commit murder, or committed murder as an agent or employee for another person.

As noted before, a few states still authorize the death penalty for offences not involving homicide. Idaho and South Dakota, for example, list kidnapping (with specified aggravating circumstances) as a capital offence and Mississippi authorizes the death penalty for felonious child abuse (rape of a female child under the age of 12).[1] As far as Amnesty International is aware, no death sentences have been imposed under the present statutes for these offences and it is thought

1. Information from the US Department of Justice *Bureau of Justice Statistics Bulletin on Capital Punishment, 1984.*

probable that the death penalty would be considered unconstitutional in such cases.

The post-*Furman* Florida statute authorized the death penalty for the rape of a minor. However, this was ruled unconstitutional by the Florida Supreme Court in 1981 and death sentences imposed on five people convicted of this crime after 1973 were vacated. In 1974 the Georgia Supreme Court vacated a death sentence imposed for armed robbery, on the grounds that it was "excessive and disproportionate" punishment for the crime.

"Felony-murder" rule

The death penalty is most commonly imposed for homicides committed during the course of an additional serious contemporaneous offence (for example, robbery, burglary or rape). These are known in the USA as "felony-murders". Four out of five death sentences imposed in Georgia, Florida and Texas are reportedly for felony-murders.

In some US states, there is no requirement to prove intent to kill in the case of the actual killer in a felony-murder. Thus, in the states where this applies, offenders who kill, even accidentally, during the commission (or attempted commission) of another felony may be found guilty of first-degree murder. In such cases the state need only prove intent to commit the underlying felony.[2] Some states where the felony-murder rule applies have laws requiring that intent to kill be found by the judge or jury before imposing a death sentence on convicted felony murderers.[3] However, in others, offenders convicted

---

2. The felony-murder rule in common law originated in England in the 17th century, and dispenses with the normal common-law definition of murder as homicide with premeditated intent to kill or inflict grievous bodily harm. It was abolished in England by the Homicide Act 1957. In its early form, a felon was considered guilty of murder for any killing (whether committed by himself, an accomplice or a third party such as a police officer) which occurred during the course of another offence. The law as it is now applied in the USA is usually limited to killings which occur during the course of a serious felony. Although a felon may still be found guilty of first-degree murder for a killing committed by a co-felon, the law on the death penalty and felony-murder has been modified in this respect.

3. The California Supreme Court ruled in 1984 (in *Carlos* v. *People*) that, under California law, the death penalty (or its alternative of life-without-parole) may not be imposed on either an accomplice or the actual killer in a felony-murder, unless intent to kill (or to aid and abet a killing) is proved, or unless the killing occurred as a direct causal result of the commission (or attempted commission) of a felony inherently dangerous to life. This ruling resulted in the vacation (voiding) of sentence of more than 40 prisoners on California's death row who had been sentenced to death under the felony-murder rule with no actual intent to kill having been found.

of felony-murder may be sentenced to death, whether or not specific intent to kill is proved.[4]

Until recently, a number of states permitted the death penalty to be imposed equally on accomplices to a felony-murder, even if they participated in only a minor way in the accompanying felony and there was no evidence of complicity in the actual killing. However, in a ruling in 1982 (*Enmund* v. *Florida*), the US Supreme Court held that the Eighth Amendment prohibited states from sentencing to death accomplices to a felony-murder unless they could show that the accomplice actually did the killing or attempted to do it, or intended that the killing take place or that lethal force be employed.

The ruling vacated the death sentence imposed on the petitioner, Earl Enmund, who had participated in an armed robbery, during the course of which an elderly couple were killed. It was found that he was not present when the killings occurred, but was waiting in a car outside the house where the robbery took place. Although he had helped to plan the robbery, there was no evidence that he had intended anyone to be killed or anticipated that lethal force would be used.

The *Enmund* ruling invalidated parts of the statutes in Florida and eight other states. However, the standard for absolving accomplices from the death penalty remains narrow. *Enmund* resulted in the vacation of sentence of only three inmates on US death rows, none of whom had planned the killings or even been physically present when they occurred.

In most states, accomplices to a felony-murder who did not commit the killing may still be sentenced to death on the broad inference that they "intended that lethal force be employed" without direct evidence of personal intent to kill.[5] Several accomplices have been executed since 1983 under the felony-murder rule. In one case there was doubtful evidence of murderous intent: the defendant was not present when the killing occurred, but was sentenced to death after the court held that he should have known that an accomplice (with whom he had left the murder victim) was dangerous and capable of killing (see case of Roosevelt Green in Chapter 3).

Trial proceedings in capital cases

The Supreme Court rulings in the 1970s set the standards for trials of capital defendants. These standards were intended to eliminate the

4. These states include Florida, Georgia, Mississippi, Nevada, South Carolina, Tennessee and Washington.

5. Only Illinois, Virginia and Maryland statutorily limit the death penalty to the actual killer in a felony-murder.

22

arbitrary and discriminatory aspects of the pre-*Furman* statutes. The rule now prevailing in all capital cases is that there must be a "two-phased" trial in which the question of guilt or innocence is determined separately from sentence. Where a defendant is convicted of capital murder the trial court must conduct a separate sentencing hearing to determine whether a sentence of death or life imprisonment should be imposed. The sentencing hearing usually takes place before the trial jury.

If a defendant pleads guilty to a capital offence there is no trial of guilt or innocence, but a sentencing hearing is usually held, either by the judge alone or, as in some states, before a jury empanelled for that purpose.[6] In a few states, such as Alabama, a jury must decide on the question of guilt or innocence of a capital charge, even if the defendant pleads guilty.

States differ as to how mitigating and aggravating circumstances are assessed at the sentencing stage of capital trials. Georgia, Florida and Texas provide examples of three different systems that are commonly used in other states.

Georgia

Where a defendant is convicted of an offence carrying the death penalty, the judge or jury must consider any mitigating circumstances and 10 aggravating circumstances listed in the statute. Only such evidence of aggravation as the state has made known to the defendant before the trial is admissible. There are no statutory mitigating circumstances listed and defendants may introduce any mitigating factors they consider relevant.

Sentence of death may be imposed only if the jury finds at least one of the 10 statutory aggravating circumstances present, but they need not impose a death sentence in such cases. The judge is bound by the jury's decision to impose death or life imprisonment. Where a death sentence is passed, the trial transcript, together with the judge's comments on the sentence, is then passed to the Georgia Supreme Court, which reviews the conviction and sentence.

Florida

The Florida statute lists eight aggravating and seven mitigating circumstances which must be considered at the sentencing stage. If a

---

6. Prosecutors may also reach a pre-trial agreement with the defendant not to seek the death penalty if the defendant pleads guilty to a capital offence. In such cases no separate sentencing hearing will be held on conviction and an automatic life sentence will be imposed. This practice is known as "plea bargaining" and is described in more detail in Chapter 3.

statutory aggravating circumstance is found, death is presumed to be the proper sentence unless one or more mitigating circumstances are found and judged to outweigh the aggravating circumstances. The jury weighs the evidence but only advises the trial judge as to sentence; the judge need not follow its recommendation. The recommendation need not be unanimous. Where a death sentence is imposed, the judge must write a report stating the reasons why the sentence was passed. This is then referred to the Florida Supreme Court, which reviews both conviction and sentence.

Texas

Murder as a capital crime is defined in the Texas statute as one of five forms of aggravated murder: murder of a peace officer or fire officer acting in the course of his or her duties; murder in the course of committing or attempting to commit a specified aggravated felony[7]; murder for remuneration or the promise of remuneration, or employing another to commit murder for remuneration or the promise of remuneration; murder while escaping or attempting to escape from a penal institution; murder of a person employed in the penal institution in which the murderer is incarcerated.

If a defendant is convicted of any of the above crimes, the jury must then consider three further aggravating factors listed in the sentencing section of the statute: 1 — whether the conduct of the defendant was such as deliberately to cause death; 2 — the probability of the defendant committing "criminal acts of violence that would constitute a continuing threat to society"; 3 — whether the conduct of the defendant was "unreasonable in response to provocation, if any, by the deceased victim". The state must prove each of these three issues as matters of fact beyond reasonable doubt. If the jury finds all three to be present by a unanimous decision, the judge must impose death. If the jury does not find all three statutory aggravating circumstances present, or if opinion is divided on any of them, a death sentence may not be imposed. Neither the judge nor the jury has any sentencing discretion once the three circumstances have been proved and accepted unanimously.

The defendant may introduce any mitigating circumstances which may rebut the state's finding of one of the above three aggravating circumstances. Where a death sentence is imposed, there is automatic review by the Texas Court of Criminal Appeals, the state's highest court of appeals.

Of the three statutes, Georgia's gives the jury the most discretion on whether or not to impose a life or death sentence. In Florida the

---

7. Kidnapping, burglary, robbery, aggravated sexual assault, or arson.

system is more structured: a life sentence may be imposed only after a finding that the mitigating circumstances outweigh the aggravating factors. Texas has a narrower definition of a capital crime; the sentencing provisions also appear more restrictive by limiting aggravating circumstances to matters of fact, all of which have to be proved and agreed on unanimously by the jury. However, two of the statutory aggravating circumstances in the Texas statute (whether the killing was deliberate and unreasonable in response to provocation) are likely to be present where anyone is convicted of capital murder. In practice, therefore, jury decisions to impose the death penalty in Texas depend on the controversial question of finding "proof" of future dangerousness.

Juries

In most states, juries have the final decision on whether to impose death sentences on convicted capital offenders. In California, the trial judge must review any death sentence passed but may not overrule a jury's recommendation of life imprisonment. In three states — Florida, Alabama and Indiana — juries in capital trials only make recommendations to the trial judge and have no final say in the imposing of death or life sentences. In a fourth state, Nevada, a panel of three judges imposes the sentence if the jury is not unanimous. In Arizona, Idaho, Montana and Nebraska, the judge alone decides on the sentence.

Appeal procedures in death penalty cases

Direct appeal to state supreme courts

Most states with the death penalty provide for an automatic appeal to the state's highest court in cases where the death penalty is imposed, whether or not the defendant wishes to waive this right.[8] Some states provide automatic review of the sentence only, others of both conviction and sentence. This automatic review of sentence by state supreme courts, by-passing lower state appeal courts, is unique to death penalty statutes.

In a direct appeal to the state supreme court, the defendant may challenge his or her conviction or sentence on the grounds of any legal or constitutional errors arising at the trial; the appeal at this stage is limited to the trial record.

Some state supreme courts review the case for legal error and also

---

8. Arkansas and New York were reported in 1981 as the only states not yet to have incorporated this provision into their statutes. The New York statute has since been held unconstitutional on other grounds.

compare death sentences with sentences given in similar cases, to determine whether the death sentence is proportionate to other sentences imposed. The Georgia statute provides for the most thorough review, requiring the Georgia Supreme Court to compile records of all capital cases resulting in conviction statewide after 1 January 1970. For the case under review, it requires the trial judge to submit to the court a transcript and complete record of the trial, and also to complete a standardized questionnaire about the crime and the defendant. After the Georgia Supreme Court has made a "proportionality" review upholding a death sentence, it is required by statute to cite, in an appendix to its opinion, all the cases it has considered that are similar to the one under review.

The Florida Supreme Court conducts a similar "proportionality" review by comparing a death sentence passed with other sentences in similar cases statewide. However, not all states make a direct comparison with actual cases. Neither Texas nor California provides for any form of "proportionality" review by the state supreme court; instead the court makes an assessment in more general terms of whether the sentence is appropriate in relation to the gravity of the offence.

The Louisiana Supreme Court conducts a limited "proportionality" review by comparing death sentences with similar cases within the judicial circuit where the trial is held.

If the state supreme court upholds the conviction or sentence, the defendant can petition the US Supreme Court to review the decision. Should it agree to review a case it will grant what is known as a writ of *certiorari*. It has discretion on whether or not to hear an appeal and will only consider cases where it believes a substantial constitutional issue is raised. Although petitions for *certiorari* are routinely filed by capital defendants on issues raised in a direct appeal, the Supreme Court rarely agrees to review cases at this stage.

State and federal habeas corpus appeals

After a sentence has been upheld by the state supreme court, a defendant may lodge *habeas corpus* appeals in the state and federal courts. Unlike a direct appeal to the state supreme court, a *habeas corpus* review is not confined to the trial record, but may raise other issues, such as newly discovered evidence and constitutional claims, including ineffective assistance of counsel at trial. *Habeas corpus* appeals are usually first filed in the trial court; if denied, a new petition may be filed in the state court of appeal for the district where the trial occurred. State *habeas corpus* appeals can be taken as far as the state supreme court; if this is unsuccessful, a petition for *certiorari* may again be lodged with the US Supreme Court.

A defendant who has exhausted state court review, after both direct and state *habeas corpus* appeals, may then seek a federal review by filing a federal *habeas corpus* petition. Whereas review in the state courts may be based on any claims of violation of the state statutes, or violations of either the state or federal constitution, review in the federal courts is limited to alleged violations of federal constitutional rights. These are issues raised under provisions of the US Constitution such as the Fourteenth Amendment's due process provisions, the Eighth Amendment's cruel and unusual punishment prohibition or the Sixth Amendment's provision of the right to effective assistance of counsel. A defendant must exhaust all available state remedies before filing for federal *habeas corpus* relief.[9]

Federal *habeas corpus* petitions start in the US District Courts. If denied, they may be taken on to the US Court of Appeals for the judicial circuit covering the state in which the trial was held. Final appeals on constitutional issues may be made to the US Supreme Court.

Execution warrants

Only direct review by the state supreme courts is automatic and compulsory in capital cases. Although a defendant has a right to file petitions for claims to be heard after this stage, they may be rejected without a full hearing if found to be without merit. Execution warrants may be issued at any time after a death sentence has been confirmed by the state supreme court. Warrants are usually issued by the trial judge or a member of the same judicial circuit.[10] The date for execution is set usually at not less than 28 days from the date of issue.[11] If further appeals are pending, the defendant then has to apply for a stay of execution. Several execution warrants may be issued before a prisoner has exhausted all appeals.

---

9. The defendant must give the highest state court of appeal the opportunity to rule on the merits of a claim raising a federal constitutional right, before lodging a *habeas corpus* petition in the federal district court.

10. In a few states (including Florida) the state governor issues execution warrants.

11. This varies: in some states, for example Georgia, an execution warrant may be issued from 10 to 20 days in advance of the execution date; in California warrants must be issued not less than 60 and not more than 90 days in advance of the scheduled execution.

Application of the death penalty, 1973 to 1985

The new death penalty statutes have removed the unfettered discretion existing under the old laws, which had produced widely differing penalties in a range of offences. The statutes provide a system of "guided discretion" in sentencing, and procedural safeguards intended to achieve consistency. Crimes for which the death penalty is now available have effectively been limited to murder with aggravating circumstances.

Although these provisions have removed some of the arbitrariness in sentencing, the death penalty continues to be unevenly applied, both nationally and within the states in which it is most frequently imposed. Wide discretion remains at every stage of the criminal justice process, from decisions taken at the stages of arrest and indictment through to clemency. The evidence suggests that the death penalty is applied neither fairly nor consistently, although the point at which this primarily occurs may have shifted from sentencing to other stages in the process.

As in earlier periods, only a relatively small proportion of offenders convicted of criminal homicide are sentenced to death. From 1979 to 1985 there were, annually, between 18,000 and 23,000 arrests for criminal homicide and several thousand murder convictions. However, fewer than 300 people a year were sentenced to death during this period.[1] The national death row population of some 1,300 prisoners in 1983 was a little over three per cent of the convicted

---

1. According to figures taken from Uniform Crime Reports of the Federal Bureau of Investigation (FBI), and given in the US Department of Justice *Bureau of Justice Statistics Bulletin on Capital Punishment, 1984*, during the 10-year period 1975 to 1984 inclusive, 204,000 people in the USA were victims of murder or non-negligent manslaughter; there were an estimated 198,000 arrests for these crimes. During the same period, 2,384 people entered prisons under sentence of death and 32 offenders were executed.

The 1984 *Bureau of Justice Statistics Bulletin* also states that in 1982 and 1983 there were, respectively, 9,060 and 8,218 admissions to prison for homicide, of which 284 and 280 were under sentence of death: around three per cent of the total. Homicide is defined as murder and non-negligent manslaughter.

murderers in US prisons at that time.[2] Even within the restricted category of capital murder, a small proportion of offenders are indicted on capital charges and fewer still are sentenced to death.

Government representatives have maintained that the small proportion of capital offenders who receive death sentences is evidence that the revised laws and procedures have served to single out the most heinous offenders. However, there is evidence that factors other than the gravity of the crime and culpability of the offender have led to some people being sentenced to death and others — whose crimes are similar — to life imprisonment, or less.

The likelihood of a death sentence being imposed may depend on a variety of circumstances unrelated to the crime itself, including political and other pressures on local prosecutors; a defendant's financial resources and the competence of trial counsel; the race or social status of offender and victim; where the crime was committed and, in certain areas, the very composition of juries.

Although disparities based on the above circumstances may occur in relation to crimes generally in any justice system, Amnesty International believes that the death penalty increases the potential for arbitrary and discriminatory treatment.

Trials of capital cases tend to cost more than those of other cases and usually involve prolonged appeals. This may discourage prosecutors from seeking the death penalty in all but a handful of cases, thus causing disparities right at the beginning of the judicial process. The complexity of capital trials, involving a separate trial and sentencing proceeding, creates a greater potential for error as a result of inadequate counsel than in other cases, thus increasing the disadvantages of defendants with the least resources. Given such factors and the unique severity of the death penalty, it is more likely to be reserved for offenders who have low social standing, are members of minority groups, or others with whom the community may least identify.

The various factors affecting the imposition of the death penalty are described in more detail below.

Prosecutors' discretion

Decisions made by prosecutors at an early stage of the judicial process have an important influence on the outcome of a homicide case, including the possibility of a death sentence. In cases involving potentially capital circumstances, prosecutors have wide powers of

---

2. Dave Bruck, "Condemned to Death (The capital punishment lottery)", in *New Republic*, December 1983.

discretion to decide what charges to file, how vigorously to pursue a case and whether or not to seek the death penalty. Many cases are settled well before trial through plea bargains — usually an offer by the prosecutor to accept a guilty plea to a lesser, non-capital charge (such as voluntary manslaughter or second-degree murder), thus avoiding the need to take a case to trial. In some cases defendants may plead guilty to a capital charge on the understanding that the state will not seek the death penalty.[3]

It appears that, in practice, prosecutors seek the death penalty in only a minority of potentially capital cases. For example, a study of homicides committed in South Carolina between June 1977 and December 1981 found that prosecutors had sought the death penalty in only 36 per cent of aggravated homicides for which arrests were made during the period studied (these constituted only 19 per cent of all homicide arrests, the others being non-aggravated or not linked to other felonies).[4] A study of homicide cases in Georgia found that two-thirds of all defendants convicted of capital murder after jury trials between 1973 and 1978 received automatic life sentences because of prosecutors' decisions not to seek a death sentence and to waive the penalty hearing.[5] This, together with jury sentencing decisions, meant that the death penalty was imposed in 17 per cent of all capital murder convictions in the state.[6]

Prosecutors — who are directly elected in 44 US states — may be influenced in their decisions on charging by many factors in addition to the statutory aggravating or mitigating circumstances of the case. Because of the cost and length of proceedings in capital trials, many prosecutors are reluctant to seek the death penalty in any case unless

---

3. County prosecutors (otherwise known as district attorneys) handle a case after an arrest and initial investigation by the police. They are responsible for initiating and conducting criminal proceedings on behalf of the state in a given district. Although plea bargains must be approved by a judge, the judge commonly defers to the prosecution's discretion on this issue. Prosecutors attached to the State Attorney General's office (known as state attorneys) usually represent the state in post-conviction appeals.

4. Raymond Paternoster, "Race of Victim and Location of Crime: The Decision to seek the Death Penalty in South Carolina", in the *Journal of Criminal Law and Criminology*, Vol. 74, No.3, 1983.

5. Unlike many other states, Georgia does not recognize degrees of murder. "Capital murders" referred to in the study are those which carried a potential death sentence by the presence of various aggravating circumstances.

6. David Baldus, Charles Pulaski and G. Woodworth, "Comparative Review of Death Sentences: an Empirical Study of the Georgia Experience" in the *Journal of Criminal Law & Criminology*, Northwestern University School of Law, vol. 74, No. 3, 1983, pp. 663-753.

there is particular pressure on them to do so. Others, however, will press for the death penalty wherever possible.

Their decisions may depend not only on the fiscal resources available in a given area, but on many other factors, including the level of public support for the death penalty in that constituency, community pressure or publicity in the case, and relations with defence attorneys and the police. Within the four states visited by the Amnesty International mission in June 1985, there were marked regional variations in the rate at which death sentences were sought by prosecutors in comparable cases.

Racial disparities in decisions on charging

Several studies have found significant racial disparities in prosecutors' decisions on charging, noting that the death penalty is sought far more frequently in cases where the victims were white than where they were black. One study was by William J. Bowers, Director of the Center for Applied Social Research at Northeastern University, Boston, Massachusetts. He examined charging decisions in criminal homicide cases in 20 Florida counties over a four-year period, taking into account a variety of factors such as the existence of an additional felony, the number of victims, the age and sex of the victim and other potentially aggravating circumstances. He found that legally aggravating or mitigating circumstances played a substantial role in prosecutors' decisions to seek a capital murder indictment. He also found that the victim's race had a significant "extra-legal" influence on whether or not a capital charge would be filed, and that the racial combination of a black killing a white was "virtually as strong a predictor of a first-degree murder indictment as any of the legally relevant factors except a felony circumstance".[7] A recent study has also indicated a possible tendency on the part of some prosecutors to "upgrade" cases with white victims and "downgrade" those with black victims.[8]

---

7. Bowers collected data on all first-degree murder indictments for the period from 1973 to 1976 in 21 of Florida's 67 counties (those counties selected accounting for approximately 75 per cent of death sentences imposed during the period). In addition he examined more complete data on all criminal homicide arrests in 20 counties for the period from 1976 to 1977, using local crime reporting agencies, court records and responses to questionnaires from prosecutors and attorneys. His findings were published in the *Journal of Criminal Law and Criminology*, vol. 74, 1983, and reproduced in expanded form in his book *Legal Homicide*. Paternoster, in his study of homicides in South Carolina cited above, found a similar racial disparity in decisions to seek the death penalty within the small range of capital murders committed in the state.

8. Michael L. Radelet and Glenn L. Pierce, "Race and Prosecutorial Discretion in Homicide Cases", an unpublished paper dated April 1983, presented at the 1983

These findings do not necessarily imply that prosecutors deliberately discriminate in their charging decisions. However, it has been suggested that in areas with a large white majority population strongly supporting capital punishment, there is inevitably more pressure on prosecutors to seek the death penalty in cases with white victims than those with black or victims from other minorities. Lawyers have also noted that there is more community outrage, publicity and public pressure when the murder victim comes from a middle-class background, which, again, is more likely to apply to whites than blacks.

Most lawyers to whom the mission spoke in states in the South believed that killings of or among blacks were simply not taken as seriously as those involving whites; several cited cases from their own experience where, in cases involving blacks, prosecutors and judges showed a tendency to accept pleas of manslaughter as opposed to murder, regardless of the circumstance.[9] (There is further discussion of racial discrimination in Chapter 4.)

Plea bargaining

Plea bargaining in the US criminal justice system can result in offenders whose crimes and circumstances were similar receiving widely differing sentences. Although this commonly happens in all criminal cases, those involving the death penalty give rise to particular concern about inequality of treatment because the death penalty is different in kind from all other penalties and cannot be reversed. The unequal sentences imposed on similar offenders in such cases may also amount to a failure to comply with the standards of evenhanded

---

meeting of the American Sociological Association in Detroit. The study, which also focussed on counties in Florida, matched police arrest reports with later grand jury indictments, and found that a significant number of initial police reports citing no felony circumstances in cases with white victims later appeared in court records as felony-related. The opposite occurred in a similar proportion of cases with black victims. This research has since been expanded to include a larger sample of cases and the findings reportedly continue to apply (see *Legal Homicide, op.cit.* p. 341). Similar patterns were also being investigated by researchers in South Carolina in 1983.

9. One lawyer had worked as a public defender in a rural area of southern Georgia during the late 1970s, and had looked at every case involving aggravated murder over a five-year period (some 10 cases with an equal number of black and white victims). The local prosecutor had asked for the death penalty in every case where the victim was white and in none of those with a black victim, even though several of the latter involved highly aggravated circumstances. Although the sample was too small to be of statistical value, this observation is consistent with the findings of other research.

justice required by the US Supreme Court in its rulings on the death penalty in the 1970s.

Several prisoners have been executed in recent years in cases where a co-accused, appearing equally culpable in law, received a lesser sentence as a result of plea bargaining. Charles Brooks was executed by lethal injection in Texas in December 1982 while a co-accused (whose original conviction and death sentence were overturned on a legal technicality) later received a 40-year prison sentence as a result of a plea bargain. It was not known which of the two had shot and killed the victim, a motor car mechanic. The prosecutor who had asked for the death penalty in Charles Brooks' case later tried unsuccessfully to persuade the Texas Board of Pardons and Paroles to grant him a reprieve, arguing that the extremely different sentences were unfair, since each defendant had been convicted on the same evidence for the same acts.

The threat of the death penalty can be a powerful weapon in the hands of a prosecutor, who may charge a defendant with a capital offence in the hope of persuading him or her to agree to plead guilty to a lesser charge, thus avoiding the expense of a trial. A practice of "indicting high" to "force a plea" may result in injustice if the defendant refuses to plea bargain (plead guilty to a lesser charge) and exercises the right to go to trial.[10] The defendant may then risk the death penalty by going to trial on a capital charge, even though the circumstances of the case may have justified a more lenient penalty. This may have occurred in the case of John Spenkelink, who was executed in Florida in 1979 after refusing to accept the uncontested second-degree murder plea offered him by the state.

John Spenkelink was convicted of murdering a travelling companion who he alleged had sexually assaulted and robbed him. Although the trial court acknowledged that he was trying to recover his stolen possessions, it found that the murder was committed "for pecuniary gain" and was "especially heinous, atrocious and cruel" — two aggravating circumstances for which a death sentence may be imposed under the Florida statute. However, several lawyers have expressed strong doubts about the fairness of the sentence, claiming that the murder lacked the highly aggravating circumstances which usually characterize a capital crime. Former US Attorney General

10. A study conducted for the Florida Justice Institute questioned prosecutors about their reasons for bringing capital charges. Although the "facts of the case" were among the most common reasons given, several were reported to have responded that one factor was to "indict high to force a plea" (cited in William J. Bowers, "The Pervasiveness of Arbitrariness and Discrimination under Post-*Furman* Capital Statutes", *Journal of Criminal Law and Criminology*, vol. 74, No. 3, 1983, p. 1077).

Ramsey Clark, one of the lawyers who handled John Spenkelink's final appeal, stated:

> "This should not have been a capital case . . . Here was a claim of self-defense, that the defendant had been homosexually raped and his money taken from him, that he had entered the motel room to recover his money and go his own way. The [murder victim] was older, bigger, stronger, had spent decades in prison and was in violation of parole at the time. . . . The death penalty is not normally asked for or given in such cases." (See Bowers, *Legal Homicide*, p.347).

There was also evidence suggesting that John Spenkelink was inadequately represented by his court-appointed trial attorney.[11]

John Spenkelink was only one of several prisoners to have been executed after refusing to plead guilty to lesser charges.

In cases involving multiple defendants, plea bargains are commonly offered to one defendant in return for testifying against a co-accused, to whom prosecutors are under no obligation to offer a reduced charge. It is possible that a more culpable defendant most at risk of receiving a death sentence may be more willing than others to testify for the state in return for a lesser sentence. A number of prisoners have been sentenced to death where the main evidence against them was witness testimony from a co-accused against whom there was at least equal evidence of at least equal guilt.

The US Supreme Court has ruled that a state may constitutionally extend leniency in exchange for guilty pleas at criminal trials (on the principle that recognition of guilt and remorse may justify mitigation). In capital cases, the Court has ruled only that guilty pleas may not automatically absolve offenders from a potential death sentence, since this would put unacceptable pressure on defendants to plead guilty.[12]

---

11. John Spenkelink's appeal lawyers found evidence suggesting that he had had ineffective assistance of counsel at trial. Among other things, his court-appointed attorney had failed to mention important information about the prisoner's background at the sentencing hearing. This included reports that his early problems began when he was 11 and found the body of his father who had committed suicide, and reports by prison psychiatrists concluding that his criminal behaviour was due in part to this experience and that he was amenable to treatment. An account of the unsuccessful attempts to have this newly discovered mitigating evidence considered at a final appeal is given in an article by Ramsey Clark in *The Nation*, 27 October 1979, reproduced on pp. 224-233 in *The Death Penalty in America* by Hugo Adam Bedau.

12. Statutes providing for automatic exclusion from the death penalty on entering a guilty plea have been held to be unconstitutional. The Massachusetts death penalty

In *Gregg* v. *Georgia* (1976), the US Supreme Court rejected a claim that prosecutors worked in a "standardless fashion". Justice White stated in the ruling that:

"Absent facts to the contrary, it cannot be assumed that prosecutors will be motivated in their charging decisions by factors other than the strength of their case and the likelihood that a jury would impose the death penalty if it convicts. . . . Thus defendants will escape the death penalty through prosecutorial charging decisions only because the offence is not sufficiently serious; or because the proof is insufficiently strong."

Research into the way the death penalty has been applied in practice in some states, and the cases of some executed prisoners, suggest that such standards are not always maintained.

Juries in capital trials

Juries retain considerable discretion in capital cases which go to trial, despite the "guided" sentencing provisions of the present statutes. No legal provision can classify all the characteristics of a given crime. Statutory aggravating and mitigating circumstances may be open to widely differing interpretations, especially those which are more broadly worded — such as whether the crime was "especially heinous, atrocious or cruel", as provided under the Florida and other statutes, or whether the defendant, in mitigation, was acting under the influence of "extreme mental or emotional disturbance".

One of the aggravating circumstances in which a death sentence may be imposed in Texas has been open to particular criticism. The Texas jury is required to find three factors present before imposing a death sentence. Two are whether the defendant's conduct was deliberate and whether it was unreasonable in response to provocation. Since a jury is likely to find both these factors present in most cases where a defendant is convicted of a capital offence, sentence of death usually rests on a finding on the third factor: "whether there is a probability that the defendant would commit criminal acts of violence that would constitute a continuing threat to society". In practice, therefore, defendants convicted of capital murder in Texas may live or die according to a jury's prediction about their future conduct, which inevitably involves guessing.[13]

statute was struck down by the Massachusetts State Supreme Court on these grounds in 1984.

13. The arbitrary effect of such a finding is lucidly described by Charles L. Black in *Capital Punishment: the Inevitability of Caprice and Mistake*, Second Edition, W.W. Norton & Co. Inc., 1981.

Exclusion of jurors who oppose the death penalty

Jury selection procedures in most states allow prosecutors to exclude people who oppose the death penalty from sitting as jurors in capital trials. This has been criticized by criminologists and some courts, who believe that the practice has created "death-prone" juries which are more likely to favour the prosecution than those drawn from a more representative cross-section of the community.

The provision is set down in a US Supreme Court opinion given in *Witherspoon* v. *Illinois* (1968), which held that prospective jurors who are unequivocally opposed to the death penalty may be excluded "for cause" (that is, for reasons given) at the *voir dire* stage of capital trials.[14] Until 1985, the standard for exclusion was based on a footnote to the *Witherspoon* opinion, which stated that prosecutors could exclude only those jurors who had made it:

> "unmistakeably clear (1) that they would *automatically* vote against the imposition of capital punishment without regard to any evidence that might be developed at the trial of the case before them, or (2) that their attitude toward the death penalty would prevent them from making an impartial decision as to the defendant's *guilt*." (emphasis in original)[15]

In a further ruling on the issue given in *Wainwright* v. *Witt* (January 1985), the Supreme Court reduced this requirement, by holding that prosecutors may exclude any juror whose views would "prevent or substantially impair the performance of his duties . . . in accordance with his instructions and oath" but that it was no longer necessary to show that the juror had made it "unmistakeably clear" that he would

---

14. The *voir dire* as it applies to jury selection for a trial is the preliminary examination of prospective jurors in order to determine their fitness to serve on a jury in that trial. The initial panel, or *venire*, of prospective jurors (from which the actual trial jury is chosen) is selected randomly, usually from voter registration lists within the court's jurisdiction. At *voir dire*, the defence or prosecution may seek the removal for cause of any prospective juror believed to be biased. This is usually determined by each member of the panel being questioned by defence, prosecution attorneys and the trial judge. The judge makes the final order to remove a juror for cause. (See below, "Peremptory challenges", by which jurors may be removed without reasons being given.)

15. *Witherspoon* 391 U.S. at 522 n.21, footnote to the main opinion. The *Witherspoon* decision established that states were entitled to remove jurors who would never vote for the death penalty, but not those who merely had some qualms about its imposition. The decision reversed the death sentence imposed on an Illinois defendant, because the prosecution at his trial had eliminated nearly half the *venire* of prospective jurors on the grounds that they had expressed only general scruples against the death penalty, without establishing that they would refuse even to consider its imposition in the case before them.

"automatically" vote against a death sentence in all circumstances. In the same decision, the court emphasized that the lower federal courts, if faced with appeals on the issue, should generally defer to the state trial judge, "who sees and hears prospective jurors and makes the final decision on whether they should be seated".

Although the ruling did not reverse the broad principle laid down in *Witherspoon* that only committed opponents of the death penalty may be removed for cause, defence attorneys believe that it has made it easier, in practice, for prosecutors to exclude from capital cases prospective jurors who have any reservations at all about the death penalty.

Supreme Court Justice Brennan dissented from the *Wainwright* decision (with Justice Marshall concurring in the dissent), stating that its effect would be a "jury biased against the defendant, from which an identifiable segment of the community had been excluded". He also stated that prosecutors in future would be able to assemble juries "certainly pre-disposed to impose" a death sentence, and "perhaps pre-disposed to convict".

The Eighth Circuit Court of Appeals reached a similar conclusion on possible jury bias at the conviction phase of capital trials, in a decision given in an Arkansas case in January 1985.[16] In this decision, the appeals court ruled by five votes to four that — even without the *Wainwright* interpretation — the *Witherspoon* exclusionary clause violated the defendant's right to a trial jury composed of a fair cross-section of a given community. Citing numerous research studies into jury attitudes and the death penalty, the court found that juries selected under the *Witherspoon* standard (referred to as "death qualified" juries) were more liable to be conviction-prone and less impartial on the question of guilt or innocence than juries which included those opposing capital punishment.[17] The court held that

---

16. The appeals court decision is cited as *Grigsby* v. *Mabry* 758 F. 2d 226 (1985). The case was consolidated with another Arkansas case raising an identical claim: that of Arcadia McCree. The subsequent appeal to the US Supreme Court, lodged by the state of Arkansas, became known as *Lockhart* v. *McCree* (A.L. Lockhart having replaced James Mabry as Arkansas' Commissioner of Corrections, in whose name the state appeal was brought). Like James Grigsby, Arcadia McCree was convicted of capital murder. Although he received a life sentence at the penalty stage of his trial, he claimed that the exclusion of eight prospective jurors who opposed capital punishment from the guilt phase of his trial violated his Sixth and Fourteenth Amendment rights to have his guilt or innocence determined by an impartial jury selected from a fair cross-section of the community. The appeals court failed to find a violation of the Fourteenth Amendment, but upheld the district court's finding of a violation of his Sixth Amendment right to a representative jury.

17. The appeal court ruling given in *Grigsby* v. *Mabry* (see note above) reviewed

committed opponents of the death penalty may, in future, be excluded only from the sentencing phase of capital trials.

The state of Arkansas appealed against this decision to the US Supreme Court, which agreed to review the issue. In a six-to-three decision given in *Lockhart* v. *McCree* in May 1986, the Supreme Court reversed the ruling of the Eighth Circuit Court of Appeals, holding that the Constitution did not prohibit the exclusion of committed opponents of the death penalty from serving as jurors at the conviction phase of capital trials.

The majority opinion, written by Justice William Rehnquist, expressed doubts about the value of the studies cited by the appeals court in predicting the behaviour of actual juries. The Court stated, however, that, even assuming that the studies were adequate to establish that "death-qualified" juries were "somewhat more 'conviction-prone' than 'non-death-qualified' juries", this would not violate the defendant's right to a fair trial.

The Court held that the constitutional requirement of a representative cross-section of the community applied only to the larger jury panel and not to the actual trial jury chosen, stating that it would be impossible to provide each criminal defendant with a truly representative jury. While the "wholesale exclusion" of groups distinguished solely by their race or sex would not be permissible, this did not apply to groups defined only by their "shared attitudes", such as those to a particular penalty. The Court stated also that state governments had a "legitimate interest" to instruct a single jury for both the trial and sentencing phases of a capital trial.

In a dissenting opinion in which he was joined by Justices Stevens and Brennan, Justice Marshall assailed the Court for upholding a practice which, he said, "allows the state a special advantage in those prosecutions where the charges are the most serious and the possible penalty the most severe". He pointed to the "essential unanimity" of the studies presented by the respondent, Arcadia McCree, which he believed showed "overwhelming evidence that death-qualified juries

some 15 social science studies into jury attitudes conducted over a 20-year period. In one of the more recent studies cited in the decision (Cowan, Thompson and Ellsworth, "The Effects of Death Qualification on Jurors' Predisposition to Convict and on the Quality of Deliberation" in 8 *Law & Human Behaviour* 53, 1984 — also referred to by Justice Brennan in his dissenting opinion to *Wainwright* v. *Witt*) jury-eligible residents of two California counties simulated jury deliberations, after being shown videotapes of a murder trial as well as being given detailed questionnaires about their attitudes to various criminal justice issues. The ruling said the study found that subjects favouring the death penalty were more likely to convict and that "jury panels containing a mix of WEs [*Witherspoon* excludables] and death-qualified subjects tended to view *all* witnesses more critically and remember the facts of the case more accurately than death-qualified jury panels".

are substantially more likely to convict or to convict on more serious charges than those juries on which unalterable opponents of capital punishment are permitted to serve."

Reviewing the studies into jury attitudes, Justice Marshall noted that "death qualification" had been found to exclude at least 11 to 17 per cent of potential jurors who, while opposing the death penalty, could still be impartial at the guilt phase of a capital trial.[18] Members of the excluded group — who included a disproportionate number of women and blacks — had also been shown to be "significantly more concerned with the constitutional rights of defendants and more likely to doubt the strength of the prosecution's case". "Death-qualified" jurors, on the other hand, had been found "more likely to believe that a defendant's failure to testify is indicative of his guilt, more hostile to the insanity defense, more mistrustful of defense attorneys, and less concerned about the danger of erroneous convictions."[19]

Justice Marshall added that ". . . the very process of death qualification — which focuses attention on the death penalty before the trial has even begun — has been found to predispose the jurors that survive it to believe that the defendant is guilty."[20]

Justice Marshall went on to say that the true impact of "death qualification" was probably greater than the studies showed. This was because prosecutors often used their "peremptory challenges" (those by which they may strike off jurors without cause: see below) to exclude potential jurors who, when questioned under *Witherspoon*, had expressed mild scruples about the death penalty but did not meet the *Witherspoon* standard for exclusion.[21] Justice Marshall concluded that:

"The State's mere announcement that it intends to seek the

---

18. Although prospective jurors so opposed to the death penalty that they state they are unable to assess guilt or innocence impartially — so-called "nullifiers" — may also be excluded from sitting on juries under the *Witherspoon* test, the issue on appeal related only to those individuals who stated they could not impose a death sentence on a convicted offender.

19. Marshall cited studies which had been analysed in the District Court ruling in *Grigsby* v. *Mabry*, with which the present case was consolidated. See note 15.

20. There is some support for this remark from observations made by lawyers that prosecutors sometimes seek the death penalty in order to obtain a jury more likely to convict on a capital charge. In some cases prosecutors have dropped their demand for the death penalty once a conviction has been obtained. (See "The Death of Fairness: The Arbitrary and Capricious Imposition of Capital Punishment in the 1980s", an article by Ronald J. Tabak, published by the Clearinghouse on Georgia Prisons and Jails, Atlanta, Georgia.)

21. Justice Marshall cited as an example a California appeal case in which it was reported that the "prosecutor informed [the] court during *voir dire* that if a venireperson expressing scruples about the death penalty 'were not a challenge for

death penalty if the defendant is found guilty of a capital offense will, under today's decision, give the prosecution license to empanel a jury especially likely to return that very verdict. Because I believe that such a blatant disregard for the rights of a capital defendant offends logic, fairness and the Constitution, I dissent."

The *Lockhart* v. *McCree* decision is one of the most important recent rulings on the death penalty given by the US Supreme Court. If it had upheld the lower court's decision, the convictions of many prisoners then on death row would have been reversed and states would in future have been required to empanel separate juries for the trial and sentencing phases of capital proceedings.

As an immediate consequence of the decision, new execution dates were set for prisoners who had been granted stays pending the court's ruling. They included Jay Pinkerton, a minor sentenced to death in Texas, who had been granted a stay in November 1985, minutes before his execution was due to take place. He was executed on 15 May 1986.

Peremptory challenges

In addition to excluding jurors for cause, the defence and prosecution counsel are allowed to make a number of "peremptory challenges" to prospective jurors in criminal trials. Peremptory challenges are those whereby the defence or prosecution may object to proposed jurors without needing to give any reason. There have been widespread complaints about the prosecution's use of peremptory challenges to exclude blacks from sitting on capital-trial juries, especially when the defendant is black. Since blacks are also more liable than other groups to be excluded from the initial jury pool under the *Witherspoon* provision, the combined effect is that prosecutors are often able to obtain juries from which blacks are entirely excluded. (Blacks have in general been found to be somewhat more likely to oppose, or have reservations about, the death penalty than whites.)

Georgia lawyers told Amnesty International that 80 per cent of black prospective jurors in capital trials are routinely excluded from the initial jury pool under *Witherspoon* and that, after peremptory challenges as well, the final trial jury may have no blacks, even though they constitute 20 to 30 per cent of the state's population. A Texas ACLU lawyer told Amnesty International that in Harris County, where he practised, it was the norm for black defendants

cause, I would kick her off on a peremptory challenge'". A 1982 study of Florida's Fourth Judicial Circuit had also found this practice to be common. *Lockhart* v. *McCree*, at p. 8 of the Dissent.

accused of capital crimes to be tried by all-white juries, although blacks constituted 30 per cent of the population of Houston, the state's largest city. A similar practice is common in Louisiana, where all blacks executed under the present statutes were sentenced by all-white juries. Similar complaints have been made about jury selection practice in other states.

An investigation into peremptory challenges in felony trials of black defendants in Cook County, Illinois, conducted by the *Chicago Tribune* in 1984, found that prosecutors eliminated black jurors at more than twice the rate at which they excluded whites, and that the dismissal rate was even higher in cases with white victims.

Until recently, the courts have held that the use of peremptory challenges was racially discriminatory only if defendants could prove that members of their own race were being systematically excluded by prosecutors from trial juries in a given jurisdiction. Many defendants had their appeals denied because they were unable to provide sufficient proof of the extent of this practice, beyond the circumstances of their own cases.

However, the US Supreme Court gave a new ruling on the issue in April 1986 in *Batson* v. *Kentucky*. The case concerned a black Kentucky man at whose trial the prosecutor had used his peremptory challenges to remove all four black people on the *venire*; a jury composed only of white people was selected. Because the trial court had flatly rejected the petitioner's objection to the removal of all the black *venire* people without requiring the prosecutor to explain his actions, the Supreme Court reserved the conviction and remanded the case for further proceedings.

The Court held that, although the prosecutor was ordinarily entitled to exercise peremptory challenges for any reason, the Equal Protection clause of the US Constitution forbade the exclusion of potential jurors solely on account of their race. The Court also held that defendants objecting to the use of peremptory challenges to exclude members of their own race from their trial juries could make a *prima facie* case of discrimination on the circumstances arising in their own cases alone. The onus then fell to the state to provide a "neutral explanation" for challenging the potential jurors.

The decision eased what the Court found had been a "crippling burden of proof" previously placed on defendants raising a constitutional objection to the removing of members of their own race from their trial juries. The ruling is expected to make it easier in future for defendants to challenge this practice. However, the Supreme Court ruled in June 1986 that the new standard would not apply retroactively to prisoners whose convictions had already been upheld on direct appeal at the time of the *Batson* decision. This disbarred hundreds of convicted prisoners from having their cases reviewed on the issue in federal *habeas corpus* proceedings.[22] The Supreme Court left open the question of whether *Batson* would apply retroactively to prisoners whose cases were still pending on direct appeal.

Powers of trial judges to overrule jury sentencing recommendations

The power of the trial judge to override jury sentencing recommendations has caused concern in Florida, because of the large number of cases in which judges have ignored jury recommendations of life imprisonment and imposed death sentences. Between 1973 and 1984, Florida trial judges imposed death sentences in 89 cases in which juries had recommended life imprisonment after considering aggravating and mitigating factors at a separate sentencing hearing. Amnesty International takes no position on whether sentencing decisions should rest with judges or juries in criminal trials. However, the overriding of a recommendation of life imprisonment by a consensus of jurors, reached after their consideration of the facts, undermines the principle that death sentences should not be imposed where there is doubt as to its appropriateness in a particular case. Although the Florida Supreme Court has vacated many of the death sentences imposed by judges against jury recommendations of a lesser punishment, this has not happened in all cases — at least one prisoner has been executed despite a jury's recommendation of a life sentence.[23]

In only two other states has the trial judge the final authority to impose life or death sentences after receiving the jury's recommendation: Alabama and Indiana. At the end of 1984, judges had overridden recommendations by juries of life imprisonment in two capital cases in Indiana and six in Alabama.[24]

In *Spaziano* v. *Florida* (July 1984), the US Supreme Court ruled that the power of a judge to overrule a jury's recommendation of life imprisonment in Florida was constitutional, stating that "there is no constitutional imperative that a jury should have the responsibility of deciding whether the death penalty should be imposed".

---

22. *Allen* v. *Hardy* 54 U.S.L.W. 3856.

23. Ernest Dobbert, executed by electrocution in Florida in September 1984. He had been convicted in 1974 of the murder of his two children during a period in which he was reportedly suffering from extreme mental stress. The jury voted by 10 to two for a life sentence in his case.

24. Michael A. Mello, "Legislative Repeal of the Jury Override", a memorandum dated 13 December 1984.

42

Legal representation of capital defendants

Most capital defendants cannot afford to retain their own counsel and are represented by court-appointed lawyers (private attorneys assigned by the trial court to take a particular case) or public defenders (lawyers attached to state-funded offices specializing in legal aid cases). Public defender offices are mainly in urban areas and do not exist in some states. In practice most capital defendants, especially those in states in the South, are represented by court-appointed private attorneys.[25]

Widespread concern has been expressed about the quality of legal representation of indigent defendants in capital trials. Despite the unique complexity of these trials, and the severity and irrevocability of the sentence once carried out, there is disturbing evidence that many defendants are assigned inexperienced counsel, ill-equipped to handle such cases and working with severely limited resources. Lawyers handling later appeals in such cases have expressed the belief that in many of them errors and inadequacies on the part of trial counsel have contributed significantly to the imposition of death sentences, sometimes resulting in serious miscarriages of justice.

The fees and expenses paid to court-appointed lawyers fall far below those commanded by privately-retained counsel or state prosecutors. They are widely held to be inadequate to cover the cost of preparing and trying a capital case, which requires interviewing potential witnesses, possible hiring of expert testimony and the investigation of a defendant's background, for both the trial and the penalty hearing.

A 1982 study conducted by Mary Brennan for the Florida Justice Institute found that the $3,500 maximum fee then allowed for defence services in trials of capital cases in Florida was considered highly inadequate by many lawyers interviewed: the fee was often exhausted before the trial, so that the lawyer had to give his time in court free of charge.[26] The fees paid for capital trials in Florida are, in fact, higher

---

25. Amnesty International was told that in Florida most, but by no means all, capital defendants are represented at trial by public defenders. In Georgia, Texas, Mississippi and Alabama, there is no statewide public defender system and most capital defendants are assigned private attorneys. In Louisiana and North Carolina (especially in the rural areas), defendants are usually assigned private attorneys. The State Public Defenders' Office in California reported that more than half the 336 capital cases pending as of 1 July 1983 were represented by court-appointed private attorneys; most of the others were represented by public defenders.

26. Study cited in Bowers' *Legal Homicide*. Mary Brennan interviewed judges, prosecutors and defence attorneys in an evaluation of the provision of defence service in capital cases in Florida.

than in some other states. During its 1985 mission to the USA, Amnesty International was informed that the maximum fee for assigned counsel in capital cases in Louisiana was only $1,000. The fees paid to assigned counsel in capital cases in Virginia are reported to be among the lowest in the country, averaging only $687 in 1985.[27] Amnesty International was told during its 1985 mission that the average fee for such cases in Texas was about $10,000 to $12,000, far less than the $50,000 minimum fee paid to a good privately-retained lawyer to try a capital case.

Successful law firms which can command high fees are therefore discouraged from taking on legal aid capital cases, which are usually assigned by judges to less experienced counsel. Amnesty International was told that it was not unusual — especially in rural areas — for lawyers handling capital cases to have had little or no experience in criminal law, and that many were ignorant of the special issues relating to capital punishment law. Although counsel assigned to capital cases in Louisiana must have five years' legal experience, this need not be in criminal law. The same applies in other states as well.

Concern was also expressed in several states to Amnesty International about a growing practice by judges of "contracting out" groups of indigent cases, including capital cases, to lawyers offering the lowest tender, thus accepting reductions in the time and resources available for each case. The American Bar Association (ABA) House of Delegates passed a resolution in February 1985 opposing "the awarding of governmental contracts for criminal defence services on the basis of cost alone, or through competitive bidding without reference to quality of representation". The resolution recommended that the awarding of government contracts for criminal defence services "should in addition to cost be based on qualitative criteria such as attorney workload maximums, staffing ratios, criminal law practice expertise and training supervision and compensation guidelines". However, ABA resolutions are not binding and Amnesty International is unaware of any change in state practice in this regard.

Public defenders, whose offices are often overworked and underfunded, may also lack sufficient resources to prepare and investigate a capital case. In 1983 Amnesty International was informed that one public defender in Oklahoma was handling most of the capital cases in the state; he said he had insufficient funds to investigate many of his clients' backgrounds or to interview important witnesses in some cases.

---

27. Reported by Ronald J. Tabak in a 1985 article, "The Death of Fairness: The Arbitrary and Capricious Imposition of Capital Punishment in the 1980s", published by Clearinghouse on Georgia Prisons and Jails, 2 January 1986.

The skills and resources of trial counsel can affect the outcome of a capital case in many ways, including the negotiation of plea bargains, presentation of an insanity defence and jury sentencing decisions. Court-appointed lawyers have been found less effective than privately retained counsel in negotiating pleas to lesser charges or in averting death sentences on defendants tried on capital charges. A recent study found that capital defendants in Texas with court-appointed lawyers were more than twice as likely to receive a death sentence than those with retained counsel (a ratio of 73:35).[28]

The trial lawyers representing a number of prisoners who were later executed were found to have spent very little time preparing the case for trial, often failing to interview potentially important witnesses or to raise mitigating factors at the sentencing hearing. The court-appointed attorney for Robert Wayne Williams, a black man executed by electrocution in Louisiana in December 1983, was reported to have spent a total of only eight hours preparing the case for trial. The trial lawyer representing Ernest Knighton, another black man executed by electrocution in Louisiana in October 1984, was reportedly handling 300 other cases at the same time.

Ronald J. Tabak, writing of his experience as an appeal attorney in a number of capital cases in the early 1980s, described the problems faced by "inexperienced, overworked and inadequately funded defense counsel" in capital trials. He pointed out that in many cases the court-appointed attorney representing a capital defendant is isolated in a small community which is outraged by the crime, and that some such attorneys fail to raise all their client's legal rights for fear of adverse reaction by the community or even the local judiciary. He also reported that some lawyers had lost potential paying clients while devoting resources to the trials of unpopular and penniless capital defendants. In such cases, lawyers might be disinclined to raise issues that threatened to prolong the trial. Many attorneys also devoted all their efforts to the trial and prepared no evidence or arguments for the sentencing phase.[29] The 1982 Florida Justice Institute study cited on p.42 also found that court-appointed lawyers, relying on judges for work and remuneration, often lacked the independence of other counsel and were less diligent in raising issues or objections that might prolong a case.

---

28. From Bruce Jackson's "Law and Disorder: Criminal Justice in America, 1984", cited in the September 1985 newsletter of the Illinois Coalition Against the Death Penalty. Bowers (*Legal Homicide*, p. 356) also found that court-appointed attorneys (whether private attorneys or public defenders) in Florida were less effective than retained counsel in averting death sentences at the trial stage.

29. See "The Death of Fairness", by Ronald J. Tabak, 23 December 1985, pp. 4-9, *op.cit.*

In a speech to a judicial conference in 1985, US Supreme Court Justice Thurgood Marshall strongly criticized the provision of defence services in capital cases, saying that many capital defendants "do not have a fair opportunity to defend their lives in the courtroom".[30] He said that trial lawyers:

". . . Whether appointed or retained — often are handling their first criminal cases, or their first murder cases, when confronted with the prospect of a death penalty. Though acting in good faith, they inevitably make very serious mistakes. Thus, in cases I have read, counsel have been unaware that certain death penalty issues are pending before the appellate courts and that the claims should be preserved; that certain findings by a jury might preclude imposition of a death penalty; or that a separate sentencing phase will follow a conviction. The federal courts are filled with stories of counsel who presented *no* evidence in mitigation of their client's sentence because they did not know what to offer or how to offer it, or had not read the state's sentencing statute. I kid you not; precisely this has happened time and again."

Concerned about the lack of adequate provision for defence services in capital trials, the ABA House of Delegates passed a resolution in February 1985 in which it recommended that two attorneys be appointed to represent defendants in the trial of death penalty cases, one of whom should have "substantial trial experience, which includes the trial of serious felony cases". A report prepared by the Criminal Justice Section of the ABA, which was attached to the resolution, set out draft guidelines in which it was stated that: "One of the most fundamental qualifications that should be possessed by appointed defense counsel in a death penalty case is criminal trial experience." One of the reasons given for recommending the appointment of a co-counsel was to provide both practical and emotional support for the primary counsel in such cases, in recognition of the fact that "the defense of a death penalty case is an intense experience for defense counsel because of the potential penalty involved."[31]

Although, in practice, there are sometimes two attorneys representing capital defendants, this does not happen in every jurisdiction and the ABA recommendations have not been formally adopted by

30. Remarks made at Judicial Conference of Second Circuit in Hershey, Pennsylvania, 6 September 1985.

31. Report to the ABA House of Delegates submitted by Paul T. Smith, Chairperson, ABA Criminal Justice Section, December 1984.

any state. Many defendants continue to be represented by attorneys with little or no criminal trial experience.

Problems of remedying errors on appeal

Most state government officials with whom Amnesty International raised these concerns during its 1985 mission denied that capital defendants were inadequately represented. They pointed out that lawyers often failed to raise possible defence issues for "tactical" reasons (leaving the state to prove its case against the defendants) and that serious errors would, in any event, be remedied on appeal.

However, there are procedural bars to appealing on the basis of issues which the defence counsel should have raised at the time of trial. Thus, failure to preserve a claim — by, for example, objecting at the proper time to alleged improprieties at the trial or to jury composition, trial venue or other alleged violations of a defendant's constitutional rights — may forfeit the defendant's right to have the claim considered on appeal, even though such failure by defence counsel may have jeopardized the fairness of the proceedings.

Failures such as those cited above might be grounds for appeal only if the defendant can show that errors by the defence counsel were so serious as to violate his or her constitutional right to "effective assistance of counsel". However, the US Supreme Court has laid down rigorous standards for overturning a conviction or sentence on these grounds. In *Strickland* v. *Washington* (May 1984), it held that, even if the trial counsel in a capital case were found to have erred, this would not merit a retrial unless the defendant could prove that the error had actually prejudiced the outcome of the case (see Appendix 8). Such proof is not always possible after the event and, in practice, only a minimal standard of competence by defence counsel is required by the courts. As Justice Marshall went on to point out in the speech cited above, the present standards relating to "ineffective assistance of counsel" do not even include recognition of a capital defendant's right to, and need of, a lawyer who is familiar with death penalty legislation.

The case of John Young, executed by electrocution in Georgia in March 1985, presents a disturbing example of failure by the appeal courts to remedy errors resulting from inadequate trial counsel.

John Young was convicted in 1976 of the murder of three elderly people when he was under the influence of drugs and alcohol; he was 18 at the time. The day before his last hearing, his original trial lawyer came forward and submitted an affidavit to the court in which he admitted spending "hardly any time preparing for the . . . case" due to a "myriad" of personal problems. The lawyer had, in fact, been disbarred from legal practice (on conviction of a drugs offence) days after the trial. In his affidavit, he stated that, among other things, he had completely failed to investigate his client's background or to raise any mitigating circumstances at the sentencing stage of the trial. These circumstances included the fact that, at the age of three, John Young had seen his mother being murdered while he was lying in bed with her; had afterwards been placed in the care of an alcoholic relative who turned him out on the streets at an early age; there he drifted into petty crime, child prostitution and drug abuse. The information about this early traumatic childhood would not have altered John Young's conviction had it been put to the jury, but might have affected its sentencing decision.

The US District Court and the Court of Appeals ruled that they could not consider the affidavit as new evidence because it should have been presented earlier. They failed to take into account the fact that, after his own conviction and disbarment, the trial lawyer had left Georgia and John Young's appeal counsel had been unable to trace him. Bruce Harvey, who was John Young's lawyer at the time of his execution, told Amnesty International that "the problem was not that we had new, powerful evidence; but that the courts simply would not consider it. It is, and remains to this day, the most frustrating, dehumanizing experience of my life."[32]

The fact that some defendants who are found guilty may receive lesser punishment owing to the skills of a particular defence attorney does not necessarily mean that others are unjustly condemned. However, in this instance, the failure to raise crucial mitigating evidence at the penalty phase of John Young's trial, as provided by statute, casts overwhelming doubt on the fairness of the sentence imposed.

Representation of capital defendants on appeal

In most states, state funding for the legal representation of capital defendants ceases after their sentences have been affirmed on direct

---

32. Commenting on the case in a letter to Amnesty International, Bruce Harvey said that John Young "was represented by a lawyer who was subsequently convicted on a drug charge and disbarred. This lawyer was using drugs during John's trial, was divorcing his wife, and proclaiming his homosexuality. However, immediately after his conviction and disbarment, he went 'underground', disappeared from Georgia and lived all over the United States. The day before John's last hearing, this lawyer resurfaced and signed an affidavit for us. He also appeared before the judge and — interrupting the proceeding — begged to be heard. He was not allowed to be heard. This short synopsis in no way conveys the travesty which occurred. The problem was not that we had new, powerful evidence; but that the courts simply would not consider it. It is, and remains to this day, the most frustrating, dehumanizing experience of my life."

appeal to the state supreme court.[33] Many prisoners are thus without a lawyer when their execution warrants are issued, and they may not have been able to file any post-conviction state or federal *habeas corpus* appeals at this stage. Since execution dates are usually issued about 28 days in advance of an execution, a prisoner may have only one month in which to find a lawyer to file an appeal and apply for a stay of execution.[34]

In practice, most *habeas corpus* appeals in capital cases are handled by lawyers recruited by organizations such as the ACLU or the New York-based LDF. The importance of having good legal representation at this stage is demonstrated by the relatively high proportion of death sentences which have been overturned by the federal courts since 1976 (see Chapter 7). This has been due largely to the efforts of a small network of lawyers prepared to take on capital appeals without pay, who have identified serious trial errors or important constitutional issues in many cases.

However, the growing number of prisoners exhausting their state appeals since the early 1980s has created a serious shortage of volunteer lawyers available for *habeas corpus* appeals in capital cases. The problem is especially acute in the southern states, where there are few local lawyers with either the funds or expertise to take on such cases. An ACLU lawyer in Texas told Amnesty International in 1985 that his local office was no longer able to pay the expenses of lawyers handling capital appeals. He and several other ACLU attorneys expressed concern that some prisoners in Texas and other southern states might in future be executed without having been able to obtain a lawyer or file any federal appeals.

The problem is increased by the fact that lawyers handling *habeas corpus* appeals in capital cases often have to work under onerous conditions. By the time a lawyer has been found to take on the case, he or she may have only days before a scheduled execution in which to read through the entire case record and prepare the grounds of appeal. Procedures approved by the US Supreme Court for hastening review of capital appeals in the federal courts (described in Chapter 7) mean that lawyers may have to present in the same emergency

---

33. In most states the practice is for court-appointed attorneys to file a routine petition of *certiorari* to the US Supreme Court before withdrawing from the case. Amnesty International has been told that these petitions (based on state trial error) are usually denied by the Supreme Court and it is at this point that execution warrants will normally be issued.

34. In some states execution warrants are issued at less than one month's notice; in Georgia, for example, execution warrants are issued 10 to 20 days in advance of the execution date.

petition the full merits of an appeal and all possible claims which are likely to have merit. An inexperienced lawyer may not have the capacity to identify, in so short a period, all issues having merit.

The shortage of lawyers at this stage can affect not only the chances of a prisoner pursuing appeals in the federal courts, but also preparation of material for review by the state pardons or clemency boards.

Amnesty International knows of only two states that provided funds for capital defendants pursuing *habeas corpus* appeals in 1985. The Florida legislature voted in 1985 to fund a state office of attorneys to take on post-conviction appeals in capital cases. It was established in October 1985 and provides legal assistance for capital defendants in Florida in their state and federal *habeas corpus* appeals. However, it was reported in March 1986 that the seven staff attorneys in this office were themselves having difficulties in meeting deadlines for filing *habeas corpus* appeals in such cases. This was due in part to the large backlog of pending cases and to the short time allowed for preparing cases for appeal once an execution warrant had been issued. As noted above, a death warrant may be signed at any time after a death sentence has been upheld on direct appeal to the state supreme court: although many Florida prisoners had reached this stage by the time the office was established, the lawyers were given no prior warning of when and in which cases the state governor would sign death warrants.

In California, an office funded by the California Supreme Court was established in the early 1980s to help find suitably qualified lawyers to handle death penalty cases on direct appeal to the state supreme court. Lawyers funded by this office were also handling some state and federal *habeas corpus* appeals in 1985.

Regional disparities in death sentencing

The uneven application of the death penalty is shown by the marked regional disparities in the rate at which death sentences are imposed for similar crimes. Where a crime was committed may have a greater influence on the imposition of a death sentence than the facts of the crime itself.

A study of criminal homicide cases in Georgia found, for example, that just 26, or 16 per cent, of Georgia's 159 counties were responsible for 85 per cent of death sentences imposed in the state from 1973 to 1978.[35] It also found that for both felony and non-felony-murder, death sentences were six times more likely to be

---

35. Study by Baldus, Pulaski and Woodworth, *op.cit.*

imposed in the more rural central region of Georgia than in the north, and seven to eight times more likely than in Fulton County in the north (which includes Atlanta, the state's capital and largest city). Although felony-murders were more characteristic of urban areas such as Fulton County and north Georgia, this area had the state's lowest rate of death sentencing. Death sentences were in fact far more likely to be imposed in rural areas, where homicides (especially capital homicides) were less frequent.

Similar findings were made by William J. Bowers in his study of Florida. He found that death sentences were less likely to be imposed in the southern region — including Miami, the area with the state's highest crime rate — than in comparable cases elsewhere in the state. There were marked regional disparities in both the rate at which Florida prosecutors charged offenders with first-degree murder (a potentially capital crime) and in the rate at which juries imposed death sentences on convicted capital offenders.

Similar differences are found in other states. A study of Louisiana, for example, found that juries in suburban parishes were far more likely to impose death sentences on convicted capital offenders than juries in New Orleans, where most such crimes occurred.[36] The victims in the more prosperous suburban parishes were also more likely to be white.

There is also a greater regional disparity nationwide in the imposition of the death penalty today than before. Whereas half of all executions during the 1920s and 1930s occurred in the southern states generally, and there was a high execution rate also in some other areas, just three states today — Florida, Texas and Georgia — account for more than two-thirds of all executions carried out in the USA since 1977. A fourth state, California, now has the USA's third largest death row, although no executions had been carried out under California's present (post-1972) statute at the time of writing.

Between them, these four states accounted for about half of all death sentences imposed in the USA from 1977 to 1985. Although there is a relatively high murder rate in the southern states, there are fewer capital-type murders than in some other areas, such as northern states with large urban-industrial bases.[37]

A US Department of Justice report, *Capital Punishment*, noted that nearly 63 per cent of those under sentence of death in 1984 were

36. Three-month study by the Louisiana *Times Picayune* newspaper, published in April 1985.

37. Although 42 per cent of murders reportedly occur in the south, fewer than one in five in Florida, Georgia and Texas are felony-related.

held by southern states; 21 per cent by western states; 12 per cent by north-central states and four per cent by northeastern states.[38]

Additional factors

This report has described some of the ways in which Amnesty International believes that the death penalty has been unevenly and unfairly applied. There may be other factors affecting the likelihood of a death sentence being imposed in one case as against another. In some areas, social class may contribute more to the likelihood of a death sentence being imposed than race. In general, the large majority of prisoners sentenced to death come from the very poorest sectors of society. In a study published in 1976, it was found that 62 per cent of prisoners sentenced to death since the 1972 *Furman* decision were unskilled, service or domestic workers, and only three per cent were professional or technical workers. Sixty per cent of those sentenced to death during that period were unemployed at the time the offence was committed.[39]

Men of all classes convicted of capital crimes are far more likely to be sentenced to death than women, of whom there were 22 on death row in 1985. Margie Barfield, executed by lethal injection in North Carolina in 1984, was the first woman to be executed in the USA for more than 40 years.

Very often, decisions leading to the imposition of death sentences may depend on a combination of chance circumstances. The arbitrariness of the death penalty is illustrated by two cases where the accomplices in murders by shooting were executed: in one, there was doubtful evidence of intent on the part of the subsequently executed prisoner that a killing should occur; in the other, the actual killer received a lesser sentence owing to fortuitous circumstances.

Roosevelt Green, a black man, was executed by electrocution in Georgia in March 1985, after being found guilty of involvement in a felony-murder. According to reports, he had not been present when the killing occurred. He claimed that he had gone to buy petrol when a co-defendant raped and murdered the victim, a young, white, female store worker, whom both men had taken hostage after robbing the store. In a report to the Georgia Supreme Court, the trial judge said that Roosevelt Green was only "an accomplice in a murder committed by another person and his participation in the homicidal

---

38. *Capital Punishment 1984*, US Department of Justice Bureau of Justice Statistics bulletin, August 1985.

39. Study by Marc Riedel in *Temple Law Quarterly* (1976), cited in Hugo A. Bedau's *The Case Against the Death Penalty*, ACLU, New York, 1977.

act was relatively minor". However, the Georgia Supreme Court upheld his death sentence on a finding that he should not have left the victim alone with a man he knew to be dangerous. He went to his execution protesting his innocence of the murder. His co-defendant (also sentenced to death) was still on death row in May 1986.

In 1974 two Texas prisoners, both white, were found guilty of the murder of an undercover police agent. One, Doyle Skillern, was executed by lethal injection in January 1985. His accomplice, who had fired the six shots that killed the agent while Doyle Skillern sat in a nearby car, received a life sentence. Both men were tried twice: at the first trial the jury did not know which of the two had carried out the killing. Although both defendants were found equally guilty of having planned the killing, Doyle Skillern alone was sentenced to death, under the Texas statutory provision of "future dangerousness" (see Chapter 2): he had previously been sentenced to five years' imprisonment for killing his brother. Both sentences were later overturned on a point of law. At the second trial, the full facts were presented to the jury, who sentenced both men to death. However, the death sentence imposed on Doyle Skillern's accomplice was later 'overturned under the law relating to "double-jeopardy".[40] At the time of Doyle Skillern's execution, over 10 years after the crime, his co-accused was soon due to be eligible for parole.

Proponents of the death penalty have argued that disparities based on chance, the relative skills of legal counsel or other factors are inevitable in any criminal justice system, and they point out that, if anything, the system errs in favour of guilty defendants escaping the death penalty. (Following on from this, some people have even argued that the death penalty should be made more widely available by removing some of the procedural rights afforded to capital defendants, particularly on appeal.) However, there are cases where, by the standards agreed by the US Supreme Court in setting guidelines reinstating the death penalty, that penalty has appeared particularly inappropriate or unfair. If the death penalty were intended to be reserved, not only for the worst crimes, but also the very "worst" and most culpable offenders, it is difficult to justify its imposition on people who participated in a contemporaneous offence but did not commit or plan any killing; on people whose cases had

---

40. The Fifth Amendment to the US Constitution provides, *inter alia*, that "No person shall . . . be subject for the same offense to be twice put in jeopardy of life or limb . . ." The Supreme Court has held that the constitutional protection against "double jeopardy" prohibits the state from sentencing a defendant to death after a life sentence has been set aside on appeal (*Bullington* v. *Missouri*, 451 U.S. 430 (1981), and *Arizona* v. *Rumsey*, 104 S. Ct. 2305 (1985).

strong mitigating circumstances that were not revealed at the sentencing stages of the trials; on defendants who were offered pleas to lesser charges (and turned them down) or — as described elsewhere in this report — on defendants who exhibited signs of severe mental illness or retardation, or were juveniles at the time of the offence.

There is also evidence, described in more detail below, to suggest that the death penalty is applied in a manner which persistently discriminates on racial grounds.

There must be serious doubts about the fairness and effectiveness of the criminal justice system when race, place, social class or chance consistently play a larger part in determining a death sentence than the facts of the crime or the character and circumstances of the defendant.

Racial discrimination and the death penalty

As shown above, there was considerable evidence of racial discrimination in the application of the death penalty before 1967 — especially in the southern states. The last chapter noted apparent continuing racial disparities in charging decisions in some states, and the under-representation of blacks or other minorities on juries in capital trials. In fact, there is evidence to suggest that the death penalty continues to be applied in a way which systematically discriminates on racial grounds, although disparities based on race of offender alone appear to have diminished under the present statutes.

Some 48 per cent of the nation's death row population in 1985 were blacks or members of other minorities, although they made up only 12 per cent of the population.[1] The proportion of blacks on death row is much higher in some individual states. However, statistics on race of offender alone do not necessarily indicate bias, given that roughly 50 per cent of all those arrested for murder are black.

Nevertheless, wide disparities are revealed when considering the race of the victim in cases where the death penalty has been imposed. Although blacks and whites are also the victims of homicide in almost equal numbers, the large majority of offenders sentenced to death have been convicted of murdering whites. Forty-six (92 per cent) of the 50 prisoners executed between 1977 and 1985, for example, had been convicted of killing whites, as had 77 per cent of the prisoners on death row nationally in 1985.

Furthermore, blacks who kill whites have been found more likely

---

1. The racial breakdown of the US death row population in May 1986 was as follows (percentages): Black – 41.25; White – 50.82; Hispanic – 5.83; Native American – 1.34; Asian – 0.35; Unknown – 0.41. (Figures published by the NAACP Legal Defense and Educational Fund Inc.) The proportion of blacks on death row was much higher in some states. In Alabama, for example, 67 per cent of death row inmates in 1986 were black (55 out of 82 prisoners). Over 50 per cent of death row inmates in Georgia, Illinois, Mississippi, North Carolina, South Carolina and Pennsylvania were black. In California and Texas a relatively high proportion of death row inmates were Hispanics, reflecting the relatively high proportion of the minority population in these states.

to be sentenced to death than any other category of offender; whites, on the other hand, have rarely been sentenced to death for killing blacks.

State governments have maintained that these disparities are due entirely to differences in the types of crime committed by or against members of different racial groups. This is likely to account for some of the racial disparities in sentencing, especially as regards the victim's race. National crime reporting data suggest, for example, that whites may constitute a greater proportion of felony-murder victims (the types of homicide for which death sentences are most frequently imposed) than other racial groups. Blacks, who are generally poorer and have a higher unemployment rate, are less likely to be the victims of murders which occur in circumstances for which the death penalty is available (such as murder during the commission of a robbery, or murder for pecuniary gain).

However, a number of research studies have isolated race as a factor in death sentencing, after allowing for differences in the types of homicide. The findings of some of these studies are summarized below.

Recent studies on racial disparities in death sentencing

In the late 1970s William J. Bowers and Glenn L. Pierce, Director and Assistant Director, respectively, of the Center for Applied Social Research at Northeastern University, Boston, compared statistics on all criminal homicides and death sentences imposed in Florida, Georgia, Texas and Ohio from the dates their respective post-*Furman* statutes came into effect (between 1973 and 1974) up to December 1977.[2] Death sentences in these four states accounted for 70 per cent of all death sentences imposed nationally at this time. Bowers and Pierce found that, as in other states, the large majority of homicides were "intra-racial", committed within the same racial group. Although there was a high homicide rate among both whites and blacks in all four states examined, far more killers of whites than killers of blacks were sentenced to death. They also found that,

2. William Bowers and Glenn Pierce: "Arbitrariness and Discrimination under Post-*Furman* Capital Statutes", in *Crime and Delinquency*, vol. 26, No. 4, October 1980, pp. 563-635; also reproduced in *Legal Homicide: Death as a Punishment in America 1864-1982*, by William Bowers, Northeastern University Press, 1984. Although the death penalty statutes in Florida, Georgia and Texas were not ruled constitutional until the US Supreme Court decision in 1976 (*Gregg* v. *Georgia*), the statutes themselves pre-dated this ruling, having been introduced as follows: Florida, December 1972; Georgia, March 1973; Texas, June 1973; Ohio, January 1974 (ruled unconstitutional in 1978 and amended in 1981).

although most killers of whites were white, blacks killing whites were proportionately more likely to receive a death sentence.

In Florida and Texas, for example, blacks who killed whites were, respectively, five and six times more likely to be sentenced to death than whites who had killed whites. Among black offenders in Florida, those who had killed whites were 40 times more likely to get the death penalty than those who had killed blacks. No white offender in Florida had ever been sentenced to death for killing a black person during the period studied.[3] The findings were similar in the other two states.

Researchers Samuel Gross and Robert Mauro also looked at later figures for the race of victims in criminal homicide cases in eight states from 1976 to 1980: Arkansas, Florida, Georgia, Illinois, Mississippi, North Carolina, Oklahoma and Virginia. They found that homicides with white victims resulted in death sentences from 2.3 to nearly nine times more often than in cases with black victims.[4]

As mentioned above, state prosecuting authorities have argued that these disparities result from differences in the types of homicide committed by blacks and because cases with white victims are more likely to be capital crimes. It has also been argued that, in non-felony cases, murders committed across racial lines (in which statistically more blacks kill whites than whites kill blacks), usually involving strangers, are likely to be more aggravated than those within racial groups.

The Attorney General of Florida used some of the above arguments in a case brought before the federal courts in September 1977. The petitioner was John Spenkelink (later executed) who, as a white who had killed a white, argued that more than 90 per cent of prisoners on Florida's death row at that time had killed whites, demonstrating that the application of the post-*Furman* Florida statute was discriminatory. The Attorney General argued that black murders were qualitatively different, and more likely to result from "family quarrels, lovers' quarrels, liquor quarrels and bar-room brawls".[5] The former Fifth Circuit Court of Appeals denied Spenkelink's discri-

---

3. A white man sentenced to death in Florida in 1980 for killing a black woman was the first white person in the state's history to be sentenced to death for killing a black victim only.

4. Samuel R. Gross and Robert Mauro: *Patterns of Death: an Analysis of Racial Disparities in Capital Sentencing and Homicide Victimization*, 37 Stanford Law Review, 1984.

5. *Spinkellink* v. *Wainwright* 578 F.2d 582 (Fifth Circuit 1978). The court's spelling of the petitioner's name is incorrect; the correct spelling, as given elsewhere in this report, is "Spenkelink". (The federal judicial circuits have since been changed and Florida now falls under the Eleventh Circuit.)

mination claim, stating that the data produced by the NAACP Legal Defense Fund (LDF) in support of his case was insufficient to demonstrate intent to discriminate in an individual case.

However, several studies have since attempted to measure racial factors in otherwise similar capital crimes. The study conducted by the Northeastern University team cited above went on to compare race-of-victim/race-of-offender ratios in felony-murders only, in Texas, Florida and Georgia. They found that significant disparities in the rate of death sentencing based on the victim's race persisted.

These results were consistent with the findings of a Florida study conducted in 1981 by Michael Radelet, Professor of Sociology at the University of Florida, Gainesville. He examined all homicide indictments in 20 Florida counties in 1976 and 1977, focussing only on those cases involving what he termed "non-primary" homicides (killings of strangers, usually felony-related): 326 cases. Of these "non-primary" homicides, 5.4 per cent of cases with black victims resulted in death sentences, compared to 14 per cent of cases with white victims. He also found that 53.6 per cent of cases with black victims resulted in first-degree murder indictments, compared to 85 per cent of cases with white victims.[6]

Hans Zeisel, Professor of Law at the University of Chicago Law School, also looked at arrests in Florida for felony-murders only, comparing them with the number of prisoners on death row in September 1977 (at the time of the Spenkelink appeal). He found that at that time 47 per cent of black defendants and only 24 per cent of white defendants arrested for murdering whites in a felony circumstance ended up on death row.[7]

Georgia study

Studies of the operation of Georgia's capital sentencing system, conducted in the early 1980s by Professor David Baldus, Professor of Law at the University of Iowa, provided the most detailed analysis of racial disparities in death sentencing at the time of writing. Professor Baldus, in collaboration with two colleagues, Dr George Woodworth and Professor Charles Pulaski,[8] aimed to discover why killers of white victims in Georgia during the 1970s had received the death penalty approximately 11 times more often than killers of blacks, taking into

6. Michael Radelet, "Racial Characteristics and the Imposition of the Death Penalty", 46 *American Society Review* 918 (1981).

7. Hans Zeisel, "Race Bias in the Administration of the Death Penalty: The Florida Experience", 95 *Harvard Law Review* 456 (1981).

8. At the time of writing Dr Woodworth was Associate Professor of Statistics, University of Iowa, and Professor Pulaski was Professor of Criminal Law, Arizona State University.

account the possibility that different levels of aggravation within potentially capital murders could explain the difference in sentencing.

Professor Baldus and his associates examined data on all homicide cases in Georgia from 1973 to 1979 from indictment to sentencing.[9] In an effort to assess whether race played an independent role in sentencing, they subjected each case to a series of rigorous tests, matching the known facts against all possible factors which might play a role in determining sentence. More than 230 control factors were identified, including statutory and non-statutory aggravating and mitigating circumstances, weight of evidence, the defendant's background and prior record, race of defendant and victim, geographical area, and chance.[10]

The team started with a pool of more than 2,000 cases, which they divided into groups according to rising levels of aggravation. They found that most fell into categories involving levels of aggravation so low that almost no one received the death penalty: in these cases no significant racial impact could therefore be deduced.

However, the team identified some 400 aggravated homicide cases, each of which involved potentially capital circumstances. They found that no significant racial disparities in sentencing appeared in the most highly aggravated cases (a relatively small number of homicides involving three or more statutory aggravating circumstances, such as a serious additional felony, multiple victims and torture). Although most of the victims in such cases were white, the severity of the crime at this level of aggravation was more important than the victim's race. These were also cases in which the death penalty was most frequently imposed.

However, the team identified a mid-range of cases with intermedi-

9. Baldus and his associates first measured for racial disparities in sentencing in the cases of all defendants convicted of murder from March 1973 to July 1978. (The Georgia statute has no degrees of murder and anyone tried on a murder charge may face the death penalty, provided aggravating factors are present.) The study was then expanded to cover all homicide cases resulting in murder or manslaughter convictions from 1973 to 1979, and included information on prosecutors' plea bargaining decisions as well as jury guilt and sentencing determinations. From an initial pool of 2,484 cases, the team drew a sample of 1,066 cases, which they subjected to the most rigorous series of tests. This sample comprised all cases where defendants were convicted of murder and sentenced to death or life imprisonment after a penalty hearing; 41 per cent of cases where convicted murderers received automatic life sentences without a penalty hearing, and 35 per cent of cases resulting in voluntary manslaughter convictions (some of which were originally charged as murder).

10. The data included information from official records of the Georgia Supreme Court, the Georgia Department of Offender Rehabilitation, the Department of Probations and Paroles, the Georgia Bureau of Vital Statistics, all other relevant court records and detailed attorney questionnaires.

ate levels of aggravation, in which death sentences were also imposed. These cases — in which there was most room for discretion — comprised the bulk of the 400 potentially capital cases. In this range of cases Professor Baldus found that offenders with white victims were 20 per cent more likely to receive death sentences than those with black victims, at similar levels of aggravation. In fact, the victim's race at this level was more important than several of Georgia's 10 statutory aggravating circumstances. The team also found at this level that black defendants were more likely to receive a death sentence than similar white defendants.

Professor Baldus then examined the outcome of homicide cases at each stage after arrest to see at what procedural points the racial disparities manifested themselves.

He observed that the proportion of white-victim murder cases rose sharply as the cases advanced through the system, from 39 per cent at indictment to 84 per cent at death sentencing. The proportion of black-offender/white-victim cases rose even faster from nine per cent at indictment to 39 per cent at death sentencing. He found that the two most significant points affecting the likelihood of an eventual death sentence were prosecutors' decisions on (1) whether or not to permit pleas to voluntary manslaughter, and (2) whether to seek a penalty hearing in cases where defendants were convicted of murder. Thus, racial disparities manifested themselves at every stage of the judicial process, from indictment to sentencing, with black-victim cases being more likely to result in pleas to manslaughter or life sentences on conviction of murder, than cases with white victims; black defendants with white victims were less likely than others to have their charges reduced and more likely, on conviction of murder, to receive death sentences.

In his earlier review of Georgia's Supreme Court decisions (see Chapters 3 and 7), Professor Baldus had noted that Georgia prosecutors had sought the death penalty in only 40 per cent of cases where defendants were convicted of a capital crime: the others received automatic life sentences without a penalty hearing. He found that, although cases with white victims tended to be more aggravated in general, the levels of aggravation in crimes involving black victims had to be substantially higher before the prosecutors sought the death penalty and a penalty hearing. Overall disparities in death sentencing were thus due more to prosecutors' charging and sentencing recommendations than to jury sentencing decisions.

Appeal to the federal courts on racial discrimination

The Georgia findings were used in support of an appeal to the

60

Eleventh Circuit Federal Court of Appeals brought by the LDF on behalf of Warren McCleskey, a black man sentenced to death for killing a white Atlanta police officer. Warren McCleskey claimed that the discriminatory application of Georgia's death penalty statute violated both the Eighth Amendment's prohibition of cruel and unusual punishment and his Fourteenth Amendment right to equal protection of the law.[11] In a nine-to-three decision given in January 1985, the appeals court rejected the claim that Georgia had unconstitutionally discriminated against the petitioner on account of race.

The court, which reviewed the Georgia study in some detail, did not dispute its findings, stating: "the statistics show there is a race-of-the-victim relationship with the imposition of the death sentence *discernible enough in cases to be statistically significant in the system as a whole*", but "the magnitude cannot be called determinative *in any given case*" (emphasis added). The court held that, because there was no proof that the state had *intentionally* discriminated against the defendant, there could be no constitutional violation of his rights.

The appeals court acknowledged that direct proof of discriminatory intent by the state might not be required if the statistical evidence was "so strong as to permit no other inference than that the results are the product of a racially discriminatory intent or purpose". However, it said that: "The key to the problem lies in the principle that the proof, no matter how strong, of some disparity is alone insufficient." It concluded that the 20 per cent racial disparity in sentencing among similar offenders in the mid-range of aggravated homicides was insufficient to find that the operation of the Georgia death penalty statute as a whole was unconstitutional.

Indeed, the court went on to say that:

> "The marginal disparity based on race of victim tends to
> support the state's contention that the system is working far
> differently from the one which *Furman* condemned. In
> pre-*Furman* days, there was no rhyme or reason as to who got
> the death penalty and who did not. But now, in the vast

---

11. A study by Professor Baldus of similar cases in Fulton County, where Warren McCleskey was tried, was also used in the appeal. This showed that 17 other Fulton County defendants had been charged with the homicide of a police officer between 1973 and 1979. Only two of these defendants even went to a penalty hearing: one, whose police victim was black, received a life sentence, the other, whose victim was white, got a death sentence.

majority of cases, the reasons for a difference are well-documented."[12]

Three judges, Judges Johnson, Hatchett and Clark, filed separate dissenting opinions in which they expressed the view that the evidence of discrimination among the mid-range of aggravated homicide cases was sufficient to show that the Georgia statute operated unconstitutionally. As Judge Clark pointed out, race had no effect in the large majority of cases because "the facts are so mitigated that the death penalty is not even considered as a possible punishment". Judge Hatchett found that the 20 per cent racial disparity among the middle range of cases, in which "decision on the proper sentence is most difficult and the imposition of the death penalty most questionable" was "intolerable". He said:

"To allow this system to stand is to concede that in a certain number of cases the consideration of race will be a factor in the decision whether to impose the death penalty. The Equal Protection Clause of the Fourteenth Amendment does not allow this result."

Judge Johnson, who wrote the longest dissent, addressed the question of discriminatory intent, expressing the view that a finding of intent was not necessary to show an Eighth Amendment violation. However, he said that, even if this were necessary ". . . under any reasonable definition of intent, the Baldus study provides sufficient proof. The majority ignores the fact that McCleskey has shown discriminatory intent at work in the sentencing system even though he has not pointed to any specific act or actor responsible for discriminating against him." He added that the study showed:

". . . a clear pattern of sentencing that can only be explained in terms of race and it does so in a context where direct evidence of intent is practically impossible to obtain. It strains the imagination to believe that the significant influence on sentencing left unexplained by 230 alternative factors is random rather than racial, especially in a state with an established history of racial discrimination."

Warren McCleskey appealed to the US Supreme Court against the decision in May 1985. More than a year later, in July 1986, the Supreme Court announced that it would hear the appeal. Among the issues the Supreme Court agreed to review were whether proof of specific intent was necessary to sustain a constitutional claim of racial

---

12. The 1972 US Supreme Court *Furman* decision ruled that most state death penalty laws then were unconstitutional (see Chapter 1).

discrimination; whether a "proven disparity" in death sentencing was unconstitutional "irrespective of magnitude" and whether — as Warren McCleskey's lawyers argued — the 20 per cent disparity "among that class of cases in which a death sentence is a serious possibility" so undermined the fairness of Georgia's capital sentencing system as to "violate the Eighth or Fourteenth Amendment rights of a death-sentenced black defendant in that class of cases".[13]

The Supreme Court's ruling on these questions — which was not expected to be given until at least the end of 1986 — will have an important bearing on the cases of many prisoners under sentence of death who have raised racial discrimination claims. Several prisoners in Georgia and other states whose execution dates were imminent when the Supreme Court granted *certiorari* in *McCleskey* were granted stays pending the decision.

Summary and comment

The findings of research conducted in a number of different US states since 1979 are consistent in showing that homicides with white victims are far more likely to result in death sentences than those with black victims. Although some of this disparity may be explained by higher levels of aggravation in homicides committed against whites, researchers have found that an independent racial factor remains in cases that are otherwise similar. Differential treatment was found to occur throughout the judicial process, especially at the indictment stage. Black defendants with white victims were also found to be more likely to receive death sentences than white defendants in similar situations.

There are a number of problems in providing statistical proof of discrimination, especially when this may occur through discretionary decisions taken early in the judicial process. Prosecutors' decisions to permit guilty pleas to non-capital offences (or to charge an offender with a lesser offence such as manslaughter or second-degree murder) may involve the removal of additional felonies from the charge sheet, for example. Also, in some states (for instance, Florida) aggravating circumstances accompanying a potentially capital charge need not be listed on the indictment and may be raised at the time of trial only if the prosecutor decides to seek the death penalty. Thus, the true level of differential treatment may not be readily apparent in the trial record. As noted in Chapter 3, several Florida researchers have tried to match initial police records with later court charging decisions. However, such research requires exhaustive investigation of all

---

13. Warren McCleskey's own case was found to fall within the mid-range of aggravated homicide cases.

possible circumstances that may lead to the imposition of capital or non-capital charges.

The difficulties in trying to obtain complete data on the disposition of potentially capital cases are illustrated by an order issued by a California judge on 26 June 1986. In investigating a *habeas corpus* claim that the California death penalty law discriminated against a defendant on racial grounds (in the case of Earl Lloyd Jackson) the judge ordered the state Attorney General to provide the court with a record of all cases involving potentially capital circumstances which were disposed of through plea bargains or convictions for non-capital offences since the enactment of the state death penalty law in 1977. The order asked the Attorney General and the Los Angeles District Attorney to turn over the name, case number and county where charges were brought in all cases: where a defendant was convicted of first- or second-degree murder or manslaughter after having original-ly been accused of murder with special circumstances; where a defendant was convicted of first- or second-degree murder or manslaughter where additional felonies were involved; and where defendants convicted of first-degree murder had prior murder convictions.[14] The Attorney General appealed against the order on the grounds that it would be too difficult and costly an operation, involving the compilation of data on more than 10,000 cases in numerous state counties. A motion against the order was denied by the court and the Attorney General given until May 1986 to comply. The outcome of the order and the appeal were still pending at the time of writing.

The Georgia study has tried to measure for such circumstances by obtaining data from the widest possible sources. Detailed information relating to the crime, defendant and victim was obtained, for example, from the Georgia Department of Pardons and Paroles, which keeps a record of more information than that necessarily given in the court records. Additional supplementary information was obtained from the Department of Offender Rehabilitation and the Georgia Bureau of Vital Statistics. The study, while limited to the state of Georgia, is by far the most comprehensive conducted so far.

Amnesty International finds it disturbing that the study's findings of racial disparities in the mid-range of aggravated homicide cases in Georgia were deemed by the Eleventh Circuit Court of Appeals to be of insufficient magnitude to cast doubt on the system as a whole. It is precisely in this range of cases — where prosecutors and juries have most room for discretion in their charging or sentencing decisions —

---

14. All these cases involved circumstances which made the homicides eligible for the death penalty under the California statute.

that discrimination is most likely to occur. By using as a yardstick a system that was fundamentally irrational (as its reference to the pre-*Furman* statutes suggests — see quotation from the court's decision on p.60), the court appeared to tolerate a somewhat lower level of unfairness in the present system.

If the courts are unable to resolve the question of racial discrimination on the evidence presented so far, this should be the subject of urgent examination by the executive or legislative authorities at both state and federal level.

Death sentences imposed on juveniles

On 11 September 1985 in Texas, Charles Rumbaugh became the first juvenile offender to be executed in the USA since 1964. He had been condemned to death in 1980 for a murder committed during the course of a robbery when he was 17 years old and thus still a minor. Two more juvenile offenders were executed in the first half of 1986; both were also 17 when the crimes were committed. James Terry Roach was executed in South Carolina on 10 January 1986 and Jay Pinkerton was executed in Texas on 15 May 1986. At least 32 other juvenile offenders were under sentence of death in 15 states at the time of writing. Their ages ranged from 15 to 17 when the crimes were committed.

The imposition of death sentences on minors is in clear contravention of international human rights treaties and standards. Article 6(5) of the International Covenant on Civil and Political Rights (ICCPR) states:

"Sentence of death shall not be imposed for crimes committed by persons below eighteen years of age and shall not be carried out on pregnant women."

Article 4(5) of the American Convention on Human Rights (ACHR) contains a similar provision stating:

"Capital punishment shall not be imposed upon persons who, at the time the crime was committed, were under 18 years of age or over 70 years of age; nor shall it be applied to pregnant women."

The United States Government signed both these treaties in 1977 but has not yet ratified them.

On 25 May 1984 the United Nations Economic and Social Council (ECOSOC) adopted a series of "Safeguards Guaranteeing Protection of the Rights of Those Facing the Death Penalty", which includes similar reference to the age limit of 18. Safeguard No. 3 states:

"Persons below 18 years of age at the time of the commission of the crime shall not be sentenced to death . . .".[1]

Minors are also exempt from the death penalty under the 1949 Geneva Convention concerning the protection of civilians in time of war, which has been ratified by the US Government. It provides that:

". . . the death penalty may not be pronounced on a protected person who was under eighteen years of age at the time of the offence."[2]

Despite these provisions, only nine US states with death penalty laws prohibit the imposition of the death penalty on people aged under 18: California, Colorado, Connecticut, Illinois, Nebraska, New Mexico, Ohio, Tennessee and, more recently, New Jersey.

Seventeen states have set a minimum age under 18, either in the capital statutes themselves or under laws specifying the age at which juveniles may be tried in the adult criminal courts for certain offences. The age limit at which a death sentence may be imposed in these states ranges from 10 years in Indiana and Vermont to 17 years in Texas, Georgia and New Hampshire. The others set the age limit variously from 12 to 16 years.[3]

A further 11 states have no specified minimum age limit at which the death penalty may be imposed.[4]

Although in most states youth is given as a mitigating factor at the sentencing phase of capital trials, this has not prevented death sentences from being imposed on minors. Florida, for example, which has no age limit but lists age as a mitigating factor in capital trials, has sentenced nine minors to death under its present statute, although only three remained on death row at the time of writing (most others having had their sentences reduced on appeal by the

1. ECOSOC Resolution 1984/50, 25 May 1984.

2. The Geneva Convention is not applicable to circumstances occurring other than at time of war, but is cited as evidence of the generally accepted nature of the international standard on juveniles and the death penalty.

3. Minimum age at which offenders may be tried in the adult criminal courts for specified offences, which include capital crimes: 10 years in Indiana and Vermont; 12 years in Montana; 13 years in Mississippi; 14 years in Alabama, Idaho, Kentucky, Missouri, North Carolina and Utah; 15 years in Arkansas, Louisiana and Virginia. (Vermont's death penalty law is a pre-*Furman* statute which, though still in the code, may be invalid). Minimum age specified in capital punishment statutes: 16 years in Nevada; 17 years in Georgia, New Hampshire and Texas. Sources: Victor L. Streib: "Minimum Statutory Ages for the Death Penalty", dated March 1982 and additional information collected by Amnesty International.

4. States with no specified age limit are are Arizona, Delaware, Florida, Maryland, Oklahoma, Oregon, Pennsylvania, South Carolina, South Dakota, Washington and Wyoming.

state supreme court).

Three states, Delaware, Oklahoma and South Dakota, have no minimum age and youth is not explicitly listed as a mitigating factor at the sentencing stage of capital trials.

The 32 juveniles on death row in the USA in May 1986 were sentenced to death for murders, most of which were committed under particularly brutal circumstances. Amnesty International does not suggest that criminal liability necessarily be removed from juveniles convicted of serious crimes. However, international standards prohibiting the execution of juveniles were developed in recognition of the fact that the death penalty — with its uniquely cruel and irreversible character — is a wholly inappropriate penalty for individuals who have not attained full physical or emotional maturity at the time of their actions. In a July 1985 letter appealing to the Governor of Texas for clemency in the cases of nine juveniles then on death row in Texas, Amnesty International stated: "However heinous the crime, the imposition on a young person of a sentence of the utmost cruelty, which denies the possibility of rehabilitation or reform, is contrary to contemporary standards of justice and humane treatment."[5] Amnesty International pointed out that: "While a person's level of maturity or potential for development or reform may vary widely according to circumstance, the age limit set in the above treaties is the *minimum* age at which international opinion is agreed that the death penalty should be inapplicable in all circumstances: a number of jurisdictions have set the age limit at more than 18 years."

Children and adolescents are widely recognized as being less responsible for their actions than adults, and more susceptible to rehabilitation,[6] thus rendering the death penalty a particularly inhuman punishment in their cases. Criminologists have also noted

---

5. Letter dated 11 July 1985 to Governor Mark White.

6. The reduced responsibility of children and adolescents is widely recognized in laws and practice and is discussed in numerous criminological and legal journals.

A recent US Supreme Court judgment contained the following observation: ". . . youth is more than a chronological fact. It is a time and condition of life when a person may be most susceptible to influence and to psychological damage. Our history is replete with laws and judicial recognition that minors, especially in their earlier years, generally are less mature and responsible than adults. Particularly during the formative years of childhood and adolescence, minors often lack the experience, perspective and judgement expected of adults. Even the normal 16 year old customarily lacks the maturity of an adult." (*Eddings* v. *Oklahoma*, 1982)

A Presidential Committee reporting on youth crime concluded that: ". . . adolescents, particularly in the early and middle teen years, are more vulnerable, more impulsive and less self-disciplined than adults. Crimes committed by youths may be just as harmful to victims as those committed by older persons, but they deserve less punishment because adolescents have less capacity to control

68

that arguments used to support the death penalty are especially inapplicable in the case of young people. It is recognized, for example, that children and adolescents are more liable than adults to act on impulse, or under the influence or domination of others, with little thought for the long-term consequences of their actions, and they are unlikely to be deterred by the penalty. Many young people who commit brutal crimes themselves come from brutalizing and deprived backgrounds. To impose the death penalty in such cases, whether as retribution or as an intended deterrent, violates basic principles of humanity.

Although no minor was executed in the USA for more than 20 years after 1964, such executions have been carried out with relative frequency in recent American history. Nearly 200 minors have been executed in the USA since 1900 — the large majority being black.[7] Executions dating from the 19th to the mid-20th century include more than 40 black juveniles executed in the southern states for the (non-homicide) rape of white women. The youngest person to be executed this century was George Stinney, who was black and was only 14 years old when he was electrocuted in South Carolina in 1944 for the murder of two white girls. He had no lawyer to lodge an appeal and was executed despite numerous appeals for clemency from people in South Carolina and elsewhere in the USA. The last execution of a juvenile before 1985 took place in May 1964, when James Andrew Echols (black) was executed in Texas for raping a white woman when he was 17.

Of the 32 juvenile offenders known to be under sentence of death in May 1986, six were in Texas; four in Georgia and between one and three in each of 13 other states. Four were aged 15 at the time of the crime (in Arkansas, Pennsylvania, Oklahoma and North Carolina). Five others were aged 16. Eighteen (56 per cent) were blacks and nearly all had been convicted of murdering whites. Several had spent more than eight years on death row.

The confinement of juveniles on death row and the conditions under which condemned prisoners are held is cause for additional concern.[8]

---

their conduct and think in long-range terms than adults." (Task Force on Sentencing Policy Toward Young Offenders, Confronting Youth Crime (1978); extract cited in an article by Helena B. Greenwald, "Capital Punishment for Minors: An Eighth Amendment Analysis", *JCLC*, vol. 74, No. 4, 1983.)

7. The ABA reported in 1983 that 191 juvenile offenders had been executed between 1900 and 1964 (p. 9 of Report to the House of Delegates by the Criminal Justice Section of the ABA, August 1983, on capital punishment and juveniles). Victor Streib, Professor of Law and a researcher into juvenile justice and the death penalty, gives a figure of 192 for the same period (*Oklahoma Law Review*, vol. 36: 613, 1983).

8. Conditions on many death rows, with no rehabilitation programs, long periods

Although, internationally, general practice is to exempt juveniles from the death penalty, this is not the case in the USA. The ABA noted in 1983 that death sentences were being imposed on minors with increasing frequency, in line with an increase in the number of juveniles prosecuted in the adult criminal courts. The number of juveniles on death row in the early 1980s reportedly exceeded that of any earlier period.[9]

In Maryland, a bill to exempt juveniles from the death penalty was defeated by the state senate in February 1985. However, New Jersey passed legislation in January 1986 prohibiting imposition of the death penalty on people aged under 18 at the time of the crime. (The minimum age before this provision was 14, the age at which a juvenile could be tried in a criminal court and sentenced as an adult.) However, a juvenile offender, Marco Bey, remained on death row at the time of writing. Amnesty International was informed that the revised New Jersey legislation did not apply retroactively; it believes that this, too, is contrary to international standards.[10] Article 15(1) of the ICCPR states that:

"If, subsequent to the commission of the offence, provision is made by law for the imposition of the lighter penalty, the offender shall benefit thereby."

Article 9 of the ACHR and safeguard 2 of the ECOSOC Resolution 1984/50 on the death penalty contain similar provisions. There is nothing in the text to suggest that the last sentence of Article 15(1) of the ICCPR should be understood to apply only to situations where lighter sentences become applicable before sentence is passed. Indeed, a proposal that would have rephrased the language of what became the present text so as to envisage such a restriction was

---

of confinement to cells, and restricted or no educational programs are especially unsuitable for juvenile offenders. Although rehabilitation is considered irrelevant to prisoners under sentence of death, juvenile offenders have sometimes spent years in such conditions before having their sentences reduced on appeal. Both Charles Rumbaugh and Terry Roach had spent more than eight years on death row before they were executed. The confinement of juveniles on death row also almost certainly contravenes the United Nations Standard Minimum Rules for the Treatment of Prisoners, Article 8 (d) of which states: "Young prisoners shall be kept separate from adults."

9. Although this is partly due to the length of appeals in capital cases, lawyers have also reported an increase in the number of juveniles being sentenced to death each year.

10. Amnesty International has been informed that Marco Bey is also under a death sentence for a crime committed after he reached the age of 18, which would also account for his remaining on death row.

defeated. It must, therefore, be presumed that no such restriction was intended.[11]

US domestic standards

Although most state laws allow the execution of minors, a significant body of opinion in the USA has rejected the use of capital punishment in such cases.

The ABA, which has not taken a formal position on other aspects of the death penalty, adopted a resolution in August 1983, opposing, in principle ". . . the imposition of capital punishment upon any person for an offense committed while under the age of 18". In a report to the ABA House of Delegates, the ABA Criminal Justice Section stated:

"Retribution or legal vengeance seems difficult enough for a government to justify where adult offenders are involved and vengeance against children for their misdeeds seems quite beyond justification. It has been persuasively argued that the Eighth Amendment precludes retribution for its own sake as improper. The spectacle of our society seeking legal vengeance through the execution of children should not be countenanced by the ABA."

The report went on to describe additional reasons, based on recognized criminal justice principles, for exempting juveniles from capital punishment.[12]

A bill before the US Senate to reintroduce the death penalty in federal law (see Chapter 12) was amended in 1985 to include a clause prohibiting the imposition of a death sentence on people aged under 18 at the time of the crime.

The Model Penal Code, which was drafted by the American Law Institute in 1962, also expressly rejects the imposition of death sentences on people aged under 18 at the time of the crime.

However, the US Supreme Court has thus far refused to consider whether the execution of minors is contrary to the US Constitution.[13]

A key case came before the Court in 1982, when it granted

---

11. The United Kingdom had proposed inserting the words "and before sentence is passed" after the words "commission of the offence". (UN doc A 4625 (1960), paras 11 and 20(b).

12. The resolution was adopted at the ABA's Annual General Meeting in Atlanta in August 1983. It was accompanied by the report to the House of Delegates quoted above, which discussed arguments such as deterrence, confessions, and protection of society.

13. As of May 1986.

certiorari in *Eddings* v. *Oklahoma* on the specific question of "whether the infliction of the death penalty on a child who was 16 at the time of the offense constituted cruel and unusual punishment under the Eighth and Fourteenth Amendments of the Constitution of the United States." This was the first time that the Supreme Court had agreed to hear an appeal based solely on the defendant's age. The petitioner, Monty Lee Eddings, had been sentenced to death for the murder of a highway patrol officer when he was 16.

In arguing the case before the Court, however, Monty Eddings' lawyers raised a second point of appeal, claiming that the trial court had erred in failing to consider additional mitigating circumstances. It was on this latter ground that the Supreme Court based its ruling on the case. In a five-to-four decision, the Court vacated the death sentence, holding that the sentencing judge had improperly failed to consider whether the evidence of the prisoner's "turbulent family history, of beatings by a harsh father and of severe emotional disturbance" was a factor which, together with his age at the time of the offence, would mitigate against the death sentence.[14] However, the Court did not address the question of whether the imposition of a death sentence on a minor was in itself unconstitutional. Justice O'Connor, concurring with the decision, stated: "I . . . do not read the Court's opinion . . . as deciding the issue of whether the Constitution permits the imposition of the death penalty on an individual who committed murder at age 16."

Since the decision in *Eddings*, the Supreme Court has denied *certiorari* in several other capital cases which have been appealed to it on the grounds of the defendant's youth.

Although a number of death sentences imposed on minors have been vacated by the state appeal courts, youth has not been considered grounds for granting executive clemency in cases where execution dates have been set.

The case of James Terry Roach

James Terry Roach was executed by electrocution in South Carolina on 10 January 1986. At the age of 17 in 1977 he had pleaded guilty to the murders of two white teenagers and to additional charges, including criminal sexual assault and kidnapping. An older co-defendant, Joseph Shaw, was also convicted of the crimes and was executed in South Carolina in January 1985. A third defendant who,

14. *Eddings* v. *Oklahoma*, 1982. The trial judge in the Eddings case had refused to consider any of the circumstances of the prisoner's background, including his disturbed childhood and frequent beatings by his father. After the Supreme Court's decision, the Eddings case was remanded to the Oklahoma Supreme Court, which modified his sentence to life imprisonment.

like James Roach, was a minor when the crimes were committed, received a life sentence in return for testifying for the state. James Roach was sentenced to death, despite a finding by the trial judge that he had acted under the domination of the older man and was reported by psychiatrists to have a mental age of 12 and a personality disorder.

A few weeks before the execution, a neurologist found also that James Roach exhibited signs of the mental deterioration that characterizes Huntington's Disease, a hereditary illness from which his mother suffered. In appealing for clemency, his lawyers pointed out that the evidence of Huntington's Disease raised a serious question about his mental competence to be executed. Although the disease — which develops fully only in adulthood — was not apparent at the time of James Roach's trial, it was pointed out that the early stages of the disease might have affected his mental state at the time of the crime.

James Roach was the only juvenile offender sentenced to death at that time to have pursued and exhausted all US state and federal appeals (Charles Rumbaugh had dropped his final appeals when he was executed by lethal injection in Texas after more than eight years on death row). In December 1985 lawyers brought a complaint on his behalf to the Inter-American Commission on Human Rights (IACHR) on the grounds that his execution would violate US obligations under international customary law and the human rights charter of the Organization of American States (OAS).[15] Amnesty International also filed a complaint with the IACHR, stating that James Roach's execution would violate customary international law, including treaties signed by the US Government. The Commission subsequently urged the US Government and the Governor of South Carolina to grant a stay of execution pending its consideration of the complaint.[16]

---

15. The complaint alleged that the execution of minors was prohibited under the American Declaration of the Rights and Duties of Man (OAS Charter), whose applicability is recognized by the USA. The petitioners claimed that the execution of minors is prohibited under articles relating to the right to life, special protection of children and the prohibition of cruel and unusual punishment — Articles I, VII and XXVI of the Declaration. The petitioners also claimed that the execution of minors violates international customary law, which is based on treaty laws, other recognized international standards and international practice.

16. The IACHR asked that the stay be granted ". . . for humanitarian reasons and to avoid irreparable damage". It noted also that "such action would be in keeping with the spirit of major human rights instruments and universal trends favourable to abolition of the death penalty." (Letter to G. Shultz, Secretary of State, dated 12 December 1985.) The IACHR reiterated its appeal in a further letter to the US Secretary of State dated 23 December 1985.

In a letter to Governor Riley appealing for clemency in James Roach's case, Amnesty International pointed out that, as a signatory to the American Convention, the USA had an obligation under the Vienna Convention on the Laws of Treaties, to do nothing that would defeat the object and purpose of signed treaties.[17] Amnesty International noted that all jurisdictions within the USA had a similar obligation to adhere to international standards. Amnesty International also said that "a strong case can be made that the prohibition reflects a rule of customary international law".

On 9 January 1986 the General Secretary of the OAS, João Clemente Baena Soares, cabled Governor Riley requesting him to "follow the current tendency of almost all the countries of this hemisphere" and stay the execution; he cited "humanitarian reasons" as well as Article 4 of the ACHR. The United Nations Secretary General, Javier Pérez de Cuéllar, also appealed for clemency.

However, Governor Riley declined to grant clemency or a temporary stay of execution pending the outcome of the international appeal. In a public statement released on 3 January 1986, he gave the reasons for his decision; he stated that:

". . . The question of his age at the time the crimes were committed was considered at every level of the trial and appellate process. The trial judge considered a number of mitigating factors in determining the appropriate sentence to be imposed. Those factors included his mental and emotional state, his acting under the domination of another person; his age and mentality; and his being below the age of eighteen. It is therefore clear that the Court considered these mitigating factors in reaching its decision of imposing the death penalty, and in this situation the Court was the appropriate body to make the sentencing decision. . . . As for the question of the effect, if any, of international law in this situation, that, in my judgement, is a matter for the courts to decide."

A final appeal to the US Supreme Court, on the grounds of the defendant's youth at the time of the crime and other mitigating circumstances, was also denied without a hearing on 9 January 1986, the day before the execution.

The IACHR was still considering the complaint before it at the time of writing.

International practice

More than 40 countries that retain the death penalty have statutes

---

17. See note 1 to Chapter 14.

74

which specifically prohibit the imposition of death sentences on people who were under 18 at the time of the crime, and executions of minors are extremely rare.[18] The large majority of member states of the United Nations report that they have never in recent years condemned to death people under 18.[19]

Out of the thousands of executions recorded by Amnesty International throughout the world between January 1980 and May 1986, only eight in four countries were reported to have been of people who were under 18 at the time of the crime: three in the USA, two in Pakistan and one each in Bangladesh, Barbados and Rwanda. (There were also unconfirmed reports of executions of juveniles in Iran.)

The data available therefore indicates that there is almost universal adherence in practice to international norms prohibiting executions of juveniles.

The ICCPR, which prohibits the imposition of death sentences on people under 18 at the time of the crime, had been ratified by 81 countries in 1985. Nineteen American states had ratified the ACHR, which contains a similar provision.

Minors on death row in the USA, July 1986

M = male; F = female; B = black; W = white

State	Date of birth	Date of offence	Age at offence	Sex/ race
ALABAMA				
Davis, Timothy	18.03.61	20.07.78	17	M/W
Jackson, Carnel	03.02.63	16.01.80	16	M/B
ARKANSAS				
Ward, Ronald	--.11.69	--.04.85	15	M/B

18. Hartman, Joan, "The Domestic Effects of International Norms Restricting the Application of the Death Penalty", in the *University of Cincinnati Law Review*, vol. 52, 1983.

19. This observation was made by the Secretary General of the UN Economic and Social Council in his Report on Capital Punishment (UN Doc. E 5242, 1973). Out of 72 countries which submitted information to the UN on the imposition of death sentences for the later period from 1973 to 1978, only two reported having sentenced anyone who was under 18 at the time of the crime, and no executions of such prisoners were reported to have been carried out during this period. For the period from 1979 to 1983 there were no reports to the UN of death sentences or executions of minors, although one non-reporting country is known to have carried out one such execution in 1982.

State	Date of birth	Date of offence	Age at offence	Sex/ race
FLORIDA				
Livingston, Jesse		--.02.85	17	M/B
Magill, Paul	21.02.59	23.12.76	17	M/W
Morgan, James	28.11.60	06.06.77	16	M/W
GEORGIA				
Burger, Christopher	30.12.59	05.09.77	17	M/W
Buttrum, Janice	17.01.63	03.09.80	17	F/W
High, Jose	17.08.59	27.07.76	16	M/B
Legare, Andrew	24.03.60	27.05.77	17	M/W
INDIANA				
Cooper, Paula		--.05.84	16	F/B
Thompson, Jay	28.10.63	08.03.81	17	M/W
KENTUCKY				
Stanford, Kevin	23.08.63	07.01.81	17	M/B
LOUISIANA				
Prejean, Dalton	10.12.59	02.07.77	17	M/B
Rushing, David		01.04.83	17	M/W
MARYLAND				
Trimble, James	--.11.63	--.07.81	17	M/W
MISSISSIPPI				
Jones, Larry		02.12.74	17	B/M
Tokman, George	19.02.63	24.08.80	17	M/W
MISSOURI				
Lashley, Frederick	10.04.64	09.04.81	16	M/B
NEW JERSEY				
Bey, Marko		--.04.83	17	M/B
NORTH CAROLINA				
Brown, Leon	--.12.67	--.09.83	15	M/B
Oliver, John	13.12.63	12.12.78	14	M/B
Stokes, Freddie	--.08.64	28.12.81	17	M/B
OKLAHOMA				
Thompson, Wayne		--.--.84	15	M/W
PENNSYLVANIA				
Aulisio, Joseph	13.03.66	26.07.81	15	M/W
Hughes, Kevin	05.03.62	01.03.79	16	M/B
TEXAS				
Burns, Victor	18.09.63	28.03.81	17	M/B
Cannon, Joseph	13.01.60	30.09.77	17	M/W
Carter, Robert	10.02.64	24.06.81	17	M/B
Garrett, Johnny	24.12.63	31.10.81	17	M/W
Graham, Gary	05.09.63	13.05.81	17	M/B
Harris, Curtis	31.08.61	12.12.78	17	M/B

Sources: LDF statistics, May 1986; Victor L. Streib, "Persons under sentence of death as of March 1 1986 for crimes committed while under age eighteen" (Cleveland-Marshall College of Law, Cleveland State University, Ohio).

Execution of the mentally ill

Under US law, a person claiming mental illness or insanity at the time of the commission of an offence is exempted from criminal liability if it is found that the defendant's state of mind was such that he or she could not be held legally responsible for the crime. Most US states with death penalty laws have also adopted, by case law, statute or implication, the common-law rule prohibiting the execution of an insane prisoner (a separate question from that relating to a prisoner's mental condition at the time of the crime).[1]

Both these principles are widely recognized internationally as regards the imposition or carrying out of the death penalty. A report on capital punishment issued by the United Nations Secretary-General on 26 April 1985 states:

"With regard to mental illness, the majority of countries reported that this precludes the possible sentencing or execution of capital offenders."[2]

Safeguards adopted by the UN Economic and Social Council in 1984 provide that sentence of death shall not be carried out on "persons who have become insane".[3]

At least two prisoners who reportedly exhibited signs of mental illness at the time of their crime have been executed in the USA (see

---

1. An article in *The Yale Law Journal*, Vol.88, 510, 1979, "Insanity of the Condemned", reported that at that time four states had adopted in their case law the common-law rule against executing the insane; 25 states had enacted statutory procedures explicitly requiring that convicted prisoners not be executed while insane; six state statutes simply required the transfer of any insane convicted prisoners from prison to a state mental hospital; two states provided only that the state governor was empowered to suspend executions. Texas and Vermont were apparently without any current statutory provisions or case law on the execution of insane prisoners.

2. *Capital Punishment Report of Secretary General*, E/1985/43, 26 April 1985 (The UN Secretary General's report on capital punishment is issued every five years in response to questionnaires from governments.)

3. Safeguard 3 of Resolution 1984/50 on Safeguards Guaranteeing Protection of the Rights of Those Facing the Death Penalty adopted by the UN Social and Economic Council on 25 May 1984. In discussing mental illness and the death penalty, several UN surveys have also noted that a large proportion of member

below). In at least one case, the question of insanity was an issue at trial but the court found the defendant mentally competent to stand trial (see the case of Arthur Goode below). In a third case (that of David Funchess), a prisoner was executed despite new evidence being produced which raised doubts about his mental competence to stand trial.

Until recently, there was no obligation upon US states to provide funds for indigent defendants to seek the help of psychiatrists in preparing an insanity defence at their trials.

However, on 26 February 1985 the Supreme Court ruled by eight votes to one that states must provide indigent criminal defendants with free psychiatric assistance in preparing an insanity defence if the defendant "demonstrates to the trial judge that his sanity at the time of the offense is to be a significant factor at trial". In *Ake* v. *Oklahoma*, 1985, the Court overturned a death sentence imposed by an Oklahoma court on a man convicted of murder whose trial lawyer had pleaded that the defendant was suffering from paranoid schizophrenia. The state had refused to provide a psychiatrist to assist him in presenting his insanity plea. The judgment, which applies to all criminal defendants, is one of the few Supreme Court rulings in recent years to increase due process protection for capital defendants. (This ruling does not apply to convicted prisoners raising insanity claims at the time of execution.)

As noted above, most US states with death penalty laws forbid the execution of insane prisoners either by statute or case law. The provision, rooted in English common law, is based on several principles. These include recognition that there is no retributive or deterrent purpose to be served by executing someone who is incapable of comprehending the nature of the punishment or why it is to be imposed; that an insane prisoner may not be competent to pursue any outstanding appeals; that execution of a convict who has become mentally ill may deprive the prisoner of the opportunity for preparing for death by atoning for his or her crimes and (depending on the inmate's religious beliefs) making peace with God. Some states provide that a prisoner found to be mentally unfit for execution must be transferred to a psychiatric hospital for treatment until he or she has recovered his or her sanity and is deemed fit for execution.

The procedure used to determine insanity in condemned prisoners varies according to state. Some states require that reasonable insanity claims be examined by a state judge, who may hold a full hearing into

states with capital punishment laws provide for the exclusion from the death penalty of people suffering from mental illness or those who have become insane at the time of execution.

the matter.[4] In others, the state governor makes a final determination of insanity claims after receiving psychiatric reports. In many states, a sanity test will be made only if the prisoner awaiting execution appears to the prison warden to be insane. Thus, the initial evaluation of insanity, and the decision to refer a case for further assessment, often lies entirely at the discretion of prison administrators.[5] In some states, even after referral, decisions on insanity claims may be discretionary. The Georgia statute, for example, provides that:

". . . upon satisfactory evidence being offered to the Governor, showing reasonable grounds to believe that a person convicted of a capital offense has become insane subsequent to his conviction, the Governor may, *in his discretion*, have the convicted person examined by such expert physicians as the Governor may choose." (emphasis added)

The statute goes on to state that:

"The Governor may, if he determines that the convicted person has become insane, have the power of committing him to the custody [of a mental institution] until his sanity has been restored . . ."

This suggests that there is no obligation under the Georgia statute to suspend the execution of an insane prisoner. However, in June 1986 the US Supreme Court, which had not previously taken a position on this question, ruled that the Eighth Amendment prohibits the state from executing an insane prisoner (see Alvin Ford's case below).

In recent years several prisoners appearing to be suffering from serious mental illness have been executed or have come close to execution. There has been criticism at the lack of procedural safeguards and clear standards for assessing insanity in many states. Attention has focussed on Florida, where several condemned prisoners have raised insanity claims.

In Florida, at the time of the Supreme Court ruling on Alvin Ford,

4. About half the states with death penalty statutes require claims to be examined by a court judge. Only six states require trial after a reasonable claim has been made. In other states this may be at the discretion of the judge or the judge may be required only to arrange a medical examination of the prisoner in order to make his final determination ("Insanity of the Condemned", *The Yale Law Journal*, vol. 88, 533, 1979).

5. Seventeen states permit insanity determinations only if the convict awaiting execution appears to the warden or the sheriff in charge of custody to be insane. Two other states imply that the warden must raise the issue of insanity because he or she is solely responsible for initiating the insanity hearing (*ibid* — note 31, p. 539).

the state governor made a final determination of an insanity claim raised by a condemned prisoner. The Florida statute provided that, on receiving an insanity claim, the governor must appoint three psychiatrists to examine the prisoner. The test for determining mental fitness for execution was whether the prisoner "understands the nature of the death penalty and why it is to be imposed on him".[6] After receiving the psychiatrists' reports, the governor made an independent decision, of which there was no review. The governor gave no written findings and no hearing was held. The question of insanity could not be raised independently in the state judicial system.

The case of Alvin Ford gave rise to particular concern about the Florida procedures.

Alvin Ford (Florida)

Alvin Ford, now aged 33, was sentenced to death in 1975 for the 1974 murder of a Florida police officer. In 1983 his lawyers asserted that he had become too mentally ill to be executed and that his mental health had started to decline in December 1981, when his first execution warrant was issued — after he had spent six years on death row. Numerous letters from the prisoner, covering the period from July 1981 to November 1983, showed signs of his mental deterioration over a prolonged period which his lawyers believed could not have been faked. (He imagined, among other things, that messages were being sent to him over the radio; that at one point hostages, including members of his family, were being held in the prison; and that a court ruling had resulted in the vacation of his death sentence.) From December 1981 until August 1982, he was examined by a psychiatrist who found him to be suffering from paranoid delusions, including "auditory and visual hallucinations". In November 1983 a psychiatrist from Washington, DC, hired by the defence counsel, examined him and found him to be suffering from severe psychosis, causing him to be mentally unfit for execution within the terms of the Florida statute.

On an application by his attorneys, three psychiatrists appointed by the governor examined Alvin Ford on 19 December 1983. All three psychiatrists were present at the examination, which reportedly lasted about 30 minutes. One of the psychiatrists declined to look at Alvin Ford's records or psychiatric history in making his assessment. No witnesses were interviewed.

In their reports, two of these psychiatrists found the prisoner to be "psychotic", but not to the point where he did not understand that he was going to be executed. One of them found, apparently without regard to the documented history of his condition, that his mental

---

6. Fla. Stat. Section 922.07 (1983).

disorder, "though severe, seems contrived and recently learned".

Despite the divided opinion of the psychiatrists on Alvin Ford's mental state, the governor concluded that he was sane enough to be executed. He signed a death warrant on 30 April 1984, setting the date for execution for the end of the following month. In May the Washington psychiatrist hired by Alvin Ford's defence counsel again examined him and found that his condition had "seriously worsened so that he now has, at best, only minimal contact with the events of the external world".

An appeal on the condemned man's behalf was lodged with the federal courts, contending that it would be unconstitutional for the state to execute a prisoner showing evidence of insanity, without holding a judicial hearing into the claim.[7] The appeal argued that the Florida statute fell below minimum procedural standards of due process required for deciding insanity claims. Eleven hours before the execution was due to take place, the Eleventh Circuit Court of Appeals granted a stay of execution, pending its ruling on his appeal.

The circuit court subsequently turned down the appeal. However, in December 1985 the US Supreme Court agreed to hear the case. Until then, the Supreme Court had never ruled on whether it was unconstitutional to execute a prisoner who appeared insane or whether specific procedures were required to determine such a claim.

The Supreme Court's ruling on the matter was given in *Ford* v. *Wainwright* in June 1986. It ruled by five votes to four that the Eighth Amendment prohibited the state from carrying out a sentence of death on a prisoner who is insane. Justice Marshall, who wrote the majority opinion,[8] referred to the widely accepted common-law restriction on executing an insane prisoner, stating:

". . . today, no less than before, we may seriously question the retributive value of executing a person who has no comprehension of why he has been singled out and stripped of his fundamental right to life . . . Whether its aim be to protect the condemned from fear and pain without comfort of understanding, or to protect the dignity of society itself from the barbarity of exacting mindless vengeance, the restriction finds enforcement in the Eighth Amendment."

The Court also held that Florida's statutory procedure for determining the mental competence of a condemned prisoner was inadequate

---

7. The appeal was brought by Alvin Ford's mother acting as "next friend", because he himself was incapable of authorizing an appeal or consulting an attorney.

8. Justice Marshall was joined in his opinion by Justices Brennan, Blackmun, Powell and Stevens. Justice O'Connor concurred with that part of the ruling which found the procedures for determining insanity claims in Florida to be inadequate.

on the grounds that it denied the prisoner any opportunity to challenge the opinions of the state-appointed psychiatrists and placed the final decision wholly within the executive branch. However, the Court did not specify which procedural arrangements would be necessary to ensure that a condemned prisoner's insanity claim was fairly assessed. It suggested that the procedures for determining whether a prisoner was mentally competent to stand trial could provide guidance.

As noted above, most US states already had laws forbidding the execution of insane prisoners, although the procedures for determining insanity claims varied. Thirteen other states whose capital punishment laws also placed the final decision on insanity claims with the state governor are expected to change their procedures as a result of the *Ford* ruling. Other states (such as those where a decision to refer a case for a sanity determination lies entirely at the discretion of the prison administration) may be affected as well (see notes 1, 4 and 5).

At least one other Florida prisoner exhibiting signs of insanity, whose case would have been affected by the *Ford* ruling, was executed before the Supreme Court's decision was handed down. This prisoner, Arthur Goode, had also challenged the Florida procedures for determining insanity, but his petition for *certiorari* was summarily denied by the Supreme Court some 20 months before it granted *certiorari* on the same issue in Alvin Ford's case.

Arthur Goode (Florida)

Arthur Goode, who had a documented history of mental disturbance from the age of three, was executed in Florida on 5 April 1984. From the age of 15 he was receiving injections of the hormonal drug Depo-Provera for sexual problems. In 1972, at the age of 18, he was arrested for paedophilia. After several more arrests he was admitted to a mental hospital but escaped in 1976 and killed (by rape and torture) a 10-year-old boy in Florida. Despite his history, and a determination by a psychiatrist who examined him before trial that he was mentally incompetent, three court-appointed psychiatrists found him competent to stand trial on a murder charge in 1977. Assisted by a court-appointed attorney, he represented himself at his trial, during which he "brought out evidence to assure his own conviction, testified in gory detail as to his guilt, and argued to the jury that he should be convicted and sentenced to death".[9] The Eleventh Circuit Court of Appeals admitted that it had "serious doubts as to Goode's

9. Quote from Appeal to Eleventh Circuit Court of Appeals (*Goode* v. *Wainwright*, No. 704 F.2nd.593 at 601).

competence" but upheld his conviction.[10] The Governor of Florida and three state-appointed psychiatrists held him to be mentally fit for execution.

An appeal to the federal courts on Arthur Goode's behalf (which, like the Ford appeal, challenged the Florida sanity test procedures) was turned down by the Eleventh Circuit Court of Appeals on 4 April 1984, the day before the execution. On the same date, the US Supreme Court summarily dismissed his petition for *certiorari* and his application for a stay of execution.

Morris Odell Mason (Virginia)

Morris Mason, a black farmworker aged 32, was executed in Virginia on 26 June 1985. He had been sentenced to death in October 1978 after pleading guilty to the murder of an elderly white woman during an alcoholic rampage in May 1978. The woman had reportedly burned to death after Morris Mason had raped her, nailed her to a chair by the palm of her hand and set the house on fire.

Morris Mason had a long history of mental illness and had spent time in three state mental institutions where he was diagnosed as mentally retarded and suffering from paranoid schizophrenia (he was found to have an IQ of 66 and a mental age of eight). At the time of the murder he was on parole from a prison sentence he had been serving after a conviction for a minor arson offence. According to his lawyers, in the week before the killing he had twice sought help from his parole officer for his uncontrollable drinking and drugs abuse — only the day before the crime he had apparently asked to be placed in a "half-way house"; however, no facilities for this were available in Virginia.[11]

Virginia law requires the transfer of any convicted prisoner found to be insane to a mental health facility. However, the prison warden is solely responsible for initiating a sanity hearing in the case of a condemned prisoner.[12] This is then ruled on by a state judge, who may order that the prisoner be examined by two physicians. This procedure was not applied in Morris Mason's case.

Although three psychiatrists had independently found Morris Mason to be suffering from paranoid schizophrenia over an eight-year period before his trial in 1978, the trial court had denied his

10. *Ibid.*

11. A "half-way house" is a hostel where offenders are placed under supervision as an alternative to prison. They may do outside work but must report back to the hostel each night. In some states, prisoners on parole are placed in half-way houses before their proper release.

12. VA Code 19.2.177 (1975). See also "Insanity of the Condemned" (*op. cit.*), note 31, p. 539.

request for the assistance of a psychiatrist in evaluating his sanity. His court-appointed attorney did not have funds to hire a private psychiatrist and Morris Mason was found competent to stand trial. In June 1985 his lawyers appealed for a review of his case — and a stay of execution — in the light of the February 1985 *Ake* v. *Oklahoma* decision, in which the US Supreme Court had ruled that states must provide indigent defendants with free psychiatric assistance in preparing an insanity defence at their trials (see above). However, the Supreme Court denied his appeal and application for a stay of execution on these grounds.

The Governor of Virginia also turned down appeals for clemency, lodged by Morris Mason's lawyers on the grounds of his mental retardation and history of mental illness.

Gary Eldon Alvord (Florida)

Gary Alvord, now aged 40, was due to be executed in Florida on 29 November 1984. He had spent most of his adult life in mental institutions in Michigan before escaping to Florida, where he murdered three women in 1973. Three days before his scheduled execution, he was examined by a panel of state psychiatrists, who advised the governor that he was insane and should not be executed. The governor ordered him to be removed to a state mental hospital for treatment under Section 922.07(3) of the Florida statute. This provides that a condemned prisoner found mentally unfit for execution should remain in hospital until such time as the "proper official of the hospital" determines that he has been "restored to sanity". At the time of his removal to hospital, he had spent more than 10 years on death row.

Florida mental health workers subsequently expressed concern about the ethical principles of treating a patient for the express purpose of rendering him mentally fit for execution. In December 1984, the Florida State Hospital Human Rights Advocacy Committee[13] declared that it "fully supports hospital staff who refuse on ethical grounds to provide mental health treatment to Mr. Alvord for the purpose of making him competent to be executed". The committee noted that this conformed to the position taken by the American Psychiatric Association that "a physician serving the state as executioner, either directly or indirectly, is a perversion of medical ethics".[14]

---

13. An independent body appointed by the state governor which has a statutory function to serve as a third party in matters concerning the rights of patients treated in the Florida State Hospital. Similar committees are attached to each state institution under the Department of Health and Human Services.

14. See Chapter 10.

84

In a letter to the Statewide Human Rights Advocacy Committee, the committee recommended that no prisoner found to lack the mental capacity to be executed be sent to a state treatment facility for mental health without his sentence being commuted to life imprisonment. It further recommended that the state legislature be urged to revise Section 922 to "include detailed standards on the determination of competency to be executed and to include in those standards a right to judicial review of competency determinations".[15]

The Florida Mental Health Association also adopted a public policy position in which it opposed the execution of the mentally ill and the "appointment of government psychiatrists to determine mental capacity to be executed". The Association also urged all mental health professionals to refuse to determine a prisoner's competency for execution.

An Amnesty International Declaration on Doctors and the Death Penalty, adopted by the organization in March 1981, opposes any form of participation by doctors in capital punishment as a violation of medical ethics (see Chapter 10). Participation is deemed to include, among other things, the determination of mental fitness for execution. (For full text see Appendix 11.)

David Livingstone Funchess (Florida)

David Funchess, a black Vietnam War veteran aged 39, was executed in Florida on 22 April 1986. He had been sentenced to death in 1975 for killing two white people during a bar robbery in 1974. Years after his conviction he was diagnosed as suffering from Post Traumatic Stress Disorder (PTSD), a psychiatric disorder now known to affect a number of Vietnam War veterans, but which was not recognized at the time of David Funchess' trial and early appeals.[16]

David Funchess had joined the Marine Corps of the US army in 1965 at the age of 18 and was sent to South Vietnam in 1967, where he was involved in some of the heaviest fighting of the war. He was badly wounded in a land-mine explosion and spent three months in a naval hospital in Japan. Although his military record had been excellent — he received five medals for bravery during his tour of duty — early signs of depression manifested themselves at this stage

---

15. These recommendations were contained in a letter to the Statewide Human Rights Advocacy Committee from Peter D. Ostreich, Chairperson of the Florida State Hospital Human Rights Advocacy Committee, dated 6 December 1984.

16. PTSD was first recognized as a clinically identifiable disorder in 1980, when it was included in the *American Psychiatric Association (APA) Diagnostic Standards Manual*, 3rd Edition. The disorder is caused by massive internalized stress and has been found to occur in hostage and kidnap victims, as well as in many Vietnam War veterans.

and he was transferred from Japan to a naval hospital in the USA. There he was diagnosed as suffering from a psychoneurotic depressive condition but was returned to duty after a month. His military record deteriorated and, after frequently going absent without leave, he received a dishonorable discharge in 1971.

David Funchess was first diagnosed as suffering from PTSD in 1982 by a leading expert on the disorder, a psychologist, who examined him in prison. The psychologist found that, although David Funchess was reluctant to dwell on them, his wartime experiences, together with the murder of his brother shortly before his tour of duty in South Vietnam and certain earlier incidents in his childhood, had combined to cause a depressive reaction characteristic of a severe form of PTSD. The psychologist stated that the disorder was produced by massive internalized stress, which could erupt, on occasion, into uncontrollable outbursts of aggressive behaviour. The symptoms included long-term suppression of emotions, dissociation from reality, mental impairment and memory loss.

However, the full extent of David Funchess' disorder was not revealed until lawyers from the newly created state-funded appeals office[17] conducted a further investigation of his case in the month before his scheduled execution. For the first time they interviewed members of his family and friends, who gave evidence of the stark contrast in his condition before and after he had served in South Vietnam. They testified that, despite a very poor and often brutal family background, he had been a quiet, intelligent and ambitious teenager, who did well at school. He joined the Marines shortly after graduating from High School, apparently believing that a career in the army would enable him to progress in life. Described by his sisters as having had a bright and easygoing personality, he returned from Vietnam addicted to heroin and in a state which one described as "shell-shocked". He was unable to tolerate noise, suffered from frequent "flashbacks", sleeplessness and recurring nightmares. His family said that he would not enter a house or room without first crouching down with an imaginary machine-gun as if ready for combat. Unable to spend time indoors he would often build what his sisters described as "foxholes" and sleep in them under the house. Later he took to sleeping in cars. His family and friends believed that part of his drug addiction was due to the continuing pain from his war injury (prison medical records indicate that he still suffered some pain from this years later). Unable to find regular employment after

17. The Office of the Capital Collateral Representative, established in October 1985 to provide free legal assistance to capital defendants pursuing post-conviction appeals (see Chapter 3).

leaving the army, he drifted into vagrancy and petty crime.

Although David Funchess was given a routine mental competency test at the time of his trial, he had by then apparently suppressed most of his war memories and did not relate them to the public defender who represented him at trial. This lawyer later testified to the appeal lawyers that he had been unaware of the existence of PTSD and had had neither the information nor funds to seek a private psychiatric evaluation of David Funchess. The trial lawyer conducted no investigation into the defendant's history or background, nor did he interview his family about his mental condition on returning from Vietnam. This was largely because — like many other lawyers at that early stage of the operation of Florida's death penalty statute — he mistakenly believed that he was limited in what could be presented in mitigation only to those specific factors listed in the statute, which did not include mitigating circumstances relating to the defendant's character or background.[18] "Had I known that I could have used any evidence whatsoever in mitigation, I would have thoroughly investigated David's background," the lawyer stated. "Because of my personal understanding of how the statute worked, which I believe was almost universally shared at the time, I did not do so."

Although the new evidence did not pertain to David Funchess' sanity at the time of his execution (which was not at issue), his appeal lawyers argued that it raised serious doubts about his mental competence to stand trial in 1975. This view was supported by a second psychologist, who examined him in April 1986 and who had extensive training and experience in the diagnosis, effects and treatment of PTSD. The psychologist who had examined him in 1982 said that, based on his experience with other PTSD cases, "a different verdict or sentence may well have been the outcome" had these findings been presented to the court and jury at the time of the original trial and hearing on mitigation. Both psychologists found that David Funchess' disorder could have been substantially alleviated, had it been recognized and properly treated earlier.

---

18. The Florida death penalty statute at that time had required the trial court at the sentencing hearing to consider mitigating circumstances "as enumerated in subsection 7" (the section listing seven statutory mitigating circumstances). This led lawyers to believe that they were limited to presenting evidence relating only to those circumstances listed in subsection 7. After the US Supreme Court's ruling in Lockett v. Ohio (1978) that the courts must consider any evidence presented in mitigation at the sentencing stage of a capital trial (see Chapter 1), the Florida legislature amended the statute to delete the words "as enumerated in subsection 7". In the same amendment, the legislature permitted the introduction of any matter deemed relevant to "the nature of the crime and the character of the defendant".

However, a motion for a retrial presented to the courts on 20 April 1986 was denied without a hearing. A stay of execution pending a hearing on the claim was also denied. An appeal for clemency to the state governor, which included medical and psychological reports and detailed affidavits from the Funchess family and others, was also turned down.

Appeals in death penalty cases

Most state authorities claim that the appeals available to defendants, including automatic review of death sentences by the state supreme courts, serve to redress any errors or unfairness in sentencing that might occur during the trial of capital cases.

A relatively high proportion of death sentences imposed since the early 1970s have been overturned on appeal, after procedural errors or flaws at trial level had been found or on constitutional grounds. Twenty per cent of the capital cases reviewed by the Georgia Supreme Court from 1973 to 1978 resulted in vacation of sentence or conviction, as did 45 per cent of the 270 cases reviewed by the Florida Supreme Court up to September 1984 (a large part of the latter being reversals of death sentences imposed by trial judges against jury 'recommendations of life imprisonment).[1] The California Supreme Court found procedural flaws or errors which resulted in its vacating 36 of the 39 death sentences reviewed from 1978 to 1985.

The relatively high rate of reversal in such cases reflects the unique complexity of capital trials, which may raise separate issues of the fairness of proceedings at both the trial and the sentencing hearings. In many cases, the appeal courts have vacated only the death sentence, either reducing it on appeal or sending the case back to the trial court for a new sentencing hearing. In some cases the conviction itself has been overturned and the case sent back for retrial.

Some 60 per cent of death sentences imposed nationally from 1973

---

1. The Georgia figure was cited in a study of the Georgia Supreme Court decisions by Baldus, Pulaski and Woodworth (see note 5 below). The Florida figure of 270 cases reviewed by the Florida Supreme Court was taken from a report issued by the Florida Capital Punishment Project, 30 September 1984. (Of these cases, 148 were affirmed, 47 reduced to life imprisonment, 38 returned for a new trial, 35 for resentencing and two reduced to second-degree murder or dismissed.) In an earlier report, Michael Radelet and Margaret Vandiver examined 145 capital cases decided by the Florida Supreme Court up to December 1983. Just over 48 per cent resulted in the vacation of sentence, of which more than half were cases in which the trial judge had overridden jury recommendations of life imprisonment: "The Florida Supreme Court and Death Penalty Appeals", published in the *Journal of Criminal Law and Criminology*, vol. 74, 1983.

to 1980 are estimated to have been overturned by the state or federal courts of appeal.[2] Many of the death sentences during this period were vacated as a result of US Supreme Court rulings in the mid to late 1970s, in which a number of state laws (such as those providing for mandatory death sentences or limiting the consideration of mitigating circumstances) were held to be unconstitutional. Later Supreme Court rulings have tended to uphold state death penalty laws, thus narrowing the grounds for future appeals on broad constitutional issues. Nevertheless, a significant proportion of cases is still likely to be overturned on their merits: 36 per cent of death sentences imposed between 1977 and 1984, for example, were reversed on state or federal appeal.[3]

Limitations of appellate review

Although the appeals process has clearly served to remedy error in a number of cases, it has by no means eliminated unfairness in all of them. Some trial errors resulting from inadequate defence counsel, for example, may not be remedied because of procedural limits to raising new claims at post-conviction hearings. As indicated earlier, several prisoners have been executed despite apparent defects in the conduct of their trials and doubts about the fairness of the sentences imposed.

It is also doubtful whether the appeals courts are able to redress — or even identify — underlying inconsistencies in the system, especially where these result from discretionary decisions taken at an early stage of the judicial process.

Some state supreme courts are required to take into account general consistency in sentencing by comparing death sentences with penalties imposed in similar cases. However, as noted earlier, only a small proportion of potentially capital crimes are actually charged as such, because prosecutors have decided not to seek the death penalty or to accept pleas by defendants to lesser charges. This inevitably limits the range of cases available to the courts for comparative review.

The Georgia statute probably provides the most thorough review, requiring the Georgia Supreme Court to keep a record of all capital cases resulting in conviction statewide after 1 January 1970 (including

2. The percentage and grounds of reversal of death sentences in capital cases during this period are described in "Capital Punishment as a System", by Jack Greenberg, published in *The Yale Law Journal*, vol. 91, 908, 1982.

3. Figure given in US Justice Department *Bulletin on Capital Punishment, 1984*.

those resulting in life sentences).[4] For the case under review, the trial judge is required to submit to the court a transcript of the trial and also to complete a standardized questionnaire about the crime and the defendant. After the Georgia Supreme Court has made a "proportionality" review upholding a death sentence, it is required by statute to cite, in an appendix to its opinion, all the cases it has considered that are "similar" to the one under review.

However, a study of cases reviewed by the Georgia Supreme Court from 1973 to 1978 revealed that, in practice, it compared death sentences only with other capital felony convictions that were appealed.[5] Since approximately two thirds of defendants convicted of a capital crime in Georgia during the period studied had received automatic life sentences, because of agreements whereby prosecutors would not seek the death penalty, these cases were unlikely to be appealed. The cases actually reviewed by the court thus included a disproportionate number of death sentences, excluding the larger proportion of cases resulting in life imprisonment. The tendency of the court was thus to cite "similar" cases by looking almost exclusively at those in which death sentences had been imposed and was a precedent-seeking exercise rather than a true comparative review. The study found that, from 1973 to 1978, the Georgia Supreme Court had conducted comparative sentence reviews in over 120 death penalty cases. In only two of these did it vacate death sentences on the grounds that they were "excessive or disproportionate"; most cases were overturned on a finding of procedural error in the conduct of the trial or sentencing hearing.

Failure to conduct a true comparative review of death sentences may mean that general inconsistencies and arbitrariness remain unchecked. Although both the Georgia and the Florida Supreme Courts compare death sentences on a statewide basis, this does not appear to have corrected the considerable regional disparities in sentencing among similar offenders in these states (see Chapter 3). A

4. After reviewing a case for procedural irregularities, the Georgia Supreme Court is required, by statute, to determine "whether sentence of death is excessive or disproportionate to the penalty imposed in similar cases, considering both the crime and the defendant": Ga. Code of Criminal Procedure, 1981, Article 2. 17-10-35. Legislation in more than 20 states with death penalty statutes requires the state supreme court to conduct some form of "proportionality" review of death sentences, although the procedures for doing so are not usually as precise as in the Georgia statute.

5. David C. Baldus, Charles Pulaski and George Woodworth, "Comparative Review of Death Sentences: An Empirical Study of the Georgia Experience" in *Journal of Criminal Law and Criminology*, Northwestern University School of Law, vol. 74, 1983.

regional comparison of death sentences reviewed and affirmed by the Georgia and Florida Supreme Courts up to 1977 showed that death sentences were affirmed by the courts more or less in direct proportion to the frequency with which they had been imposed in each region, thus doing nothing to redress the regional imbalance in death sentencing.[6]

Amnesty International does not have information on later decisions by the Georgia and Florida Supreme Courts. However, the Georgia court in particular would seem to have the capacity to conduct a more effective comparative review of sentencing in capital cases, since it is required to keep a detailed record of all capital convictions after 1969. Although review of the convictions alone cannot eliminate arbitrariness resulting from earlier charging decisions, it may, nevertheless, reduce some of the disparities in sentences imposed on similar offenders tried in different judicial circuits.

Some states, including Texas and California, do not conduct any form of proportionality review of death sentences by comparing them with other cases. In a decision given in January 1984 in *Pulley* v. *Harris* (California), the US Supreme Court ruled that there was no constitutional requirement for the state appeals courts to conduct such a review. The Supreme Court also upheld the Louisiana statute, which provides for a limited proportionality review by requiring the state supreme court to compare death sentences with similar cases only within the judicial circuit in which the trial is held. This does not enable the court to take account of any regional disparities in the application of the death penalty in the state, despite evidence that there are considerable differences in sentencing among Louisiana's 40 judicial circuits.

Appellate review of death sentences has also not served to remedy racial disparities in death sentencing. This is largely because most cases reviewed by the appeal courts involve white victims (95 per cent of capital convictions in Florida up to 1977 and 88 per cent of those in Georgia for the same period were for homicides in which the

---

6. From a study by William J. Bowers and Glenn L. Pierce, reproduced in *Legal Homicide*, pp. 254-257. The study found that the more likely a region was to impose death sentences for potentially capital crimes, the more likely it was to have the sentence affirmed on review by the state supreme court. The appellate review process in Florida was found, if anything, to reinforce the overall regional differences in death sentencing in the state. The Florida Supreme Court's rate of affirming death sentences, for example, was lowest for the southern region of Florida where (despite this area having one of the highest incidences of felony-murder) death sentences were less likely to be imposed than for comparable crimes in any other region of the state.

victims were white). Any imbalance resulting from prosecutors' decisions not to press capital charges in similar cases with black victims, or differences based on the race of the offender at this earlier stage of the judicial process, would not be revealed to the state courts, which review only convicted capital felonies.

As shown in Chapter 4, the federal courts have also failed thus far to remedy disparities in the application of the death penalty.

Length of appeals in capital cases

State and federal authorities have frequently criticized the length of appeals in capital cases, claiming that delays by lawyers and the lodging of repeated "frivolous" appeals have impeded the course of justice in many cases. Although state courts started sentencing people to death under the new laws from the early 1970s, only four prisoners were executed before 1982, three of whom had dropped their final appeals. Up to 1982, most death row inmates were still pursuing individual appeals or their cases were pending the outcome of appeals on constitutional issues brought in related cases. The prisoners executed from 1977 to 1985 had spent an average of six years on death row, and in some cases much longer.

However, the notion that capital appeals are unnecessarily prolonged or frivolous appears to be largely unjustified. During the 1970s, state capital punishment laws were continually being revised and tested in the US Supreme Court and this accounted for many delays in the execution of sentences during this period. As noted above, the Supreme Court rulings on mandatory penalties and other practices resulted in the vacation of a large number of death sentences. Had these prisoners foregone their appeals, many would have been executed under procedures subsequently found to be unconstitutional.

Much of the delay in the carrying out of death sentences occurs at state level. It is not uncommon for an appeal to the state supreme court to take several years, since the compulsory review of all death sentences at this stage has created a heavy case load for these courts and there is a backlog of cases in many states. There may also be delays in the preparation of trial transcripts for appellate review. Some delays occur at other stages also. Florida's Governor holds a clemency hearing in each case after the state supreme court has upheld a death sentence (see Chapter 8). It was reported in August 1984 that the average length of time between affirmation of a death sentence by the Florida Supreme Court and the clemency hearing was just over 14 months.[7] This was before the prisoner had lodged any

7. A report on clemency in Florida, issued by the Department of Sociology, Florida State University, dated 1 August 1984.

state or federal *habeas corpus* appeals on constitutional issues.

Attempts to speed up capital appeals in the federal courts

Despite the demonstrable merit of many capital appeals, by 1980 the state authorities — and the US Supreme Court — had become increasingly concerned about the long delays between the imposition of death sentences and executions. In 1983 the Supreme Court approved measures for shortening the procedure for considering federal *habeas corpus* appeals in such cases.

After the state supreme court has affirmed a death sentence on direct appeal, a defendant may then file *habeas corpus* petitions in the state and federal courts.[8] As noted earlier, many prisoners are unable to lodge *habeas corpus* appeals before their execution dates are set (which may be at any time after the sentence has been affirmed by the state supreme court). If a claim having possible merit is raised at this stage, the district court may grant a stay of execution, pending its adjudication of the appeal. If a federal district court denies a writ of *habeas corpus*, it may grant the defendant leave to appeal against this decision to the US Court of Appeals. Until 1983 it was the usual practice of the federal appeals courts to grant a further stay of execution in such cases, pending a separate hearing on the merits of the appeal.

However, in a decision given in *Barefoot* v. *Estelle* in July 1983, the US Supreme Court ruled that the federal appeals courts may expedite their handling of *habeas corpus* appeals in capital cases by summarily considering the merits of the appeal at the same time as deciding upon a motion to stay the execution. Although the Court stated that the merits of the appeal must be considered and a separate hearing held if this could not be done summarily, it permitted the circuit courts to adopt procedures for dealing with such cases expeditiously by setting early dates for hearings.

In the same decision, the Court ruled that the federal district courts should grant leave to appeal only upon a "substantial showing of a denial of a federal right", and that second or subsequent petitions on

8. These are appeals on constitutional grounds against conviction or sentence. As noted in Chapter 2, a defendant must exhaust available state remedies before filing for *habeas corpus* relief in the federal courts. This means that the defendant must have given the state's highest appeal court an opportunity to rule on the claim before filing a *habeas corpus* petition in the federal district court. Many appeals on federal constitutional claims are summarily denied by the state courts and proceed immediately to the federal courts. In cases where the state courts are deemed already to have addressed the issue in an earlier ruling, a defendant may file directly in the federal district court.

the same issues should be dismissed without a hearing.[9]

The ruling upheld the procedure used in the case of the Texas prisoner Thomas Barefoot. His execution date was set after the US district court had denied his petition for a writ of *habeas corpus* but had granted him leave to appeal against its decision to the Fifth Circuit Court of Appeals. The appeals court decided to deal with the case expeditiously, allowing his lawyers only two days to prepare the briefs for a single oral hearing in which the court ruled against the merits of the appeal at the same time as denying the application for a stay of execution.[10]

The *Barefoot* ruling endorsed a practice that was already being used in some judicial circuits. It allowed the federal courts to hear and decide *habeas corpus* appeals in capital cases within the month before an execution, rather than granting stays so that the case might be heard during the normal course of the court's business. As noted earlier, many prisoners do not have legal counsel when their dates of execution are set and must then find a lawyer. This may reduce the time still further for preparing and filing appeal briefs. Although the expedited procedures are not used in all cases, many *habeas corpus* appeals — sometimes raising important constitutional questions — are now dealt with under emergency conditions, often passing through several stages in the courts within days, or even hours, of an execution.

The result of this practice is that capital defendants in many cases now have less time than other defendants to have their *habeas corpus* appeals considered. Under the federal rules of procedure applying to normal felony cases, for example, the defence attorney has 10 days

---

9. There is also a general rule, applying to all criminal cases, that all claims of a violation of a federal constitutional right should be filed in the first *habeas corpus* petition. Subsequent petitions, even when raising new issues, may be dismissed on grounds of "abuse of the writ" unless the defendant can show good cause for failure to present the claim earlier.

10. Although the federal district court denied Thomas Barefoot's petition for *habeas corpus* relief, it did grant him leave to appeal on finding that a substantial constitutional issue had been raised. He had claimed that the use of psychiatric testimony at the sentencing stage of his trial to predict "future dangerousness" (one of three factors which a Texas jury must rule on before imposing a death sentence — see Chapter 2) was unconstitutional. His appeal was supported by a brief from the American Psychiatric Association, which stated that psychiatric opinion in response to hypothetical questions of this nature was unreliable. Although the federal appeals courts denied his appeal, a stay of execution was subsequently granted by the US Supreme Court, pending its ruling on the expedited procedures used in Thomas Barefoot's case. In its July 1983 decision upholding these procedures, the Supreme Court also denied the merits of the appeal, ruling that the use of psychiatric testimony to predict future dangerousness was constitutionally permissible. Thomas Barefoot was executed by lethal injection on 30 October 1984.

after the district court enters its judgment in which to file notice of appeal, more time while the record on appeal is assembled and another 40 days to prepare the opening brief once the record of appeal is filed. After receiving the state's reply, the court allows defence counsel two weeks in which to submit a response. There is usually another month after this before oral argument takes place.[11]

The Fifth Circuit (covering Texas, Louisiana and Mississippi), in particular, tends to use expedited procedures for handling *habeas corpus* appeals in capital cases. An example is the case of Johnny Taylor, who was executed in Louisiana on 29 February 1984, seven days after the state supreme court had denied his first application for *habeas corpus* relief. The federal district court denied his appeal on 27 February and the US Court of Appeals affirmed the denial on the same day. The US Supreme Court denied *certiorari* on 28 February. Johnny Taylor had found a lawyer to take his case only 14 days before his execution date. The attorney was in his first year of practice and had no experience of handling death penalty cases. Amnesty International was told that a claim of ineffective assistance of counsel at trial may have been sustained on appeal, had the appeal lawyer had more time to raise this issue.[12]

Some other circuits have adopted fairer rules. For example, the US Court of Appeals for the Seventh Circuit (covering Illinois, Indiana and Wisconsin) has adopted a rule guaranteeing counsel to all indigent death row inmates whose *habeas corpus* claims are not frivolous. It also provides 28 days for filing an opening brief, although even this rule provides substantially less briefing time than is allowed in ordinary criminal cases.[13]

The US Supreme Court has also expedited its own procedures in capital cases and no longer routinely grants stays of execution pending final appeals on constitutional issues. Instead, it will grant a stay only if it concludes that an appeal, even if not yet filed, is likely to merit a full hearing by the Court. To avoid delays in executions, it will often also hold emergency sessions to consider stay applications and the grounds of an intended appeal. The Court has generally shown itself increasingly unwilling to consider late or last-minute appeals, even though a prisoner might have been unable to raise a constitutional claim at an earlier stage of the case through lack of legal counsel.

---

11. Procedure described in *The Death of Fairness* by Ronald J. Tabak, *op. cit.*, p. 24.

12. Information from Richard Brody of the LDF; also given in *The Death of Fairness* by Ronald J. Tabak, *op. cit.*, p. 26.

13. Information from *The Death of Fairness*, *op. cit.*, pp. 27-28.

Several US Supreme Court justices have expressed concern about what has been described as a "rush to judgment" in the final stages of capital appeals. In a speech to a judicial conference in September 1985, Justice Thurgood Marshall, referring to the expedited procedures used for handling *habeas corpus* appeals in capital cases, said:

".... The Supreme Court has allowed this process, which usually takes months to years, to occur in a matter of hours. It has taken from the capital defendant, whose life is on the line, the basic right guaranteed to parties in run-of-the-mill civil litigation."

He noted that non-capital litigants, for example, had time to study the opinions of the lower courts and prepare appeals and that even civil litigants had 90 days in which to file petitions for *certiorari* to the US Supreme Court.[14]

The procedures for handling final appeals in capital cases have led to the execution (or near-execution) of several prisoners under circumstances which appear to contravene basic standards of fairness, as the following cases illustrate.

Charles Brooks

Charles Brooks was executed by lethal injection in Texas on 7 December 1982. The date had been set after the US District Court had denied his first application for *habeas corpus* relief on 5 November 1982. On 2 December an attorney from the LDF, using funds from his own New York law firm, took up the case and studied 3,000 pages of trial documents. On 6 December he applied to the US Court of Appeals for a stay of execution (pending the court's consideration of an appeal he had prepared). On the same date, the Texas Attorney General filed an emergency motion to the same court, opposing a stay; the stay was denied and Charles Brooks' attorney appealed to the US Supreme Court. At 8.35pm on 6 December, after several hours' deliberation in an emergency session, the Supreme Court refused to grant a stay by a six-to-three vote. At 11.35pm, Charles Brooks' lawyers appealed to a judge of the Fifth Circuit Court of Appeals to reconsider its refusal to grant a stay. The judge agreed to reconvene the panel by telephone. Some 20 minutes later, at a few minutes to midnight, the court again refused to grant a stay and Charles Brooks was executed just after midnight.

---

14. From remarks made at the Judicial Conference of the Second Circuit in Hershey, Pennsylvania, 6 September 1985. Other US Supreme Court justices, including Justices Brennan and Blackmun, have also expressed concern about the rushed procedures used by the Supreme Court in capital cases.

Charles Brooks was executed before he had completed the first round of federal *habeas corpus* appeals; his application for a stay of execution had been denied by the US Court of Appeals without its considering the merits of his appeal. It appears, therefore, that the procedures used in his case were contrary to those approved by the US Supreme Court in its subsequent decision in *Barefoot* (in which the court stipulated that a petitioner must be given an opportunity to address the merits of an appeal, even if this was considered in the same hearing as an application for an execution stay).

James Autry

James Autry was scheduled to be executed by lethal injection in Texas on 5 October 1983. On 3 October the US Supreme Court denied his application for a stay by a five-to-four vote, even though he had not had an opportunity to file a formal appeal with the court. The day before his execution a new set of lawyers from the ACLU in Texas and Washington took up his case. They found that a recent appeal ruling in another judicial circuit raised a constitutional issue of direct relevance to James Autry's case. The Ninth Circuit Court of Appeals had ruled in a California case that the state appeal court must compare death sentences with similar cases to determine "proportionality". An appeal against this decision by the State of California was currently pending a ruling by the US Supreme Court. Since the Texas statute also failed to provide for a proportionality review, the outcome of the California appeal had a direct bearing on James Autry's case. Both the US District Court and the Fifth Circuit Court of Appeals refused to grant a stay on the new issue: the decision by the Fifth Circuit Court was given just over an hour before the execution was due to take place. Meanwhile, an ACLU lawyer in Washington sat in the night entrance to the US Supreme Court, drafting a final appeal to the Court on this question. He delivered the appeal to a clerk of the Court at just after midnight, Washington time. Half an hour later, US Supreme Court Justice Byron R. White (responsible for handling emergency appeals from the Fifth Circuit) granted a stay of execution on the "proportionality" question, just 23 minutes before James Autry was due to be executed. He had by then been strapped to a stretcher and was undergoing the first stage of the lethal injection process — a needle had already been inserted and a saline solution was being dripped into his veins. Had a stay been granted in the first place, the appeal could have been considered in the normal course of the court's business. As it was, only a supreme effort in a race against the clock by James Autry's volunteer lawyers prevented a potentially serious miscarriage of justice.

It transpired that the stay was to be only temporary. The US

98

Supreme Court overturned the Ninth Circuit Court of Appeals' ruling in the California case in January 1984 and James Autry was executed that March.

Alpha Otis Stephens

Alpha Otis Stephens, who was black and had been convicted of murdering a white, was executed in Georgia on 12 December 1984. At the time of his execution, the Eleventh Circuit Court of Appeals was reviewing two cases in which it was alleged that the Georgia death penalty statute discriminated against certain offenders on racial grounds. Alpha Stephens had been granted a stay of execution by the US Supreme Court in December 1983, after lodging an appeal on the same issue. However, on 27 November 1984 the Supreme Court suddenly lifted the stay by a six-to-three vote, even though the appeals court had not yet ruled on the analogous cases before it. The Supreme Court gave no explanation for its decision (the only written opinion given was a vigorous dissent by one of the opposing judges). However, lawyers for Alpha Stephens believe that the decision was based on a finding that the prisoner should have raised the racial discrimination issue at an earlier stage of his appeals (the grounds on which a lower court had denied his application for a stay in 1983 by a tied six-to-six vote). The Court's decision was, nevertheless, extraordinary, since it had reportedly granted the earlier stay of execution specifically "pending the decision of the United States Court of Appeals for the Eleventh Circuit in *Spencer* v. *Zant*" (one of the racial discrimination cases still pending before that court).[15] Moreover, the circumstances of the Stephens case were directly comparable to those leading to the granting of a stay by the court in the case of James Autry, several months earlier.

Amnesty International expressed concern to the Georgia Board of Pardons and Paroles because the stay in the Stephens case "was lifted on what appear to be essentially technical grounds, while the merits of a related issue have not yet been decided" and said that it would be "contrary to the interests of justice" to allow the execution to take place under the circumstances.[16]

Roosevelt Green

Roosevelt Green was executed in Georgia on 9 January 1985, after

15. Quote from the Supreme Court given in *Stephens* v. *State Board of Pardons and Paroles*, No. D-14767, filed October 1984: a case in which Alpha Stephens had unsuccessfully challenged the procedures for considering clemency used by the Georgia Board of Pardons and Paroles.)
16. In a letter dated 10 December 1984 to the Georgia Board of Pardons and Paroles appealing for clemency or an executive reprieve.

the US Supreme Court had denied his application for a stay by a tied four-to-four vote, when one of the nine judges was temporarily absent. Roosevelt Green had sought a stay pending an appeal which he, too, had lodged on the grounds that the Georgia statute was discriminatory: he was black and had been convicted of complicity in the murder of a white female store cashier who had been kidnapped. Four of the judges ruled that a stay should be granted pending the outcome of the related cases then being considered by the Eleventh Circuit Court of Appeals.

An execution stay had earlier been denied by the federal court of appeals in Roosevelt Green's case. The Supreme Court's decision was procedurally correct, since a tied vote automatically affirms a lower court's decision on the granting or denying of stays. However, the interests of justice were clearly not served in executing a prisoner against the recommendation of an equal number of the judges of the nation's highest court.

Roosevelt Green had reportedly not been present when the killing by an accomplice occurred. He went to his death protesting his innocence of the murder.

*

The major racial discrimination case pending before the Eleventh Circuit Court of Appeals when Alpha Stephens and Roosevelt Green were executed was *McCleskey* v. *Kemp*. The McCleskey appeal was denied by the court in January 1985.[17] However, in July 1986, the US Supreme Court granted *certiorari* in the case, agreeing to review the circuit court's decision. Several Georgia prisoners whose executions were pending when the Supreme Court granted *certiorari* in the case consequently won stays of execution. Georgia lawyers told Amnesty International that — pending the Supreme Court's ruling — no further executions would be carried out in Georgia cases in which the racial discrimination question had been raised. This was too late, however, to affect the cases of Alpha Stephens and Roosevelt Green. (The Supreme Court's decision in *McCleskey* was not expected to be given until the end of 1986 at the earliest.)

---

17. A decision by the court in *Spencer* v. *Zant*, referred to above, had been deferred pending *McCleskey*, which presented more detailed evidence on the racial discrimination claim.

Executive clemency in capital cases

Most state constitutions give the executive authorities the power to grant clemency in capital cases by commuting death sentences to life imprisonment. The procedures vary. Traditionally, the power to grant clemency has been vested solely in the state governor, as remains the case in many states. In others, the responsibility for reviewing cases for clemency has been transferred to state boards of pardons and paroles.[1] In some states, the pardons and paroles boards make recommendations to the state governors, who retain the final authority to grant or deny clemency. In others, the board has the sole power to grant clemency and the governor has no role in the decision. Most state governors or clemency boards also have the power to grant stays of execution.

Although state procedures rarely require that a prisoner await the final decision on judicial appeals before seeking clemency, it is usually considered only after the prisoner has effectively exhausted all legal appeals.

The practice differs in Florida, where clemency is considered relatively early in the judicial process. The Governor of Florida holds a clemency hearing with members of his cabinet in each case after a death sentence has been confirmed by the state supreme court; that is, before any state or federal *habeas corpus* appeals have taken place. A copy of the conviction and sentence is sent to the governor within 30 days of the Florida Supreme Court's decision in such cases (although the clemency hearing itself may take place much later).

Material supplied to the state governors and clemency boards usually includes information on the legal background to the case (including, in some cases, the entire trial record), with additional information about the prisoner's personal history and criminal record. Petitions from other sources may also be considered, including, in some states, those from the victim's family. Some states

---

1. The boards of pardons and paroles are usually appointed by the state governor to serve a fixed term, which usually extends beyond the governor's period in office. In some states — for example, Louisiana — the board serves only for the term of office of the appointing governor.

hold a hearing, or interview witnesses, before a final decision is taken; others may decide on the basis of written submissions only. In some cases, the prisoner may be interviewed personally before a final decision is reached.

Information supplied to the clemency authority will usually include submissions from prosecutors as well as representations on behalf of the prisoner. In Florida, counsel for the defendant and the prosecution (the latter being a lawyer from the state Attorney General's office) will always appear at the clemency hearing to give oral argument for and against clemency.

In Louisiana, a clemency hearing takes place at the prison, usually the day before the execution date. The hearing is attended by the prosecutor or district attorney as well as the prisoner's lawyer, and often also by relatives of both the prisoner and the victim.

Concern has been expressed because clemency decisions in many states are made so close to the execution date, in an atmosphere of intense emotional pressure and public attention. The Louisiana pardons board itself expressed concern about this, but said that prisoners did not apply for clemency until all legal appeals had failed, although they were free to do so at any time after conviction. However, Amnesty International was told that in many states clemency will not be considered while legal appeals are pending.[2] As shown above, final decisions in capital appeals often are not given until days or even hours before the execution is scheduled to take place.

Criteria for considering clemency

Relatively few applications for clemency had been made in capital cases during the period covered by this report, as most prisoners were still pursuing their legal appeals. Most of Amnesty International's observations are based on the practice in the four states visited by its 1985 mission. These states had probably reviewed more cases for clemency than others, owing to the larger number of prisoners reaching this stage and the provision for early clemency review in Florida.

At the time of Amnesty International's mission in June 1985, the Governor of Florida had held more than 100 clemency hearings in capital cases and had granted clemency in only six cases (none since

2. For example, the Rules of the Georgia State Board of Pardons and Paroles provide in part that "After receiving an application the Board will decide whether or not to consider commutation. This decision will be made after it appears that all appeals through the courts have ceased or have been exhausted." (Rule 475-3-.10(2)(b).

1982). Clemency had not been granted in any of the cases reviewed by the pardons boards in Texas or Louisiana at that time. The Georgia Board of Pardons and Paroles had considered seven applications by mid-1985 and had granted clemency in only one case. This was a case in which the actual killer had testified for the state and received a 10-year sentence for manslaughter, while the prisoner sentenced to death had played only a relatively minor role in the crime.

No reasons were given for granting or denying clemency in Louisiana, Texas and Georgia. Each member of the Boards of Pardons and Paroles makes an independent, discretionary decision which, in Louisiana and Georgia, is recorded by a simple majority vote.[3] In Louisiana, the recommendation is passed to the state Governor, who has the final authority to grant clemency; in Georgia, the board's decision is final; in Texas, each board member's recommendation is recorded separately and passed to the state Governor for a final decision on clemency.

In Florida, the Governor alone takes a decision on clemency, although his decision to commute a death sentence must have the approval of at least three members of the cabinet, which meets to vote on the matter not less than 10 days after the clemency hearing. If clemency is denied, the Governor's decision is final and no reasons are given. Amnesty International was told that in most cases a prisoner will know that a negative decision has been made only when an execution warrant is issued, which may be long after the clemency hearing.

There are no written guidelines or criteria for considering clemency in the states visited by the mission. Several board members pointed out that they had purposely not established written guidelines because they did not wish to be restricted in the matters which they could take into consideration.

However, Amnesty International has found that, in practice, the authorities take a very narrow view of the role of executive clemency. Although data on other states is insufficient to draw comparisons with earlier periods, it has been shown that, in Florida, a much smaller proportion of death sentences imposed under the present laws have been commuted through executive clemency than in any period since 1924.[4] The state authorities appear to take the view that the present

---

3. There are five board members in Louisiana and Georgia and seven in Texas. Four of the Georgia board members in 1985 were white and one (the only woman) was black. Three members of the boards of Louisiana and Texas were black.

4. A memorandum issued by the Capital Punishment Project of the University of Florida on 1 August 1984 reported that the six commutations granted by Governor

system of judicial review ensures that death sentences are fairly imposed, and has largely dispensed with the need to exercise the prerogative of mercy. In responding to appeals for clemency, several state governors have said that they were not prepared to interfere with the final decisions of the courts, on the grounds that the cases had already been extensively reviewed on appeal. Some governors have suggested that clemency would be considered only if there were new evidence in a case or irregularities in the legal process. In reply to an Amnesty International appeal in 1984, the Governor of Louisiana wrote: "It is my intention to intervene only if I determine that there are glaring inconsistencies with the legalities and facts of the case."[5]

The Boards of Pardons and Paroles in Louisiana, Texas and Georgia emphasized that they were not judicial bodies whose function was to review the legalities of the court decisions, but that they took wider considerations into account. However, they appeared to be influenced almost entirely by factors such as the severity of the crime, the legal culpability of the defendant and the general "correctness" of the conviction. Mitigating circumstances in the offender's background or other factors affecting the fairness of the sentence did not appear to be taken into account.[6] One member of the Georgia pardons board said that clemency would not be granted if the crime was "heinous enough for the offender to forfeit his life"; another said that, in his view, "the only consideration is whether the crime is of sufficient magnitude to take a life".

In Georgia, clemency was denied in several cases where the legal process, while technically correct, had clearly produced — or failed to remedy — an unjust result.

Graham represented only 5.2 per cent of the 115 cases reviewed at that time. The memorandum stated that this was a "lower per cent of commutations than that of any Florida Governor since records became available in 1924." The memorandum gave the percentage of executive clemency commutations granted out of all capital cases which reached their final disposition during each governor's administration since 1924. Figures given for the latter part of the pre-*Furman* period were: Governor Johns (1953-1955), 25.0 per cent; Governor Collins (1955-1961), 23.7 per cent; Governor Bryant (1961-1965), 37.5 per cent. (The last execution in Florida before its death penalty statute was vacated with the 1972 *Furman* decision was in 1964.)

In Georgia, clemency was reportedly granted in more than 25 per cent of cases considered from 1949 to 1963. Amnesty International has been unable to obtain information on the proportion of cases nationally in which clemency was granted before 1972.

5. Letter dated 26 March 1984 from Governor Edwin Edwards to a Swedish member of Amnesty International.

6. The Texas Board of Pardons and Paroles emphasized that the issue was not the degree of guilt or innocence, but whether other factors — perhaps unknown to the

One such case was that of John Young, executed in March 1985 for a murder committed when he was 18. His trial lawyer had clearly been negligent in failing to put before the sentencing jury mitigating circumstances on the defendant's background (including his having witnessed the murder of his mother when he was three and his subsequent neglected childhood). However, his appeal was dismissed on the procedural ground that testimony from the trial lawyer about his failure to conduct an adequate defence was submitted too late (see Chapter 3). Information submitted to the clemency board included statements about John Young's background from relatives and acquaintances who, though available, had not been called by his lawyer to testify at his trial, and an affidavit from a child psychologist about the likely traumatic effect of John Young's childhood experiences on his character and development.

The Georgia board had granted neither clemency nor stays of execution in the cases of Roosevelt Green and Alpha Otis Stephens, even though an appeal on an issue of direct relevance to their cases (racial discrimination in the application of the Georgia death penalty statute) was still pending a decision by the US Court of Appeals. In both cases, stays of execution had been denied or vacated by the US Supreme Court in circumstances which appeared unjust (see Chapter 7).

In the Green case, the tied vote by the Supreme Court on the denial of a stay of execution indicated doubt, which should have been grounds for at least an executive stay of execution by the clemency board. Other circumstances in this case might also have constituted grounds for clemency, since Roosevelt Green was convicted as an accomplice to a murder committed by a co-felon and, according to reports, had not been present when the killings occurred.

In the Stephens case, the Supreme Court lifted a stay it had earlier granted, without explanation, even though the circumstances under which it had granted the previous stay (the pending appeal on racial discrimination) were unchanged. In a letter to the Georgia Board of Pardons and Paroles dated 10 December 1984, Amnesty International expressed the view that it would be "contrary to the interests of justice to allow [Alpha Stephens'] execution to take place" in the circumstances, and appealed for clemency or, if this were not granted, a reprieve in the case "as a minimum measure toward serving the interests of justice."

---

jury — affected the fairness of the sentence imposed. To this extent, this board had a clearer concept of the role of clemency than the others. However, its members were unable to elaborate on which factors might be taken into account and clemency had been denied in several cases which appeared to Amnesty International to meet this criterion.

In each of the above three cases, the clemency process clearly failed to redress unfairness. When asked about these cases at the meeting with Amnesty International's mission in 1985, the Georgia board said it would not "interfere" with the decisions of the courts.

In none of the states visited were disparities in sentences among similar defendants in the same case considered grounds for commuting death sentences (although, as mentioned above, clemency had been granted to a co-defendant in a Georgia case where the principal offender had received a relatively minor sentence). In a Texas case of a murdered police officer, clemency was denied to Doyle Skillern, who did not shoot the victim, while his accomplice, who had fired the six fatal shots, was given a life sentence (see Chapter 3). Amnesty International raised this case with members of the Texas Board of Pardons and Paroles, who stated that the board had taken into account the fact that Doyle Skillern had a prior conviction for homicide (he had served a five-year prison sentence for killing his brother). However, information from the prisoner's lawyer suggested that more fortuitous circumstances had produced the disparate results in this case, rather than the trial court's perception of Doyle Skillern as the more dangerous offender.

The boards of the four states visited said that, in general, they considered the cases of co-defendants separately, without regard to differences in sentencing. It appeared that the clemency review process did not serve to remedy a lack of evenhandedness in the application of the death penalty in such cases.

Clemency was denied also in the cases of three juvenile offenders executed in Texas and South Carolina, despite international standards prohibiting the imposition of death sentences on people aged under 18 at the time of the crime. In these cases, the two governors relied on state laws setting the age at which a death sentence might be imposed, and on the fact that a defendant's youth was a mitigating circumstance considered at the sentencing stage of capital trials.

The limited view taken of the role of executive clemency in such cases is illustrated by the decision taken in the case of James Terry Roach, who was executed in South Carolina in January 1986 for two murders committed when he was aged 17 (see Chapter 5). The Governor of South Carolina declined to commute the death sentence imposed on him despite evidence that he had acted under the domination of an older person and was mentally retarded. Although the Governor based his decision on the fact that these and other mitigating circumstances had been considered by the trial court, he failed to take into account later evidence of a hereditary illness which raised doubts about the prisoner's mental competence to be executed.

The Governor also declined to grant an executive stay of execution in the case pending the outcome of a complaint to the IACHR, stating that the question of international law was a matter for the courts.

Clemency was denied in several other cases where prisoners showed signs of mental illness which brought into question their competence to be executed in accordance with international standards (see cases in Florida and Virginia, described in Chapter 6).

Divided opinions of the clemency boards

Most of the recommendations made by the Boards of Pardons and Paroles in Louisiana and Texas were majority rather than unanimous decisions. (The Georgia board gave no information on this point.)

Amnesty International was told that the Texas board had not made a unanimous recommendation against clemency in 1985 and that several of its decisions were narrowly divided. In Louisiana, a prisoner was executed after a recommendation against clemency was carried by one vote; the same prisoner had lost his appeals to the Louisiana Supreme Court and the US Court of Appeals, also by one vote, and the US Supreme Court had denied *certiorari* in the case by a single vote.[7]

The fact that so many opinions are divided indicates that there may be honest differences of opinion in the application of standards to individual cases. It suggests that there may be lingering doubts in the minds of members of clemency boards over whether particular prisoners should be executed. On the principle that any benefit of doubt should favour the condemned prisoner who faces the extreme penalty, it would seem fairer to grant clemency in all cases where opinion is divided.

On the question of divided court opinions, it is interesting to note that two former governors of New York made a practice of commuting death sentences in cases where the state appeals court's decisions were divided.[8]

Conclusions

After studying the practice of executive clemency in the USA, Amnesty International has reached the following conclusions:
□ The power to commute death sentences to life imprisonment has long been regarded as an important function of the executive

---

7. Robert Wayne Williams, a black man convicted of the 1979 killing of a supermarket security guard. He was executed by electrocution in December 1983.
8. Governors Alfred E. Smith and Herbert Lehman, in the 1920s and 1930s.

prerogative of mercy. By its very nature, executive clemency has a role in mitigating sentences which have been legally imposed by the courts but are unduly harsh. In exercising its discretion, the executive is not bound by the rules of the courts, but may take a wider range of factors into account.

☐ The state authorities appear to take a very narrow view of the role of executive clemency, believing that the decisions of the courts should stand unless there are irregularities or errors in the legal process.

☐ Several prisoners have been denied clemency despite factors that would seem to constitute especially strong grounds for exercising mercy. The clemency authorities appear to have lost sight of their traditional role to provide a final safeguard against the unfair imposition of death sentences by considering all the circumstances of the cases.[9] Clearer guidelines and criteria may help to broaden the concept of clemency.

☐ Reliance on the decisions of the courts cannot always ensure that the highest standards of fairness prevail. The appellate courts are bound by procedural rules which may prevent them from considering new evidence or information withheld at an earlier stage of the proceedings. Other information excluded from the trial and appeals process may include factors such as: excessive differences in sentencing among similar co-defendants; subsequent development of physical or mental illness; or testimony about an offender's background that may be available only at the clemency stage. All these factors may properly be considered grounds for exercising compassion in mitigating a death sentence.

☐ Amnesty International further believes that the observance of recognized international standards, contained in treaties signed by the USA, should be a minimum ground for granting clemency in cases involving the death penalty. Where state laws fall short of such standards and an execution is pending, the executive authorities, through the exercise of the prerogative of mercy, cannot disclaim all responsibility for meeting these standards.

---

9. The traditional role of executive clemency and its various functions, including the amelioration of unfair or unduly harsh sentences, is described in a number of articles and comments by those having knowledge of the process, cited in "A Matter of Life and Death: Due Process Protection in Capital Clemency Proceedings" by Deborah Leavy in *The Yale Law Journal*, vol. 90, No. 4, March 1981.

The cruelty of the death penalty

The experience of being under sentence of death

Amnesty International opposes the death penalty fundamentally, on the grounds that it is the ultimate form of cruel, inhuman and degrading punishment. It believes that the experience of being under sentence of death is itself cruel, inhuman and degrading. Long before execution, the condemned prisoner is forced to contemplate the prospect of being taken away to be put to death at an appointed time. During each appeal, the prisoner may suffer an agonizing conflict between the desire to live and remain in hope and the need to prepare for the possibility of imminent death. This has produced enormous stress in many condemned inmates and may have led to some prisoners dropping their legal appeals.[1]

Criminologist Robert Johnson, who interviewed death row inmates in Alabama in the 1970s, found that many of of them were intensely preoccupied with the thought of execution, speculating about the mechanics of electrocution (the method used in Alabama) and its likely impact on the body, which they visualised in great detail. The prisoners expressed anxiety about how they would behave during the walk to the death chamber and whether they would break down; whether they would feel pain as the electrical current surged through the body; how the memory or image of the execution would affect their families. For many prisoners these and similar thoughts had become a total obsession. Some prisoners had recurring nightmares in which they went through the execution process in vivid detail.[2]

Johnson noted that a condemned prisoner's contact with family

---

1. Lawyers acting for several prisoners who dropped their appeals confirmed this: they said stress and the conditions on death row had caused the prisoners to drop their final appeals and demand to be executed.

2. Robert Johnson, *Condemned to Die: Life under Sentence of Death*, Elsevier Books, New York: Oxford, 1981. The research was based on tape-recorded interviews with 35 of the 37 men confined on death row in Alabama in 1978. Extracts from the taped conversations with inmates given in the book include the following: ". . . I already have an understanding of electricity, you know, it's not hard for me to imagine what an experience it would be . . . Just think about the

and friends often deteriorated in the face of the prospect of permanent separation and a sense of the futility of pursuing relationships. He found that loss of contact with the outside world and the isolated conditions under which the condemned inmates were confined on death row produced widespread feelings of abandonment, leading to what he termed "death of the personality"; in some instances this happened long before the execution. This condition was characterized by severe depression, apathy, loss of a sense of reality and both physical and mental deterioration.[3]

Many of the stresses and anxieties suffered by condemned inmates are an inevitable consequence of the penalty itself. However, the prolonged isolation, enforced idleness and other deprivations experienced by death row inmates in some US states may exacerbate the inherently cruel and dehumanizing experience of being under sentence of death (see Chapter 11).

Condemned prisoners may also suffer the prospect of imminent execution each time a death warrant is signed. This may occur two or three times during the course of a prisoner's various appeals. The prisoner may then have to undergo at least part of the "death-watch" procedure (described below), during which he or she is removed to an isolated cell adjacent to the death chamber to await execution. Several prisoners have received last-minute reprieves only hours, or even minutes, before the scheduled execution. Amnesty International has been told that the "death-watch" procedure is one of the greatest single causes of stress among condemned inmates, several of whom are reported to have broken down mentally during this period.

Preparing for execution

The preparation for an execution itself may cause acute anguish. A condemned prisoner whose execution date is imminent is moved

---

insides of your body, you know, how such organs could be burned . . . Think about the precious brain that is in your head, you know? Think about your eyes. What will become of them through such hundreds of volts being ran through your body? It's just really unpredictable what all can happen through such an experience and what it will be like to go through it, to die right there, strapped in the chair . . . The body sears when the currents start going through the body. This makes a guy shiver to think of it. Does he feel it? What does he feel to start off with? When the current goes through, does he, is he, unconscious right when it strikes him? Or what really happens? . . . you know, I think about it quite a bit, and it does go through my mind. And I wonder what's really going to happen . . . I go to sleep and I dream of me sitting down in that chair. I mean, it's such a fearful thought. Me walking down the tier, sitting down on it [the electric chair], them hooking it up and turning it on . . . I don't know. I can wake up, my heart's beating fast, I'm sweating like hell, just like I'd rinsed my head in water . . . I feel I'm gonna have a heart attack."

3. In later interviews with the same death row inmates, Johnson found a loss of mental acuteness, confusion and some psychosis in 70 per cent of the cases.

from the general death row population to an isolated cell adjacent to the death chamber. Most or all of the prisoner's personal possessions are removed at this time and he or she is placed under special observation — this is known as the "death-watch" procedure. In some states the procedure is initiated from the moment an execution warrant is signed; in others, the condemned inmate may be removed to the "death-watch" cell from several days to 24 hours before the scheduled execution.

In Florida, the steps preceding execution (by electrocution) are contained in a confidential memorandum, "Execution Guidelines During Active Death Warrant", distributed to prison personnel by the Superintendent of Florida State Prison (Appendix 14).

According to these guidelines, phase one of the "death-watch" procedure begins from the moment a death warrant is read to the condemned inmate, four weeks before the execution date. At this point the prisoner is moved from the general death row area to one of three cells in "Q" Wing, which leads directly to the death chamber. Most of the prisoner's personal possessions are removed; all association with other prisoners and contact visits with the condemned inmate's family and friends is withdrawn (although the inmate may still have contact visits with his or her attorney). The prisoner has no out-of-cell exercise during this period and is placed under close observation.

Phase two of the procedure begins four days before the execution, when the prisoner is placed under constant observation by a prison officer positioned in front of the cell. The regulations provide that, during this period, all visits, including those with the prisoner's attorney are changed to non-contact; the prisoner's remaining property is removed and sealed for storage; the prisoner is measured for clothing to be worn during the execution; the prisoner must specify in writing his or her funeral arrangements and designate the "recipient of any personal property".

On the fourth, second and final day before the execution, an "execution squad drill" takes place and the electrician tests the execution equipment and generator. The day before the execution the electrician makes up a solution of ammonium chloride (which acts as a conducting agent) in which he soaks the sponge which will be placed on the prisoner's head just before execution. On the same day the Chief Medical Officer of the Corrections Department prepares a death certificate, in which cause of death is given as: "legal execution by electrocution".

The prisoner is allowed a final contact visit with relatives at around 1am on the execution day. A "last meal" is served at 4.30am. Between 5am and 6am, the prisoner's head and right leg are shaved;

the prisoner is showered and changed into his or her execution clothes. At 5.50am, conducting gel is applied to the prisoner's crown and right calf: this is similar in consistency to petroleum jelly and its purpose is both to help conduct electricity and reduce the burning of the flesh.

At 7am the prisoner, held in restraints, is escorted into the execution chamber by three prison officials. He or she is then strapped into the electric chair, secured at the arms, legs, chest and lap. The electrician will then attach an electrode to the prisoner's right ankle, which is wired to an electrical panel behind the chair. The prisoner is then permitted to make a final statement. After this, the ammonium-soaked sponge and the head-set and electrodes are placed on the prisoner's head and secured tightly around the jaw so that the head is held upright and rigid against the chair. A leather hood, which is part of the head-set, is then pulled down to completely mask the condemned prisoner's face. A masked executioner, standing in a booth just behind the chair, then pulls the switch and the electrical current is applied.

A stay of execution may be granted at any point in the proceedings, until the electrical current is switched on. According to the Florida regulations, an outside open telephone line must be available in the execution chamber for the purpose of receiving information about stays. The guidelines require that the superintendent in charge of the procedure go to the telephone immediately after the prisoner has made his last statement to inquire whether there has been a last-minute stay of execution.

According to the Florida guidelines, 10 people are present in the death chamber during an execution, including prison guards, two electricians, the executioner, a physician and a physician's assistant.

A condemned inmate may struggle during the preparation for execution. This happened in the case of Florida death row inmate Daniel Morris Thomas, who was executed on 15 April 1986. According to lawyers, he remained calm as he was led to the execution chamber but began to struggle as four officers began to strap him into the chair. A report by lawyers said that this resulted in a "rather uneven conflict which culminated with seven white men — guards, medical assistant, *and the attending physician* — brutally subduing and restraining Mr Thomas, physically forcing him into the restraints which would hold his body motionless for the minutes before his death . . ." (emphasis in original).[4] Press reports state that the struggle in the death chamber lasted for seven minutes before the

---

4. From Motion to Vacate Judgment and Sentence filed before Circuit Court of Fourth Judicial Circuit, Florida, in the case of David Funchess, 20 April 1986.

112

electric current was applied.

The procedures issued by the Texas Department of Corrections for execution by lethal injection, require that the condemned inmate be removed to the unit where the execution is to take place not more than 72 hours or less than 24 hours before execution. The prisoner is kept under constant observation during this period. All visits are terminated by 6pm on the day before the execution. A last meal is served between 6.30pm and 7.30pm on the day of the execution. The inmate is showered and changed into his or her execution clothes between 8pm and 8.30pm. The condemned prisoner is removed from the holding cell at midnight. Just outside the execution chamber, the inmate is secured to a hospital "gurney" (a wheeled stretcher) which is then "rolled from the cell area into the Death House". There a "medically trained individual (not to be identified)" inserts an intravenous catheter into the inmate's arm. The inmate is then permitted to make a last statement. After this, prison officials begin the flow of a neutral solution and, subsequently, introduce by syringe a solution of sodium thiopental to cause death. There may be a lapse of some 30 minutes between the insertion of the catheter and the actual administration of the fatal solution. The executioner(s) are separated from the execution chamber by a wall, through which the intravenous lines run.

An article in the *Los Angeles Herald* of 25 March 1984 described the procedures for execution by lethal gas in California, where 196 prisoners died in the gas chamber in San Quentin Prison from 1938 to 1967.[5] The article was based on accounts by eye-witnesses and officials involved in the executions, including Joe Ferretti, a former "death-watch" officer who had officiated at 126 executions and who was brought in to train new executioners in the early 1980s, in preparation for a resumption of executions in the state by this method (see below: Methods of execution). The gas chamber in California is a vacuum-sealed, eight-sided steel tank situated in a corner of a room outside the cell block which houses death row. Inside the gas chamber there are two steel chairs from which cheesecloth bags containing 16 cyanide pellets are suspended. During the execution, the bags are lowered by a remote controlled lever into vats of acid. Joe Ferretti said that during his period as "death-watch" officer a condemned prisoner was moved into a holding cell next to the gas chamber at about 4pm on the day before the execution. While still in the holding cell a harness with a stethoscope was strapped round the prisoner's chest. Once the prisoner was strapped into the chair in the

---

5. Article by Michael A. Kroll, "The Fraternity of Death", *Los Angeles Herald*, 25 March 1984.

113

gas chamber, a rubber tube was fastened to the stethoscope so that
a doctor could monitor the prisoner's heartbeat from outside the
chamber. The door to the tank was then sealed and the execution
began.

Joe Ferretti, who kept notes on many of the executions he presided
over, and other witnesses said that several of the condemned
prisoners were dragged, or carried, screaming into the gas chamber.
One prisoner cut his throat with a concealed piece of glass and was
taken into the chamber bleeding profusely. He managed to free his
arm, which was slippery with blood, from one of the straps on the
chair and died shouting and struggling to free his other arm: this was a
double execution and the other prisoner sat strapped to the chair
beside him. Describing the 1949 execution of Leandress Riley, a
one-eyed, nearly deaf black man who was sentenced to death for the
murder of a laundryman, Joe Ferretti said he was carried struggling
into the gas chamber. The prisoner, who weighed only 80lb, managed
to slip out of the restraining straps and ran round the gas chamber
screaming and beating on the glass window behind which the
witnesses were seated. The procedure had to be stopped and resumed
three times before the execution could be completed. Recalling the
execution, former prison warden Louis Nelson said: "the fact that the
fellow is crying and baying like a dog, you just can't deal with it at that
point. You've got to carry out the job at hand."

At the time of writing, only two people had been executed by lethal
gas since the death penalty was reinstated. One of them, Jimmy Lee
Gray, was executed in Mississippi in September 1983. He was
removed to a holding cell a few feet away from the gas chamber about
an hour before the execution was due to be carried out. The gas
chamber in Mississippi is a six-sided stainless steel cubicle which is
clearly visible from the holding cell. A few minutes before the
execution, the prisoner was placed in the gas chamber and strapped
into a chair, after which a prison guard pulled a lever which released a
cyanide pellet into a bucket of acid, which produced the lethal gas.

Death warrants are commonly signed two or three times during the
various stages of a prisoner's appeals. Amnesty International was
informed that some 30 to 40 prisoners in Florida have been through at
least part of the "death-watch" procedure before getting stays of
execution. At least one prisoner in Florida is reported to have
developed signs of mental illness as a result of this experience.[6]

At least two prisoners in Texas received stays of execution minutes
before their scheduled execution by lethal injection. One of them,

6. Alvin Ford reportedly first developed psychotic symptoms when his first
execution warrant was issued in 1982 and he was placed in the "death cell".

James Autry, was already strapped to a stretcher and undergoing the first stage of lethal injection when he was granted a temporary stay.

Methods of execution

The most common methods of execution in the USA are electrocution, lethal injection (injection of poison) and asphyxiation by gas. A few states provide for execution by firing-squad or hanging.

Lethal injection — first introduced in Oklahoma and Texas in 1977 — had been adopted as a sole or alternative method of execution in 16 states by May 1986. Charles Brooks in Texas was the first person to be executed in this manner, in December 1982. As noted above, at the end of 1985 the gas chamber had been used in only two cases since the death penalty was reinstated in the 1970s: Jesse Bishop, executed in 1979 in Nevada (which now uses the lethal injection method) and Jimmy Lee Gray in Mississippi in 1983. California, which has the USA's fourth largest death row and also provides for execution in the gas chamber, had not yet carried out any executions under the present laws by the end of May 1986.[7]

Electrocution was first introduced as a method of execution in the USA in 1888 (in New York State) on the grounds that this would be more humane than hanging. This became the preferred method of execution in the USA until the introduction of lethal injection in the 1970s. Electrocution produces visibly destructive effects as the body's internal organs are burned; the condemned prisoner often leaps forward against the restraining straps when the switch is thrown; the body changes colour; the flesh swells and may even catch fire; the prisoner may defecate, urinate or vomit blood. Eye-witnesses always report that there is a smell of burned flesh.[8] However, it has been argued that, despite the violent physical effects of electrocution, no pain is experienced by the prisoner and unconsciousness, if not actual death, is instantaneous.

This has been disputed by scientists and doctors. In a dissenting opinion given in *Glass* v. *Louisiana* (1985), US Supreme Court Justice Brennan reviewed the considerable accumulated evidence of electrical scientists, eye-witness testimony and medical research, suggesting that electrocution causes "unspeakable pain and suffering"

---

7. As of May 1986, 15 states prescribed death by electrocution, 16 by lethal injection, seven by the gas chamber, four by hanging and three by firing squad. Eight of the above states prescribed death by more than one method. (See Appendix 1.)

8. There are many eye-witness accounts of the physical effects of electrocution, including testimony to the US congressional debates on the death penalty in 1968 and 1972.

far beyond the mere extinction of life.[9] The opinion cited the findings of research scientists that:

"The [electric] current flows along a restricted path into the body and destroys all tissue confronted in this path . . . [i]n the meantime the vital organs may be preserved; and pain, too great for us to imagine, is induced . . ."[10]

The opinion also quotes from a renowned French electrical scientist who concluded after extensive research that:

"In every case of electrocution . . . death inevitably supervenes but it may be [a] very long and, above all, excruciatingly painful [death] . . . The space of time before death supervenes varies according to the subject. Some have a greater physiological resistance than others. I do not believe that anyone killed by electrocution dies instantly, no matter how weak the subject may be. In certain cases death will not have come about even though the point of contact of the electrode with the body shows distinct burns. Thus, in particular cases, the condemned person may be alive and even conscious for several minutes without it being possible for a doctor to say whether the victim is dead or not . . . [This] method of execution is a form of torture."[11]

In 1946 Willie Francis, a 17-year-old black youth, survived an attempted execution by electrocution in Louisiana. After the electric charge failed to kill him he was removed from the chair and returned to his cell. He is reported to have stated afterwards that: "My mouth tasted like cold peanut butter. I felt a burning in my head and my left leg, and I jumped against the straps. I saw little blue and pink and

---

9. From *Glass* v. *Louisiana*, 1985, opinion by Justice Brennan, dissenting from denial of *certiorari* by the US Supreme Court. The defendant, Jimmy Glass, condemned to death in Louisiana, had appealed to the Supreme Court, claiming that execution by electrocution violated the Eighth and Fourteenth Amendments to the US Constitution on the grounds that it causes the "gratuitous infliction of unnecessary pain and suffering and does not comport with evolving standards of decency". As well as reviewing the major research during this century into electrocution as a method of killing, the dissenting opinion also describes the physical effects of electrocution, contained in testimony given to the House and Senate Judiciary Committees during debates on capital punishment in 1968 and 1972.

10. Footnote to the opinion, citing N. Teeters, "Hang by the Neck", p. 448.

11. Footnote to the *Glass* opinion gives as a reference for this statement, made by French scientist L.G.V. Rota, as quoted by C. Duff, in *A Handbook on Hanging*, pp. 119-120 (1974).

green speckles." A new death warrant was signed and he was executed a year later.[12]

Laws providing for execution by lethal injection have been enacted on the grounds that this provides a more humane and less painful form of execution than other methods. However, this has also been disputed by medical opinion.

Execution by this method involves the continuous intravenous injection of a lethal quantity of a short-acting barbiturate in combination with a chemical paralytic agent. In Texas, a combination of three drugs is used (sodium thiopental, pancuronium bromide and potassium chloride), each of which is fatal when administered in sufficient quantities but one of which is used to render the subject unconscious before the fatal dose takes effect. The solution is administered by medically trained technicians from behind a wall through which four intravenous lines run into the death chamber.

A number of doctors have described the problems which may arise when administering lethal injections. It has been pointed out that there may be special difficulties with diabetics or former drug users, whose veins may be hard to reach (which applies to many prison inmates). This reportedly accounted for the problems experienced in the execution of Stephen Morin, an alleged former heroin addict (see below). According to medical testimony, in some cases minor surgery may be required to cut into a deeper vein.[13] There is also a risk, if the prisoner struggles, or the vein is hard to locate, of the substance entering an artery or muscle tissue, which medical opinion agrees can be extremely painful (this may have happened in the case of James Autry — see below). Doctors have also said that skill is required in determining the correct dosage, which may be especially difficult in the case of prisoners with a history of alcohol or drug abuse. Greater quantities may be needed in such cases than would normally be given. If there is an imbalance in the solutions, or the drugs are mixed together too soon, the solution may thicken, causing the catheter to clog and slow down the execution.[14]

Other methods of execution may also be prolonged or cause acute suffering, either in the preparations or during the execution. The

12. From reports in the daily *Washington Post* newspaper, 14 December 1984, and the US weekly *Guardian* newspaper, 4 May 1983.

13. This had not occurred in the relatively few executions by lethal injection which had been carried out by the time of writing.

14. The testimony of doctors on lethal injections is contained in numerous articles and medical journals, including the 6 February 1985 edition of the *Medical Tribune* (an international medical weekly published in the USA), and the article "Lethal Injection; An Uneasy Alliance of Law and Medicine", by Thomas O. Finks, published in *The Journal of Legal Medicine*, vol. 4, Number 3, 1983.

anguish which may be caused to the condemned prisoner during the preparation for gassing in California has been described above. Eye-witness accounts and medical reports indicate that lethal gas causes a slow and painful death by asphyxiation as the brain and heart are deprived of oxygen.[15] Howard Brodie, a journalist, described an execution by gassing he witnessed in California in 1967. The prisoner had struggled and screamed before entering the gas chamber. Later, Brodie said, "As the gas hit him his head immediately fell to his chest. Then his head came up and he looked directly into the window I was standing next to. For nearly seven minutes, he sat up that way, with his chest heaving, saliva bubbling between his lips. He tucked his thumbs into his fist and, finally, his head fell down again". The prison warden was reported as saying of the same execution that "It seemed to take ten years. He kept gasping for air". According to the records, it took 12 minutes for the prisoner's heart to stop beating.[16]

Execution by hanging, also, may not kill instantly. British physiologist Harold Hillman, writing in the British science journal *New Scientist* on 27 October 1983, described execution by hanging in Britain before its general abolition there in 1969. He stated that after the trap-door on which the condemned prisoner is placed had been opened: "the weight of the prisoner's body below the neck causes traction and tearing of the cervical muscles, skin and blood vessels. The upper cervical vertebrae are dislocated, and the spinal cord is separated from the brain: this is the lesion which causes death . . . The respirating and then the heart rate slow and then stop, and death supervenes." He went on to say that "it is impossible to know for how long the condemned person feels pain, and the standard practice of hooding prevents observation of the face. Animals in an analogous situation often squeak. Their facial muscles go into spasm . . . and they close their eyes."

The cruelty of execution is illustrated by some recent cases in the USA in which the prisoner did not die instantaneously and suffering appeared to have been prolonged.

John Louis Evans was executed by electrocution in Alabama in April 1983 after having been convicted of murder in 1977. According to eye-witness accounts, it required three separate charges of 1,900 volts over 14 minutes before he was officially pronounced dead.[17]

15. This evidence was referred to in a dissenting opinion in *Gray* v. *Lucas* (1983).
16. The execution of Aaron Mitchell, described in "The Fraternity of Death", *Los Angeles Herald*, 25 March 1984.
17. Most states require a number of witnesses, including authorized press representatives, to be present at an execution. A detailed account of John Evans' electrocution is contained in an affidavit by Russell Canan, his attorney who witnessed the execution.

During the first electrical charge, the electrode on his leg burned through and fell off; prison guards repaired it after doctors had said he was not dead. During the second charge, smoke and flame erupted from his left temple and leg. The third jolt was given after doctors had put a stethoscope to his chest and said they were still not certain he was dead. This was the first execution in Alabama for 18 years. Amnesty International subsequently wrote to the Governor of Alabama expressing its unconditional opposition to the death penalty and stating that "prolonged suffering was manifestly inflicted in this case".

Alpha Otis Stephens was executed by electrocution in Georgia in December 1984. The *New York Times* newspaper reported on 13 December that the first two-minute charge of electricity failed to kill him and that he "struggled for breath for eight minutes" before a second charge was applied. The same report stated that, after the first charge, applied at 12.18am, "His body slumped when the current stopped . . . but shortly afterward witnesses saw him struggle to breathe. In the six minutes allowed for the body to cool before doctors could examine it, Mr Stephens took about 23 breaths." The second, fatal, charge was applied at 12.28am, after the two doctors who had examined him said he was still alive.

The execution of William Vandiver by electrocution in Indiana on 16 October 1985, was reported to have taken 17 minutes, requiring five charges of electricity before he was pronounced dead. An official from the Department of Corrections was reported in the *Washington Post* newspaper on 17 October to have said that the equipment had not malfunctioned in any way.

James Autry was executed by lethal injection in Texas on 14 March 1984. He had previously been scheduled for execution in November 1983 and at that time had been strapped to a stretcher and was undergoing the first stage of the lethal injection process (a saline solution was being dripped into his veins) when his execution was stayed. The US news magazine *Newsweek* reported on 9 April 1984 that at his execution in March, James Autry "took at least ten minutes to die and throughout much of that time was conscious, moving about and complaining of pain". A staff prison doctor, who was present at the execution, was later reported to have said that the catheter needle may have become clogged, slowing down the execution. Other witnesses said that some of the solution had apparently entered the muscle tissue, which can cause pain.[18]

In the execution of Stephen Morin by lethal injection in Texas on

---

18. A prison doctor who witnessed James Autry's execution suggested that the catheters may have clogged, slowing the execution. He said that this may have been

13 March 1985, technicians are reported to have taken more than 40 minutes searching the prisoner's limbs for a suitable vein in which to insert the needle.

Jimmy Lee Gray was executed by lethal gas in Mississippi on 2 September 1983. At just after 12.11am, the executioner flipped a lever causing the lethal gas from cyanide crystals to enter the gas chamber. Reports state that, after gas rose from the floor, the prisoner had convulsions for eight minutes and gasped 11 times, striking his head repeatedly on a pole behind him. Some of the witnesses said that he did not appear to be dead when deputies asked them to leave the witness room. As they filed out, Warden Eddie Lucas was asked if Jimmy Lee Gray were dead. "No question," he said. Dennis Balske, the prisoner's lawyer and a witness to the execution, said his client appeared to suffer a "painful death".[19]

due to the narrowness of James Autry's veins. From articles by Dennison Demac in the *Medical Tribune*, 6 February 1985. A Texas prison spokesperson, Jay Byrd, is reported in an article in the same journal of 6 February 1985 to have said about James Autry's execution that ". . . every individual is different in reaction to a chemical. For some reason, if the drugs are mixed too closely together, the combination may thicken, flow more slowly and so delay death. It's possible the [pancuronium bromide (Pavulum, Organon)] was added too soon after the sodium thiopental."

19. Reports from *Reuters*, 2 September 1983, the *San Francisco Chronicle*, 2 September 1983 and the *Delta Democrat Times*, Mississippi, 2 September 1983.

WASHINGTON: The gallows in Walla Walla Prison, where eight inmates were on death row in October 1986. The state's death penalty statutes provide for execution by hanging or lethal injection. No prisoners have been executed in the state since 1963. Three other states provide for execution by hanging: Delaware (five prisoners on death row — no executions since the 1940s); New Hampshire (no prisoners on death row — no executions since 1939); and Montana (five prisoners on death row — no executions since the 1940s); Montana also authorizes execution by lethal injection. © *Gamma-Liaison*

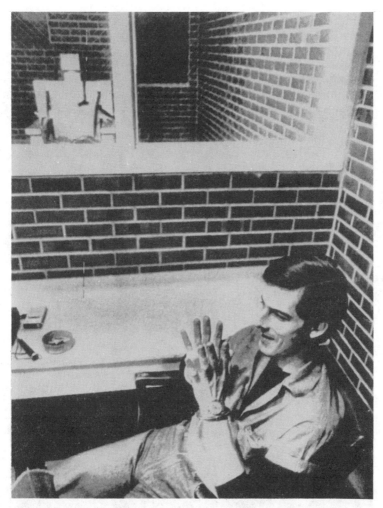

ALABAMA: John Louis Evans, sentenced to death in 1977 for murder and robbery, was photographed in 1979 with Alabama's electric chair visible in an adjoining room. At his execution in April 1983, he had to be given three charges of electricity before he was pronounced dead, after 14 minutes. After the first charge, the electrode on his leg burned through and fell off. During the second, smoke and flame erupted from his left temple and leg. The third charge was given after doctors had put a stethoscope to his chest and said they were still not certain he was dead (see page 117). © *Popperfoto*

122

TEXAS: The death needle used in executions by lethal injection. The method involves the continuous injection of a lethal quantity of a short-acting barbiturate
in combination with a paralytic agent. In Texas, a combination of three drugs
is used, each of which is fatal when administered in sufficient quantities but one
of which is used to render the prisoner unconscious before the fatal dose takes
effect. The solution is administered by medically trained technicians from behind
a wall. © *Gamma-Liaison*

123

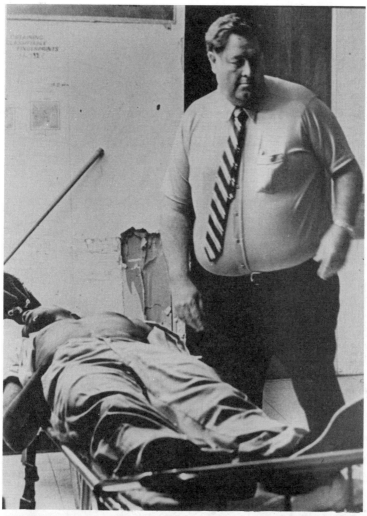

TEXAS: The body of Charles Brooks lies on a "gurney" (wheeled stretcher) outside the death chamber soon after his execution by lethal injection in Huntsville prison in December 1982 — he was the first prisoner in the USA to die by this method. He was convicted of murder. His co-defendant in the case (whose original conviction and death sentence were overturned on a technicality) later received a 40-year prison sentence as a result of a plea bargain. It was not established which of the two had been the actual killer. Charles Brooks was executed before he had completed the first round of federal *habeas corpus* appeals — his application for a stay of execution was denied by the US Court of Appeals without its considering the merits of his appeal (see pages 32, 96 and 141). © *Huntsville Item*

124

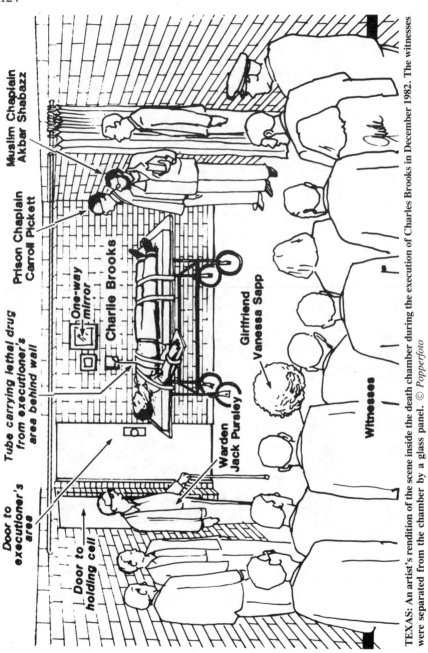

Door to executioner's area

Tube carrying lethal drug from executioner's area behind wall

Prison Chaplain Carroll Pickett

Muslim Chaplain Akbar Shabazz

One-way mirror

Charlie Brooks

Door to holding cell

Warden Jack Pursley

Girlfriend Vanessa Sapp

Witnesses

TEXAS: An artist's rendition of the scene inside the death chamber during the execution of Charles Brooks in December 1982. The witnesses were separated from the chamber by a glass panel. © *Popperfoto*

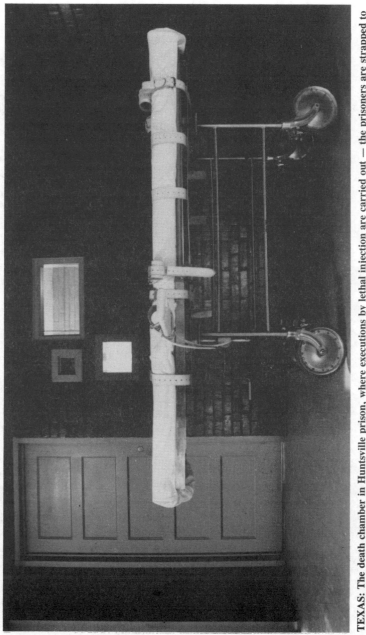

TEXAS: The death chamber in Huntsville prison, where executions by lethal injection are carried out — the prisoners are strapped to the "gurney" before the injection process begins (see Chapter 9). © *Gamma-Liaison*

126

LOUISIANA: The electric chair in the state penitentiary's "death house"... witnesses sit in the adjoining room and watch executions through

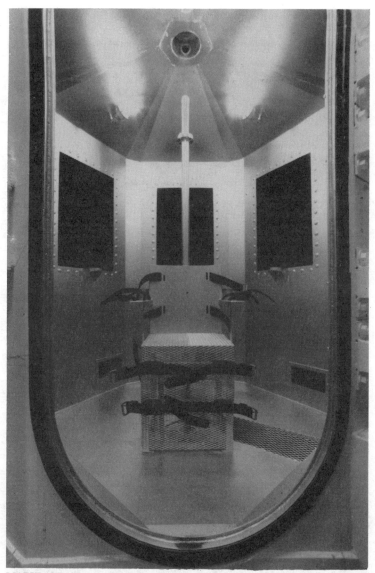

MARYLAND: The gas chamber in Maryland Penitentiary; 19 prisoners are on death row in the state — there have been no executions since 1961. Six other states provide for execution by lethal gas (the figure in brackets is the year of the last execution): Arizona (1963), California (1967), Colorado (1967), Mississippi (1983), Missouri (1965), and North Carolina (1961 by lethal gas; 1986 by lethal injection).
© *Gamma-Liaison*

LOUISIANA: Two death row inmates play chess between cells in Louisiana's Angola State Penitentiary. © *Ted Jackson/Times-Picayune*

ILLINOIS: Death row in Menard Penitentiary, one of two prisons housing the state's 98 condemned inmates in October 1986. The Illinois statute provides for execution by lethal injection but there have been no executions since 1962. © *Gamma-Liaison*

FLORIDA: Starke State Prison's "R" wing, which houses Florida's 247 prisoners on death row — the largest in the country. Sixteen prisoners were executed between May 1979 and October 1986. © *Gamma-Liaison*

CALIFORNIA: San Quentin Prison, which houses the country's third largest death row: 190 prisoners in October 1986. State law provides for death by lethal gas but the prison's gas chamber *(inset)* has not been used since 1967. © *Popperfoto*

132

GEORGIA: Jerry Banks, who spent five years on death row before all charges against him were dismissed. Three months later his wife asked for a divorce and he killed her and himself. The children were later awarded damages by the state for its mishandling of the case (see page 173).

Charles Brooks

James Dupree Henry 8 0

John Young

Roosevelt Green

TEXAS: Charles Brooks, the first death row prisoner in the USA to die by the lethal injection method (see previous photos and pages 32, 96 and 141). © *AP*

FLORIDA: James Dupree Henry, executed in September 1984, had been convicted and sentenced to death for an accidental killing during a robbery (see page 175 and Appendix 4).

GEORGIA: John Young was executed in March 1985 for the murder of three people. Important mitigating evidence was not put before his trial jury (see page 46). © *Popperfoto*

GEORGIA: Roosevelt Green was electrocuted in January 1985 for murder. He was reportedly not present at the killing and had not intended that it should occur — but the court ruled that he should have known his accomplice was dangerous and capable of killing. The accomplice was still on death row in October 1986 (see page 98). © *AP*

134

John Spenkelink

Daniel Thomas

James Terry Roach

Doyle Skillern

FLORIDA: John Spenkelink, electrocuted in May 1979, had been sentenced to death for capital murder after he had refused a prosecution offer of a guilty plea to a lesser charge (see page 32). © Doug Magee

FLORIDA: Daniel Thomas reportedly struggled as guards began to strap him into the electric chair in April 1986. Witnesses say an attending doctor and a medical assistant helped in "brutally subduing and restraining" him (see page 111).

SOUTH CAROLINA: James Terry Roach, electrocuted in January 1986, was 17 at the time of the crime (rape and murder). Psychiatrists said he was mentally retarded, and the trial judge found that he had acted under the domination of an older man (see page 71). © Jeff Amberg/The State

TEXAS: Doyle Skillern, an accomplice sentenced to death for murder, was executed in January 1985 — soon afterwards the actual killer, who received a life sentence, became eligible for parole (see page 52). © AP

Alvin Ford

Morris Mason

Jerome Bowden

David Funchess   D O R

FLORIDA: Alvin Ford won a stay of execution after the US Supreme Court ruled that Florida's procedures for determining insanity at the time of execution were inadequate (see page 79). © *UPI/ Bettmann Newsphotos*

VIRGINIA: Morris Mason, a black farmworker aged 32, was executed in Virginia in June 1985. He had a long history of mental illness but the trial court denied his request for the assistance of a psychiatrist in evaluating his sanity (see page 82). © *Richmond News Leader*

GEORGIA: Jerome Bowden, 33, diagnosed as mentally retarded, was electrocuted in June 1986, after a trial from

which the prosecutor had peremptorily excluded all blacks (see footnote on page 184).

FLORIDA: David Funchess, a Vietnam War veteran, was electrocuted in April 1986 — even though evidence of his severe mental disorder only came to light years after his 1975 conviction for murder (see page 84).

Jimmy Lee Gray

James Autry

Alpha Otis Stephens S CTR

Stephen Morin

stayed after he had been strapped down and a saline drip was being fed intravenously (see page 118). © *Popperfoto*

GEORGIA: Alpha Otis Stephens reportedly struggled for breath for eight minutes after the first charge during his electrocution in December 1984 (see page 118).

TEXAS: Stephen Morin was executed by lethal injection in March 1985 — medical technicians are reported to have taken more than 40 minutes to find a suitable vein in which to insert the needle (see page 118).

MISSISSIPPI: Jimmy Lee Gray is reported to have had convulsions for eight minutes and to have struck his head repeatedly on the pole behind him during his execution by lethal gas in 1983 (see page 119). © *Popperfoto*

TEXAS: James Autry is reported to have suffered a painful death when executed by lethal injection in March 1982. A previously scheduled execution was only

Jay Thompson

Paula Cooper

© AFP

Ronald Ward

Juvenile offenders on death row in October 1986

ARKANSAS: Ronald Ward, aged 17, was sentenced to death in September 1985 for the murder of three white people when he was 15. © AP

INDIANA: Paula Cooper, aged 16, was sentenced to death in July 1986 for the murder of a woman of 78, and Jay Thompson was sentenced to death in March 1982 for the robbery and murder of an elderly couple when he was 17.

The imposition of the death penalty on people who were under 18 at the time of the crime is in clear violation of the International Covenant on Civil and Political Rights and the American Convention of Human Rights. The US Government signed both treaties in 1977 but has not yet ratified them. International standards prohibiting the execution of juveniles were developed in recognition of the fact that the death penalty is a wholly inappropriate punishment for people who have not yet attained full physicial or emotional maturity at the time of their actions, are more liable than adults to act on impulse or under the domination of others, with little thought for the long-term consequences of their actions, and are unlikely to be deterred by the penalty. At the time of writing 32 juvenile offenders were known to be on death rows in the USA (see Chapter 5).

ARIZONA: A condemned cell in Arizona State Prison, Florence. In October 1986 Arizona, whose statutes provide for execution by lethal gas, had 65 prisoners on death row — the last execution in the state was in 1963. © *Doug Magee*

DOCTORS: Doctors and other medical professionals have used extended stethoscopes like these to monitor the condition of prisoners while they are being executed in sealed gas chambers. World and US medical professional bodies have condemned the participation of doctors in executions (see Chapter 10). © *Jackson Hill*

LOUISIANA: The mother of Robert Wayne Williams pleads unsuccessfully for his life at a hearing of the Louisiana Board of Pardons and Parole. An all-white jury had convicted him of murder and robbery — his court-appointed lawyer was reported to have spent a total of only eight hours preparing his case. He was electrocuted in December 1983 (see page 44). © *AP*

Involvement of doctors and other health professionals in the death penalty

There has been concern that the involvement of doctors and other health professionals in some US executions has been contrary to medical ethics, which require dedication to the preservation of life and the principle that a physician must do no harm.[1] The introduction of execution by lethal injection, in particular, has caused concern among members of the medical profession, many of whom are disturbed that drugs and practices developed for medical purposes are being used to kill people. There is concern also that, even without doctors personally giving lethal injections, other health professionals may be required to do so, and that doctors and other health professionals may be required to assist in such activities as determining mental and physical fitness for execution, giving technical advice, prescribing the drugs, supervising the procedure or examining the prisoner during the execution so that it can continue if the prisoner is not yet dead. Some of these concerns apply not only to lethal injection but also to other forms of execution.

None of the statutes authorizing lethal injection as a method of execution require that a doctor personally administer the drugs. Most provide that the execution be carried out by "medically trained" technicians attached to the state prisons departments.

However, shortly after the enactment of the Oklahoma statute (the first to introduce lethal injection in 1977), the Oklahoma Corrections Department issued regulations in which it required that a doctor actively supervise the execution process by inspecting the catheter and monitoring equipment to determine that the fluid would flow into the vein. The regulations also stipulated that the toxic drugs be ordered by the Medical Director of the Corrections Department. The Oklahoma Corrections Department has since revised these procedures, eliminating the role of its Medical Director in ordering the drugs or supervising the execution. This change in procedure took place after a number of US medical associations had issued

---

1. These principles were first codified in the Hippocratic Oath.

140

statements declaring that direct participation by doctors in lethal injections was ethically unacceptable.

At its annual meeting in July 1980, the House of Delegates of the American Medical Association (AMA) adopted a resolution stating, among other things, that:

"A physician, as a member of a profession dedicated to the preservation of life when there is hope of doing so, should not be a participant in a legally authorized execution."

The resolution added that: "A physician may make a determination or certification of death as currently provided by law in any situation", on the grounds that this did not constitute participation in the act of execution.

In November 1980 the Texas Medical Association adopted a policy statement declaring that: "A physician may be present at a chemical execution for the sole purpose of pronouncing death". Several other state medical associations including those of Idaho and New Mexico, also adopted resolutions affirming the AMA position.[2] Some associations, such as the North Carolina Medical Society, have gone further and urged other health care workers and physicians' assistants to refuse to participate in executions.[3]

There has also been international concern at the possible effects of lethal injection on doctors' involvement in executions. On 11 September 1981 the Secretary General of the World Medical Association (WMA), Dr André Wynen, issued a press release stating that:

"Acting as an executioner is not the practice of medicine and physician services are not required to carry out capital punishment even if the methodology utilizes pharmacologic agents or equipment that might otherwise be used in the practice of medicine. A physician's only role would be to certify death *once the state had carried out the execution*." (emphasis added)

The substance of this text was confirmed at the World Medical Assembly of the WMA, held in Lisbon from 28 September to 2 October 1981.

2. Although the Oklahoma State Medical Association has not adopted a resolution against physicians participating in executions, it subscribes to the AMA policy prohibiting participation (letter to Amnesty International USA from Oklahoma State Medical Association, 1 October 1985).

3. A resolution adopted by the North Carolina Medical Association in 1983 endorsed the 1980 AMA resolution and extended its prohibition to "those who may perform services as agents of physicians".

Although the position taken by the WMA is unambiguous in stating that a doctor's only role should be to certify death after an execution has been carried out, there has been controversy in the USA as to how far doctors may be involved in monitoring executions without breaching medical ethics. Most of the statutes authorizing lethal injection (and those providing for other forms of execution) either require the presence of one or two doctors at an execution, or state that their presence may be required by the executioner. The Oklahoma regulations, while eliminating the active participation of doctors in the routine administration of lethal injection, do not bar medical observation and supervision of an execution, or direct intervention by a doctor to help with the administration of the drug should difficulties arise. Some Oklahoma physicians have reportedly volunteered to participate in executions for these purposes.[4]

Particular concern arose from the role played by a doctor in the first execution to take place by lethal injection: that of Charles Brooks in Texas in December 1982. Dr Ralph Gray, then Medical Director of the Texas Department of Corrections (TDC), examined Charles Brooks before the execution to see whether his veins were large enough to accept the catheter needle used to inject the lethal drug. Dr Gray also acknowledged later that the drugs had come from his own supply and that the "medical technicians" who administered the injection were from his staff. Dr Gray was present — with another doctor — throughout the execution, during the course of which he monitored the prisoner's heartbeat through a stethoscope, indicating at one point that the execution should continue for a few more minutes.

The local Texas county medical society[5] subsequently considered a complaint charging that Dr Gray's involvement in the execution had violated the policy guidelines issued by the Texas Medical Association (TMA). In ruling on the complaint in February 1984, the society concluded that Dr Gray's actions did not constitute participation in the execution, as proscribed by the TMA, and that no breach of medical ethics had occurred. The society stated in its opinion that the policy statement issued by the TMA in 1980 "was intended to prohibit a physician's direct participation in an execution by lethal

4. This was reported in an article by Ward Cascells, M.D. and William J. Curran, J.D., S.M. Hyg., "Doctors, the Death Penalty and Lethal Injections", in *The New England Journal of Medicine*, 9 December 1982.

5. The Walker-Madison-Trinity County Medical Society, whose jurisdiction included Huntsville, where the prison at which the execution took place was situated. The complaint was brought by Charles Sullivan, Executive Director of CURE: Citizens United for the Rehabilitation of Errants, a prison reform organization now based in Washington DC.

142

injection, such as by actual insertion of an intravenous catheter or actual introduction of the lethal agent(s)".[6]

The TMA did not itself conduct an inquiry into the matter. However, Amnesty International has learned that there was some concern within the association that the role played by doctors in Charles Brooks' execution had come closer to active participation than the guidelines intended. After the county society ruling, the TMA sponsored a bill before the state legislature providing that no doctor employed by or under contract to the TDC should be required, as a condition of service, to be present at or participate in an execution. The bill defined participation as including "not only personal preparation of convicts and the mechanism for their execution, but also supervision of the activities of non-physician personnel".

The bill was not voted on by the legislature for lack of time. However, Dr Armand Start, who replaced Dr Gray as Medical Director to the TDC in 1983, appears to have acted to minimize the participation of doctors in executions. He has reportedly not been present at any of the executions carried out after that of Charles Brooks, and is brought into the execution chamber only afterwards, in order to certify death.[7]

However, during the executions that followed — those of James Autry in March 1984 and Stephen Morin in March 1985 — technicians were partially unsuccessful or had difficulty in administering the drugs, with the result that the executions were prolonged and possibly painful (see Chapter 9). This creates a serious dilemma for both the medical profession and the state authorities: doctors, being dedicated to preserving life and health are required by their own ethical standards not to participate in executions; however, without their participation, the prisoner may suffer more, by having the drugs administered by less experienced personnel. This must undermine still further the notion that lethal injection is an acceptable and "humane" alternative to other execution methods.

Even without the direct administration or supervision of lethal injections by doctors, the latter may in some cases be called on to perform other tasks in preparing for executions. For example, the authorization of a licenced doctor may be necessary in some states to order drugs used in an execution. Doctors may also be called on to train technicians to prepare the substances or administer the drugs.

---

6. Statement from the Walker-Madison-Trinity County Medical Society, dated 16 February 1984.

7. A staff prison doctor is reported to have witnessed the execution of James Autry.

The TDC policy calls for lethal injections to be performed by a "medically trained individual" designated by the Director of the department, who is not under a doctor's direction, and who shall not be identified. This may itself be in breach of medical standards, which require that medically trained personnel such as nurses or technicians may administer drugs only under the direct authority or orders of a doctor.[8]

Amnesty International believes that no medical knowledge or training should be used to inflict harm, and that nurses, technicians or other individuals who receive such training should be bound by the same ethical principles as doctors. In a letter to the *Washington Post* of 22 December 1984, Eunice R. Cole, President of the American Nurses Association Inc., cited a statement issued by the American Nurses Association Committee on Ethics which concluded:

"Regardless of the personal opinion of professional nurses regarding the morality of capital punishment, it is a breach of the nursing code of ethical conduct to participate either directly or indirectly in a legally authorized execution."

Most states which provide for other forms of execution require the presence of one or two doctors at an execution. A number of these doctors appear to have participated actively in several reported cases of electrocution when they monitored the condemned prisoner while the execution was being carried out, checked the heartbeat and indicated whether or not further electrical charges should be applied (see Chapter 9).

These practices are in clear violation of the WMA standard that a doctor's only role should be to certify death after the state has carried out an execution.

A "Declaration on the Participation of Doctors in the Death Penalty", formulated by Amnesty International's Medical Advisory Board, was adopted by the organization in 1981. It says that "the participation of doctors in executions is a violation of medical ethics" and calls upon doctors not to participate in them. Participation in an execution is deemed to include, among other things:

☐ determining mental and physical fitness for execution;

---

8. Commenting on the use of medically trained personnel or "volunteer medical technicians" to carry out executions by lethal injection, Drs Ward Cascells and William J. Curran state: "The licencing laws and ethical standards for nurses and medical technicians would sanction no such independent action. Such personnel are authorized to perform medical interventions with patients only under a physician's specific order or valid standing orders . . ." ("The Ethics of Medical Participation in Capital Punishment by Intravenous Dry Injection", *The New England Journal of Medicine*, 24 January 1980.)

☐ giving technical advice;

☐ prescribing, preparing, administering and supervising doses of poison in jurisdictions where this method is used;

☐ making medical examinations during executions, so that an execution can continue if the prisoner is not yet dead.[9]

Amnesty International believes also that the participation of doctors and other health professionals in executions is contrary to the Principles of Medical Ethics relevant to the Role of Health Personnel, particularly Physicians, in the Protection of Prisoners and Detainees against Torture and Other Cruel, Inhuman or Degrading Treatment or Punishment, adopted by the UN General Assembly on 18 December 1982. Principle 3 states: "It is a contravention of medical ethics for health personnel, particularly physicians, to be involved in any professional relationship with prisoners or detainees the purpose of which is not solely to evaluate, protect or improve their physical and mental health."[10]

Role of psychiatrists or mental health personnel

The same ethical principles that apply to doctors and other health professionals would apply also to psychiatrists or other mental health workers. As noted under Chapter 6, most states provide that a condemned prisoner found to be insane be given psychiatric treatment until he or she is rendered mentally fit for execution. This is contrary not only to the standards cited above, but also to the position taken by the American Psychiatric Association (APA).

In a resolution approved by its Board of Trustees in June 1980, the APA stated:

"The physician's serving the state as an executioner, either directly or indirectly, is a perversion of medical ethics and of his or her role as a healer and comforter. The APA strongly opposes any participation by psychiatrists in capital punishment . . . in activities leading directly or indirectly to the death of a condemned prisoner as a legitimate medical procedure."[11]

Concern has also been expressed about the role played by

9. Amnesty International Declaration on the Participation of Doctors in the Death Penalty, adopted by Amnesty International's International Executive Committee on 12 March 1981 (see Appendix 11).

10. UN Resolution 37/194, principles 1, 2, 3 — see Appendix 5.

11. American Psychiatric Association's position statement on medical participation in capital punishment, in the *American Journal of Psychiatry*, November 1980, p. 1,487: reference cited in an article by Ronald Bayer in the *Journal of Prison Health*, vol.4, No.1, Spring 1984.

psychiatrists in testifying for the state in capital trials in Texas as to the "future dangerousness" of defendants facing a possible death sentence. One of three questions that a Texas jury must rule on affirmatively before imposing a death sentence is "whether there is a probability that the defendant would commit future acts of violence that would constitute a continuing threat to society" (see Chapter 2). At the time of writing, a Texas psychiatrist had reportedly testified for the prosecution in more than 100 capital sentencing cases; in almost every one he predicted that the defendant constituted a continuing danger to society.[12] Amnesty International believes that this participation is also contrary to the principles cited by the APA, since such testimony may contribute directly or indirectly to the imposition of death sentences in some cases. (In all but one of the cases referred to juries returned death sentences.)

In addition to the fundamental concern about the use of such testimony being in violation of medical ethics, the APA has also stated that psychiatric predictions of long-term "future dangerousness" are inherently unreliable. In an *amicus curiae* brief to the US Supreme Court in the case of *Barefoot* v. *Estelle* (1982), the APA stated that:

> "psychiatrists should not be permitted to offer a prediction
> concerning the long-term future dangerousness of a defendant
> in a capital case, at least in those circumstances where the
> psychiatrist purports to be testifying as a medical expert
> possessing predictive expertise in this area".

The APA went on to say that the large body of research into this area indicated that such predictions were "wrong in at least two out of three cases" and that "because the prejudicial impact of such assertedly 'medical' testimony far outweighs its probative value, it should be barred altogether in capital cases."[13]

In at least some instances, psychiatrists' predictions about the future dangerousness of convicted capital offenders in Texas have taken the form of answers to hypothetical questions regarding the defendant and the crime, without their ever having personally examined the defendant (this happened in the case of Thomas Barefoot).

Despite the brief from the APA, the Supreme Court ruled in *Barefoot* v. *Estelle* in July 1983 that the use of psychiatric testimony to predict "future dangerousness" was constitutionally permissible, and

---

12. Article by Larry Gostin in the *Guardian* of 6 August 1986.

13. Thomas Barefoot had claimed that the testimony of psychiatrists in predicting his future dangerousness for the state at his trial had led directly to the imposition of his death sentence by the jury.

that such testimony "need not be based on personal examination of the defendant and may be given in response to hypothetical questions".

Conditions on death row

In most states, prisoners sentenced to death are immediately put in a segregated prison unit for condemned inmates only.[1, 2] Known as "death rows", these units are usually in the maximum security sections of the main state penitentiaries. Prisoners remain there either until their sentences are commuted or vacated on appeal; or until they are executed.

Death row inmates are not serving prison sentences like other prisoners but are merely housed in prison until they are executed. Rehabilitation is considered by most state authorities to be irrelevant to such prisoners. Although court actions have resulted in conditions on death row improving considerably in a number of states in recent years, condemned prisoners in most states are far more restrictively confined than other inmates. Unlike inmates in the general prison population, most death row prisoners have no access to prison work, vocational or training programs or group educational classes. They are typically confined for many hours a day alone, in small, often poorly equipped cells, with limited occupational facilities or opportunities for social contact with other inmates.[3]

Until the early 1980s, most death row inmates were held in conditions of extreme deprivation. They were commonly confined to

1. In 1985 Maryland was the only state to place death row inmates in the general prison population, although prisoners under sentence of death there are not allowed to do prison work. Pennsylvania, which was the only state in 1981 in which condemned prisoners were kept with other inmates, has since created a separate death row.

2. There are a few exceptions to this. In Louisiana, for example, prisoners sentenced to death are transferred to death row in Angola Prison (the state penitentiary) only after their sentence has been affirmed by the Louisiana Supreme Court. Until then they are held in parish (local district) jails.

3. Farms, light industries and factories are commonly attached to state prisons, providing work for inmates in the general prison population. Such inmates spend an average of 10 to 14 hours a day out of their cells, in work or other activities in association with fellow prisoners. Although prisoners segregated for disciplinary infractions do no prison work and have little or no association with other inmates, periods of segregation are subject to regular review.

their cells for 23 to 24 hours a day with no rights to regular exercise or recreation. Their day-to-day treatment was often entirely at the discretion of the prison authorities, or the warden in charge of the unit. In some states, such as Georgia, death row prisoners had no outdoor exercise. In Alabama, condemned inmates in the 1970s were confined to their cells for 23½ hours a day and also took exercise alone in a small caged yard. Apart from a bed, wash-basin and toilet, death row cells were usually unfurnished.

From the late 1970s onwards, however, death row prisoners in several states brought legal actions in the federal courts, seeking relief on the grounds that the conditions under which they were confined violated constitutional standards prohibiting "cruel and unusual" punishment.[4] As a result, settlements known as "consent decrees" have been drawn up through negotiation between the federal district courts and state prison authorities, establishing minimum periods of exercise and other facilities.[5]

From 1979 to 1985 court settlements were obtained in Alabama, Florida, California, Georgia and Texas; a general conditions suit on Meklenberg Prison, Virginia, had a section devoted specifically to death row, and some provisions in the 1976 consent decree on the Maximum Security Unit of Parchman Prison, Mississippi, were later applied to death row. Death row litigation was pending in Illinois and a number of other states at the end of 1985.

Most of the federal court orders were individually framed to take account of particular conditions applying in an institution or unit, and did not establish absolute standards that were binding on other states or institutions. The terms of the settlements varied considerably in each state: most have provided minimum recreation periods for death row inmates, at least in line with those afforded other inmates in punitive or administrative segregation.

By 1985 the most favourable settlements had been reached in Texas, California and Georgia. After negotiations with the courts, the authorities in these states introduced a classification system for

---

4. Under the federal Civil Rights Act of 1871, prisoners may sue state or local officials directly in the federal courts where a violation of a federal constitutional right is alleged. Plaintiffs may sue for damages or — as in the case of death row inmates — an injunction for an end to the violation alleged. Most of the death row suits were what are termed "class action suits" applying to all inmates in the unit concerned. In recent years the Civil Rights Act has been used extensively by prisoners to secure improvements to general conditions in state prisons.

5. Consent decrees are legally binding out-of-court settlements, agreed through negotiation by both parties, drawn up and approved by the trial court as an alternative to pursuing costly litigation to a final judgment. Many actions concerning prison conditions are settled in this way.

death row inmates, according to the level of security required. This was the first time that a classification procedure based on the inmates' personal behaviour and prison record — applied to all other US prisoners — was applied to prisoners under sentence of death.

Under the final settlement reached in Georgia in 1983, level-A inmates, requiring less supervision, are allowed 35 hours out-of-cell time a week, and level-B inmates, 23 hours; in both cases six of the hours must be taken outdoors. The settlement also provided a dayroom and law library for the use of all death row inmates, who are also allowed to take a General Education Diploma (GED) program on request and to acquire hobby materials. Level-A inmates may also have group religious services and small group study and counselling sessions.

Under the 1980 California settlement, all death row inmates are allowed outdoor exercise for nine to 12 hours a week, may buy hobby materials for use in their cells and have individual tutoring for a high-school diploma. Grade-A inmates are allowed up to 42 hours out-of-cell time a week and group religious services.[6] Under an informal arrangement with the Warden of San Quentin Prison (which houses the death row), a group of about 15 Grade-A inmates in 1985 were given job assignments ranging from cleaning to working in a prison office.

The most far-reaching settlement was agreed in 1985 in Texas, which is believed to be the only state to offer a full work program to death row inmates (see below).

However, in many states the amount of out-of-cell time afforded to death row inmates — even after litigation — remains extremely limited. The 1980 Alabama court settlement did not increase the 30 minutes' daily exercise allowed each death row prisoner, but provided that inmates could exercise in groups rather than alone as previously.[7] The lawsuit brought on behalf of death row prisoners in Florida in 1979 dealt mainly with visiting conditions (see below) and — apart from those receiving visits — condemned inmates have only about six

6. Owing to the growing size of California's death row in San Quentin's Secure Housing Unit, a number of inmates were placed in another unit of the prison, which also houses ordinary inmates who have been put in punitive segregation. Grade-A inmates in this unit have no indoor out-of-cell time and no group religious services. Negotiations for compliance with the court order were going on at the end of 1985.

7. The Alabama settlement also gave death row inmates access to a special law library (also known as a "writ-room") attached to the unit. Inmates could use the room not only to research legal documents relating to their cases, but as a general day room. However, Amnesty International was told in 1983 that the room could accommodate only a few prisoners at a time and in practice this increased the total out-of-cell time for each inmate to an average of seven hours a week.

hours' total out-of-cell time a week, comprising twice-weekly outdoor exercise and once-weekly access to a "writ room". Death row prisoners in Mississippi, Louisiana and Illinois in 1985 had an average of only five to seven hours out-of-cell time a week, with minimal facilities for recreation and exercise. Each condemned inmate in Louisiana, moreover, had to exercise alone in a small caged area of the prison yard.

Although most of the court settlements have resulted in minimum exercise periods and better provision for inmates wishing to pursue hobbies in their cells, few have achieved any fundamental change to the regimes under which death row prisoners are held. Most of them may not engage in work, vocational or rehabilitation programs or attend educational classes run by the prison. Although death row inmates in most states may subscribe to educational correspondence courses, these require a degree of literacy and considerable self-motivation, which may be lacking in many prisoners on death row. Many inmates have complained also that the constant noise level on death row has impaired their ability to concentrate on individual study or other pursuits.

The sizes of death row cells in most states range from about 5ft by 7ft to 6ft by 9ft and fall below the minimum recommended by the American Correctional Association (ACA) for the period spent in confinement in cells.[8] Also contrary to ACA standards, many death row cells have no windows and are often arranged in tiers which have little or no natural light. The sanitary conditions in death row cells (most of which are equipped with a toilet and washbasin) are also reported to be very poor in many states, with inadequate plumbing and ventilation. Unlike other inmates, most of those on death row take all meals in their cells. Unhygienic eating conditions and cold food are common complaints by condemned inmates.

Some court settlements have included improved visiting privileges for them in recognition of the fact that contact with relatives is particularly important for prisoners under sentence of death. In several states, visiting rights are better than those for other inmates in segregation. The 1979 Florida prison suit dealt almost exclusively

---

8. *The ACA Standards for Adult Correctional Institutions* manual recommends that the floor area for a single cell occupant (including bed space) should be "at least 60 square feet, provided inmates spend no more than 10 hours per day locked in. When confinement exceeds 10 hours per day, there [should be] at least 80 square feet of floor space" (2-4129-24130 of the ACA Manual). Most death row inmates spend much longer than 10 hours a day locked in their cells, even in states such as Georgia, where inmates have won a relatively favourable conditions settlement. The ACA standards are intended to provide guidelines for prison authorities and are not binding on states or institutions. Institutions are encouraged to comply with the standards, however, and to receive accreditation from the ACA.

with visits for death row inmates who, unlike other segregated prisoners in Florida State Penitentiary, are allowed contact visits of up to six hours on Saturdays or Sundays. Grade-A prisoners in California are allowed contact visits seven days a week from 7.30am to 2pm. Once-weekly contact visits were also provided for under the court settlements in Georgia and Alabama. Many states, however, do not allow contact visits, and death row inmates are separated from their visitors by barriers. It appears also that many prisoners do not have regular visitors, partly because many prisons are in remote areas of the states. Amnesty International was told that in Florida, for example, only about half the death row population had visits from family or friends in a year.

Lawsuits filed on behalf of death row inmates in the states of Missouri and Tennessee in 1985 illustrate the poor conditions prevailing on some death rows at this time.

Missouri

The Missouri death row is in the basement of Missouri State Penitentiary, which was built in the late 19th century. The conditions of confinement were described in a complaint filed with a federal district court in August 1985.[9] The inmates then on death row were confined to their cells for an average of 23½ hours a day; they had a maximum of three 45-minute spells of solitary exercise on an indoor weight machine and outside exercise for the same period on three alternate days. These exercise periods were sometimes cancelled for no apparent reason. There was no day room or communal area on death row and the inmates had no educational or vocational programs and no access to the prison library (although law books could be ordered from a law library attached to the unit).

There was no natural light at all in the death row area and the windows in each cell were either painted or frosted over, so that the prisoners could not tell whether it was day or night. The low-wattage bulbs in each cell made it "virtually impossible to read or write". The cells, which had bad plumbing and no ventilation, were reportedly dirty, odorous and infested with flies and cockroaches. All meals were taken in the cells. The last meal of the day was served at 2.30pm, after which prisoners had nothing more until breakfast at 8am the next day: 17½ hours later.

The prisoners complained that their requests for medical attention and medication were routinely delayed or denied and that medical examinations were perfunctory. No dental care was available.

9. Class action suit *McDonald* v. *Armontrout* before US District Court, Western District of Missouri, Central Division.

The prisoners also complained at the lack of adequate facilities for receiving visitors, who were separated from them by a thick screen through which it was difficult to communicate.

The inmates sought an injunction for relief from the federal court on the grounds that their conditions constituted "cruel and unusual" punishment. In March 1986, pending settlement of the case, the Missouri prison authorities introduced a classification system for death row inmates. A consent decree was issued by the court in May 1986. The terms of the settlement included 16 hours a week out-of-cell time for "regular custody" inmates and eight hours for "close custody" inmates, better physical and mental health care, and provision for private religious services or counselling sessions. The authorities also agreed to renovate the death row area and improve the sanitation in the cells, to provide an indoor recreation area and to expand the one outdoors. Arrangements were also made to provide death row inmates with meals on the same schedule as ordinary inmates, including an evening meal.

Tennessee

A May 1985 Order and Memorandum issued by the US District Court for the Middle District of Tennessee contained the court's findings after investigation of a complaint brought by death row inmates of Tennessee State Penitentiary. The court noted that the 44 inmates then on death row were confined for about 22 hours a day to single cells measuring 35 or 44 square feet (compared to the 80 square feet minimum recommended by the ACA), that each cell contained a toilet and wash-basin and that there was room to take only three paces. The court stated that:

"the cells do not contain windows. Ventilation and odors have been a serious problem . . . Often the stale air, laden with cigarette smoke, malodorous emissions from toilets, and paint fumes, make existence in the cells extremely uncomfortable. Insect infestation is a problem . . ."

The cells looked out over four corridors, two of which had no natural lighting and two of which had "minimal" sunlight. Fluorescent lighting remained on 24 hours a day, but the single low wattage bulbs in the cells made reading difficult. The court found that "the lack of natural light has had an adverse impact on the sleep cycle of many, if not all inmates". The inmates were also unable to regulate the heating in their cells, which were too hot in summer and too cold in winter. Television sets and radios (which inmates were allowed to acquire at their own expense) created constant noise in the cell area and led to tensions between prisoners.

The inmates had access to a small yard for one hour a day and limited use of a writ room. All meals were taken in the cells. Inmates had no access to the prison gymnasium and could not visit the prison's law or general library (although they could order books). There were no educational, work or recreation programs. Apart from group religious services (which were provided for under a preliminary injunction issued by the court in December 1984), death row inmates had no group meetings of any kind. The one counsellor available for the 44 inmates on death row was also the sole counsellor for more than 80 inmates in another unit of the prison.

The court concluded that the totality of the conditions existing in the unit violated the Eighth Amendment prohibition of cruel and unusual punishment, noting that condemned prisoners could expect to spend six to 10 years on death row pursuing appeals. Although the court did not make any specific recommendations in its order, it observed that a classification system could reveal inmates who might benefit from more freedom of movement and participation in classes and group activities. The court ordered that a special monitor be appointed to draw up a plan to improve conditions in the unit. Although some minor improvements have been made since the court ruling, the Tennessee Correctional Department has appealed against the court order. A hearing was expected to take place during 1986.

Texas

As noted above, by 1985 the most substantial improvements in conditions on death row had been achieved in Texas, which had the nation's second largest number of prisoners under sentence of death: 221 on 1 May 1986. Death row in Texas is in Ellis Unit, a maximum security prison near the town of Huntsville.

As a result of litigation in the federal courts, a draft recreation plan for death row inmates was drawn up in March 1983, which gave each inmate two hours daily out-of-cell time. However, the prisoners objected that the out-of-cell time was inadequate, given the poor conditions in the death row cell area. In October 1983, after further negotiations with the court, a number of inmates were transferred from death row to the general population of Ellis Unit. The transfer was part of an interim order issued by the court to last for a trial period. It stipulated that condemned inmates classified as "work capable" should be assigned to do regular prison jobs and have the same privileges and freedom of movement as other inmates. For six months some 40 former death row prisoners lived and worked alongside other inmates, eating in a communal dining room and participating in recreation programs available to the others. The situation was monitored by a prison specialist appointed by the court.

Although Amnesty International has not seen his reports, it is informed that the program worked well and there were no serious disciplinary or security problems. However, when the order expired in mid-1984, the prisoners were returned to a separate unit of the prison housing only inmates under sentence of death. Under the final settlement reached with the court in January 1985, conditions in the unit, nevertheless, are considerably better than those formerly prevailing on death row. "Work capable" inmates (more than 100 in May 1986) are allowed out of their cells all day, with extensive outdoor recreation, opportunities to engage in a range of educational programs and weekly religious services. In addition, a sports factory, designed to provide work and training for at least 100 death row inmates at a time, was nearing completion in May 1986.

Texas inmates given "death row segregation" status have three hours' out-of-cell time for five days a week, with access to a law library and a day room. They are permitted to buy art materials and may follow a GED program and correspondence courses on request. They are also allowed group religious services and the same access to books and materials from the unit's general library as "work capable" inmates.

The settlement provided that "segregated" inmates should have their classification status reviewed every six months. On official notification of an execution date, "work capable" inmates were to be reclassified "death row segregation".

Summary and Comment

Despite the improvements made to a number of death rows in recent years, condemned inmates in most states are held in more restricted conditions for far longer periods than any other group of prisoners in the USA, simply because they are under sentence of death. Prolonged confinement and isolation in cells is imposed in nearly all cases as a matter of administrative policy. In Louisiana, Mississippi, Illinois, Florida and other states, condemned inmates have a total of only five to seven hours out-of-cell time in the 168 hours of a week. Most condemned inmates spend several years in these conditions.[10]

Although many states now provide minimum exercise periods and better facilities for death row inmates wishing to pursue hobbies in their cells, there is little social contact with other inmates and an almost total lack of organized group activity on most death rows. Texas is one of the few states to provide group educational or training

---

10. Although ordinary prisoners placed in punitive or administrative segregation for disciplinary purposes may also be confined to their cells for prolonged periods, this is subject to regular review and segregation is usually of limited duration.

courses. While other states allow death row prisoners to pursue correspondence courses, these require basic literacy and a high degree of self-motivation, which may be lacking in condemned inmates.

Amnesty International has spoken to a number of prison specialists and visitors and counsellors to US death row inmates. Most believed that the stresses and anxieties experienced by condemned prisoners were due less to physical or environmental factors than to the nature of the penalty. However, the prolonged isolation and inactivity experienced by many such prisoners was thought to exacerbate these anxieties, leading in some cases to intense preoccupation with the sentence and manner of execution. This was also found to lead to apathy and "withdrawal from reality" in many cases. Amnesty International was told that many condemned prisoners suffered from severe depression and even psychosis.[11]

It was widely agreed that greater social contact among inmates, better counselling and occupational programs could substantially improve the conditions in which condemned prisoners were confined. It was believed that such measures would not create an undue security risk, particularly given the improved classification procedures used by many states. It was pointed out that there were many prisoners serving sentences for serious crimes in the general prison population, who were not subject to the strict conditions of confinement placed on death row inmates.

Many prisoners have their death sentences vacated on appeal, often after spending years on death row. The provision of better educational and rehabilitation programs for them would increase the chances of their benefiting from such programs when returned to the general prison population. Under the present conditions in many states, prisoners who could otherwise be rehabilitated or go on to pursue useful lives in prison may suffer permanent mental or psychological damage as a result of their confinement on death row; this applies especially to juvenile offenders.

11. See also Chapter 9.

The death penalty in federal law

The death penalty is authorized under federal law only for air piracy and for crimes under the Uniform Code of Military Justice (UCMJ), the latter applying to members of the US armed forces. In November 1985 President Ronald Reagan signed into law an amendment to the UCMJ, extending the death penalty to military personnel convicted of espionage in peacetime (see below). Legislation to reinstate the formerly more general application of the death penalty under federal law was pending before Congress in early 1986. Such reinstatement has been strongly supported by the Reagan administration.

The death penalty in military law

At the time of the *Furman* decision in 1972, the UCMJ authorized the death penalty for 13 offences. These included rape, first-degree murder, felony-murder and a number of purely military offences (including espionage and desertion) which carried the death penalty only if committed in time of war.

Although no death sentences had been imposed by the military courts for some years previously, from 1979 to 1982 several members of the armed forces were sentenced to death by courts-martial for murder. However, the sentencing procedures contained in the UCMJ at that time had not been amended to comply with the US Supreme Court guidelines laid down in the 1970s. In October 1983 the Court of Military Appeals, the highest military court of appeal, vacated the death sentence imposed on a soldier serving in the US army in West Germany, who had been convicted in 1979 of the rape and murder of a civilian. The court ruled that the capital sentencing provisions of the UCMJ failed to meet constitutional requirements.[1]

As a direct result of this ruling, the President signed an Executive Order in January 1984, promulgating new regulations for imposing death sentences under the UCMJ. The revised regulations amended the Manual for Courts Martial to provide that, after convicting an

1. *US* v. *Matthews* 16 M.J. 354(CMA), 1983.

offender of a capital crime, the court's sentencing panel must weigh statutory aggravating and mitigating circumstances and rule on them unanimously before imposing a sentence of death or life imprisonment.[2] The amendments did not alter the crimes for which a death sentence could be imposed.[3]

They applied only to the trials of capital offences committed on or after 24 January 1984 and invalidated all existing death sentences imposed under military law. Seven soldiers who had been sentenced to death before this date had their sentences commuted to life imprisonment.[4]

In November 1984 Todd Andrew Dock, a soldier serving in the US forces in the Federal Republic of Germany (FRG) became the first person to be sentenced to death under the new regulations. He was convicted by a US military court in the FRG of the murder of a German taxi driver. Appeals were still pending in the case in May 1986.

A death sentence imposed by a military court must be approved by the commanding officer of the division in which the soldier was enlisted. If the death sentence is approved, the trial transcript is then reviewed by the US Army (Navy or Air Force) Court of Military Review in Washington, DC. If the review court affirms the conviction and death sentence, the case is then reviewed by the Court of Military Appeals, which is composed of three civilian judges. An amendment to the UCMJ, which came into effect on 1 August 1984, also provided the right of direct appeal to the US Supreme Court after the exhaustion of appeals in the military courts. The UCMJ requires that a death sentence be personally approved by the President before it may be carried out.

The last execution of a soldier sentenced to death under military law was in 1961.

Extension of the death penalty for espionage during peacetime

Until 1985 the death penalty was not authorized under military law for peacetime espionage (although death sentences were mandatory

2. Several organizations and individuals have questioned the validity of these amendments, claiming that, since the death penalty had been invalidated under military law, it may be reinstated only by the legislature and not by executive act, as had occurred in this case (see comment by Henry Schwarzchild, Director of the ACLU Capital Punishment Project, writing in the February 1984 issue of *LifeLines*, the newsletter of the National Coalition Against the Death Penalty). This has yet to be tested in the courts.

3. The death penalty for rape under the UCMJ had been abolished in 1980.

4. The seven comprised four army recruits, two marines and one member of the air force; five were black, one Hispanic and one white.

in the cases of members of the armed forces convicted of espionage during time of war).

In November 1985 President Reagan signed the Department of Defense Authorization Act, 1986, which had earlier been enacted by Congress. The Act, among other measures, amended the UCMJ to provide a maximum penalty of death for members of the armed forces convicted of espionage in peacetime.

The legislation was introduced into Congress after the arrest and conviction of three former US military officers on charges of passing classified information to the Soviet Union. Although the Act could not be applied retroactively to these cases, the trial had been widely publicized and had led to calls for the introduction of the death penalty for future spying offences.

The relevant provisions of the Act are very broadly framed. An offence for which death is a possible penalty is defined, among other things, as the communication, or attempted communication, to any citizen, faction, party or force within a foreign country of any information directly concerning "nuclear weaponry, military spacecraft or satellites . . . or other means of defense or retaliation against large scale attack . . . war plans, communications intelligence . . . or any other major weapons system or major element of defense strategy", where this is done with "intent or reason to believe that it is to be used to the injury of the United States or to the advantage of a foreign nation".[5]

The Act has been criticized by some members of Congress and others who believe that the death penalty would not act as a deterrent to espionage, on the grounds that those engaged in spying rarely contemplate being caught. It has been questioned, also, whether the trial of people charged with disseminating highly classified information would in all cases be able to meet the standards of openness and public scrutiny necessary to ensure that death sentences are fairly imposed.

Proposals to reinstate the death penalty under federal (civilian) law

When the 1972 *Furman* decision invalidated most existing death penalty laws, federal law authorized the death penalty for six categories of offence: treason, espionage, first-degree murder; felony-murder; rape, and kidnapping (where the victim was not released unharmed and when the kidnapping was committed during a bank robbery).

---

5. "Department of Defense Authorization Act, 1986", Title V — Defense Personnel Policy, Part D, Section 534.

Like the state laws of the time, the federal statutes contained no guidelines to control the sentencing authority's discretion in determining when death sentences were to be imposed. These federal laws have not been amended to conform to later Supreme Court rulings and are therefore considered to be unconstitutional, although most remain on the statute books.[6]

The only new civilian legislation on the death penalty passed by Congress after 1972 was the Air Piracy Act of 1974, which provides for a death sentence for those convicted of homicides resulting from aircraft hijacking. However, its provisions have not been tested in the light of later rulings by the Supreme Court and the law is believed to be unenforceable in its present form.[7]

The death penalty provisions of the espionage act were formally invalidated by the courts in 1984, when an attempt was made to bring capital charges against an individual under this section, without revising the sentencing procedures.[8]

The last execution under federal law was in 1963 (when Victor Feguer was hanged for kidnapping). Thirty-four people were executed under federal jurisdiction from 1930 to 1963. No death sentences have been imposed under the law since 1977.

A number of bills providing for revised death sentencing procedures have been introduced into Congress since 1972. Although several of these bills have been considered in detail by the House and Senate Judiciary Committees, none had by May 1986 passed through all the stages necessary to become law.[9]

In January 1985 the Senate Judiciary Committee began discussion on further draft legislation to restore capital punishment under federal law. The bill (S-239) incorporated provisions contained in several previous bills, with amendments. It was introduced by the Chairman of the Committee, Senator Strom Thurmond, and is known to have the strong support of the President and the Attorney General. Similar draft legislation was also under consideration by the House Judiciary Committee.

The Senate bill establishes procedures for imposing the death

---

6. However, the death penalty was dropped from the kidnapping statute when this section of the law was revised in other respects a few months after the *Furman* ruling.

7. Air Piracy 49 U.S.C. 1472-3.

8. *U.S.* v. *Harper* (1984) — Ninth Circuit Court of Appeals opinion holding the death penalty provisions of the espionage act unconstitutional.

9. For an act to become law, the legislation (which may originate in the House or the Senate) must be passed by both the Senate and the House of Representatives and, if adopted, signed by the President.

penalty and also specifies the offences to which it would apply. The procedures are similar to those contained in the revised state laws and provide, among other things, for a separate sentencing hearing to be held after conviction on a capital offence, in which the judge or jury would weigh aggravating and mitigating factors before deciding whether to impose a sentence of death or life imprisonment without parole.

An amendment to the bill adopted in 1985 provided that the death penalty should not be imposed on people who were under 18 at the time of the crime. The committee also adopted an amendment removing felony-murders from the list of crimes for which a sentence of death may be imposed.

Under the bill, the death penalty would apply to most of the offences which were capital offences under existing federal statutes, including treason, first-degree murder and other offences where death results, such as air piracy, explosives offences and bank robbery.

However, the bill would also extend the death penalty to a number of offences to which it did not previously apply. It would, for the first time, provide the death penalty for the attempted assassination of the President, where such attempt resulted in "bodily injury to the President or [came] dangerously close to causing the death of the President". The death penalty would be extended to murder of a foreign official, an official guest or internationally protected person, and kidnapping where death results (an offence for which death had previously been the penalty but was dropped when the kidnapping laws were revised in 1972). The bill would also create a new federal capital offence of murder committed by a federal prisoner already serving a life sentence.

The bill also contains a provision to reinstate the death penalty for peacetime espionage, although only where this concerns certain major military matters which directly affects national defence. (This is a separate provision from the amended UCMJ, which applies only to military personnel convicted of peacetime espionage.)

In February 1986 the Senate Judiciary Committee voted by 12 votes to six to pass the bill to the full Senate for debate. It was still pending before the Senate as of May 1986. An earlier bill to reinstate the death penalty (which contained similar provisions to the present bill) was passed by an overwhelming majority of the Senate in February 1984, but similar legislation failed to secure majority approval in the House of Representatives at that time.

Senate Judiciary Committee report on draft death penalty legislation

The Senate Judiciary Committee issued a report on draft legislation to restore the death penalty in federal law in 1983.[10] The provisions were almost identical to those contained in S.239. In the report, a majority of the 18-member committee supported the restoration of the death penalty on the following grounds: its deterrent value with respect to certain premeditated crimes (although it was acknowledged in the report that there was no statistical proof available); its necessity as an "incapacitating" measure for certain offenders; strong public support for the death penalty and a belief that it "serves the legitimate function of retribution". The Committee addressed the possibility of error and gave the view that "this minimal risk is justified by the protection afforded to society by the death penalty".

Three members of the Committee (Senators Edward M. Kennedy, Howard Metzenbaum and Patrick J. Leahy) submitted a minority report opposing the proposed legislation. They opposed the death penalty as a measure of public policy to reduce violent crime on the grounds that it would not serve this purpose but would result in delays and unjustified strains on the criminal justice system, outweighing any "marginal benefit that is arguably gained". They expressed the view that "real life sentences" would more effectively accomplish the goal of deterrence and protection of society without imposing the "social cost of the death penalty", including its potential for error and discriminatory treatment. They also held that the death penalty was wrong in principle, believing that the "act of premeditated execution is itself a debasing denial of the sanctity of life". They also questioned the constitutionality of the proposals to reintroduce the death penalty for crimes where death did not result.

Conclusions

The extension of the death penalty under military law and the proposals to reinstate it under federal law are in clear conflict with international standards, particularly Article 4(2) of the ACHR, which states that the application of such punishment "shall not be extended to crimes to which it does not presently apply".

These measures are also contrary to the internationally recognized objective that states should "progressively restrict" the number of offences for which the death penalty may be imposed (see reference to United Nations General Assembly resolution, in Chapter 14).

---

10. Report of the Committee on the Judiciary, United States Senate, together with Minority Views on S.1765 (September 1983) (Report No. 98-251, US Govt. Printing Office, Washington, DC, 1983).

General arguments for and against the death penalty

Deterrence

An argument commonly used in support of capital punishment is that it acts as a deterrent to violent crime. However, detailed research in the USA and other countries has provided no evidence that the death penalty deters crime more effectively than other punishments. In some countries, the number of homicides actually declined after abolition. In Canada, for example, the murder rate fell from 3.09 per 100,000 in 1975 (the year before abolition) to 2.74 in 1983.[1] A United Nations study published in 1980 found that: "Despite much more advanced research efforts mounted to determine the deterrent value of the death penalty, no conclusive evidence has been obtained on its efficacy."[2]

US studies have shown that, under past and present death penalty statutes, the murder rate in death penalty states has differed little from that in other states with similar populations and social and economic conditions.

One of the first to conduct research in this field was Thorsten Sellin, who compared homicide rates from 1920 to 1974 in groups of contiguous US abolitionist and retentionist states with similar social and demographic characteristics. He found that most of these states had similar homicide rates. The rates were unaffected by changes such as the abolition or reintroduction of the death penalty in some states. He found that, where a difference existed, abolitionist states (particularly those which had not had the death penalty over a long

1. A study published in 1983 examined short, medium and long-term homicide rates in 14 countries after they had abolished the death penalty and found that more than half the countries showed a decline in homicides after abolition. It also examined data to see whether homicide rates had fallen more slowly than other crimes, and found that this was not so. Dane Archer, Rosemary Gartner and Marc Beittel, "Homicide and the Death Penalty: A Cross National Test of a Deterrence Hypothesis", *Journal of Criminal Law and Criminology*, vol. 74, 1983, pp. 991-1013.

2. *Capital Punishment: Working Paper Prepared by the Secretariat*, Sixth United Nations Congress on the Prevention of Crime and the Treatment of Offenders, Caracas, Venezuela, 25 August to 5 September 1980. A-CONF. 87-9, para 65.

period) tended to have lower homicide rates than retentionist states.[3]

The relative homicide rates of many of the neighbouring states studied by Sellin and other researchers before 1974 remain similar in the 1980s. For example, the states of Virginia, Washington and Vermont, each of which have the death penalty, had higher homicide rates in 1983 than their neighbouring abolitionist states of West Virginia, Oregon and Maine. North Dakota, a state without the death penalty, had an almost identical homicide rate to the neighbouring death penalty state of South Dakota.

Some research has suggested that the use of the death penalty may even increase the crime rate. William J. Bowers and Glenn L. Pierce analyzed monthly homicide rates from 1907 to 1963 in New York State (which carried out more executions than any other state during this period). They found that there had been, on average, two additional homicides in the month after an execution. They suggested that this momentary rise in homicides might be due to a "brutalizing" effect of executions, similar to the effect of other violent events such as publicized suicides, mass murders and assassinations.[4] Although their findings are not conclusive, similar findings have been made by other studies.[5] A rise in homicides has occurred in other jurisdictions after executions, including Florida after 1979 (see below).

Opinion polls indicate that public support for capital punishment in the USA, which had been declining, increased significantly during the 1970s. This is believed to have been in response to a marked increase in violent crime during the past 25 years. Between 1960 and 1974, after a period of relative stability in the 1950s, the US homicide rate doubled from 4.7 to 9.8 murders per 100,000 people. The rate rose again nationally (by seven to 11 per cent, depending on region) in 1978 and 1979. There was an increase from 21,460 reported homicides in 1979 to 23,000 homicides in 1980.

One of the few studies purporting to show that the death penalty had a special deterrent effect was published by Isaac Ehrlich in 1975. He measured the aggregate number of homicides in the USA for each year from 1933 to 1969 against a range of variables he thought likely to affect the homicide rate, including unemployment and per

3. Thorsten Sellin, "The Death Penalty", *Philadelphia: The American Law Institute, 1959* and *The Sage Library of Social Research*, vol. 102, 1980.

4. William J. Bowers and Glenn L. Pierce, "Deterrence or Brutalization: What is the Effect of Executions?", *Crime and Delinquency*, Oct. 1980, pp. 453-484.

5. A monthly time-series analysis of executions and first-degree murders in Chicago, Illinois, from 1915 to 1921, produced findings consistent with those of Bowers and Pierce: William C. Bailey, "Disaggregation in Deterrence and Death Penalty Research: The Case of Murder in Chicago", *The Journal of Criminal Law and Criminology*, vol. 74, No. 3, 1983, pp. 827-859.

164

capita income rates, demographic factors, arrest, conviction and execution rates. By using a complex econometric approach, he concluded that each execution had deterred seven to eight murders that would otherwise have occurred.[6] His findings (which were contrary to all previous studies) roused considerable attention at the time, and were included in an *amicus curiae* brief filed by the US Solicitor General in a death penalty case then pending before the Supreme Court.[7]

However, the overwhelming majority of studies on deterrence conducted after 1975 discredit Ehrlich's findings. Several studies, using his method of analysis, found that his inclusion of the five years from 1964 to 1969 — when homicide rates almost doubled and executions virtually ceased — had produced a distorted statistical effect on his overall findings. When these years were removed from the analysis, the effect of executions on the homicide rate disappeared. These and other studies found that the rise in homicides after 1960 was unrelated to the decline in the use of the death penalty (see below). Ehrlich was found, among other things, to have omitted some important factors from his analysis, such as the relative rates of other crimes, the incidence of gun ownership and the length of prison terms. He had also failed to take account of the relative homicide rates in states which had never had the death penalty and those which (in the 1960s) had only recently ceased to use it. In presenting aggregate data, Ehrlich had also failed to account for possible differences between states in the causes of murder.[8]

Other studies analysing relative crime rates during this period have found that the sharpest increase after 1960 was largely confined to a few states only: those with rapidly growing urban ghetto populations

6. Isaac Ehrlich, "The Deterrent Effect of Capital Punishment: A Question of Life and Death", *American Economic Review*, 65(3): 387-417, 1975. Ehrlich's analysis was based on the theory that the act of murder depends on the relative "costs" and "benefits" perceived by the potential murderer in response to factors such as unemployment and poverty (which may lead to crimes involving homicides) and the probability of apprehension, conviction and execution. He used complex mathematical equations to measure each variable against the aggregate annual US homicide rates in an attempt to isolate the effect of executions.

7. *Fowler* v. *North Carolina*, 96 s. Ct. 3212 (1976).

8. Major challenges to Ehrlich's work include: William J. Bowers and Glenn L. Pierce, "The Illusion of Deterrence in Isaac Ehrlich's Research on Capital Punishment", *The Yale Law Journal* 85(2), pp. 187-208, 1975; Peter Passell and John Taylor, "The Deterrent Effect of Capital Punishment: Another View", *American Economic Review* 67(3), pp. 445-451, 1977; Lawrence Klein, Brian Forst and Victor Filatov, "The Deterrent Effect of Capital Punishment: An Assessment of the Estimates", in *Deterrence and Incapacitation: Estimating the Effects of Criminal Sanctions on Crime Rates*, edited by A. Blumstein, J. Cohen and D. Nagin; Washington, DC: National Academy of Sciences, 1978, pp. 336-360).

(such as Michigan, Illinois and parts of the Pacific West).[9] States in which the use of the death penalty had declined after the 1950s showed no greater increase in homicides than states which had never had the death penalty.[10] Were the death penalty to act as a unique deterrent to violent crime, a faster increase would be expected in states where the death penalty had previously been available. Moreover, other crimes increased faster than homicides during this period. Federal Bureau of Investigation (FBI) crime statistics for the years 1960 to 1970 show, for example, that while murders and non-negligent manslaughters increased by 74 per cent during this period, burglaries increased by 142 per cent, car thefts by 183 per cent and larcenies by 245 per cent.[11]

There was also an increase in the 15- to 30-year age group among the general population after 1960, following the post-war birth boom. Youths from their mid-teens to late 20s have been found more likely to commit crimes than any other sector of the population. Males between the ages of 15 and 24, for example, accounted for 44 per cent of homicide arrests during the 1970s; men aged from 18 to 30 were also most likely to be the victims of homicides. The increase in these crime-prone age groups together with the rise in urban populations (and an increase in poverty and unemployment in some areas) are believed to have contributed significantly to the overall rise in crime during this period.

Other factors leading to an increase in homicides must also include the availability of handguns, possession of which quadrupled between 1962 and 1968. Between 1961 and 1970, murders in which firearms were used more than doubled, rising from 2.5 to 6.1 per 100,000 of the population.[12]

It has also been suggested that the increased crime rate may have led to a lower rate of detection as pressures on law enforcement

9. See Daniel Glaser, "Capital Punishment — Deterrent or Stimulus to Murder? Our Unexamined Deaths and Penalties", *University of Toledo Law Review*, 10(2), pp. 317-333, 1979. (In this article Glaser examines various factors contributing to the rise in crime in the 1960s and 1970s.)

10. Brian Forst, "The Deterrent Effect of Capital Punishment: A Cross-State Analysis of the 1960s", *Minnesota Law Review*, 61(5): 743-767, 1977.

11. Figures taken from FBI Uniform Crime Reports, cited in Klein, Forst and Filatov, "The Deterrent Effect of Capital Punishment" (*op. cit.*).

12. Figures on the 1961 to 1970 increase in firearms murders given by D.P. Phillips (1973) cited in Klein, Forst and Filatov's "The Deterrent Effect of Capital Punishment" (*op. cit.*). The same article also cites a 1969 study by Newton and F.E. Zimring, indicating that the rise in handgun possession contributed to the rise in homicides in the 1960s. See also Gary Kleck, "Capital Punishment and Gun Ownership, and Homicide", *American Journal of Sociology* 84(4), 1979, pp. 882-910.

agencies grew, thus lessening the deterrent effect of any punishment. Statistics show that the rise in crime during the 1960s was accompanied by a drop in the US prison population. There is also evidence that the time served by convicted murderers in prison fell during the 1960s. A study conducted in the late 1970s found that, although the arrest rate for homicides in the USA was high compared to other crimes, the time served in prison (both for homicides and other offences that often result in homicides) had declined in the 10 years from 1960 to 1970: a higher proportion of convicted homicide offenders released in 1970 had served less than five years than similar offenders released in 1960. The research team suggested that lenient prison sanctions, rather than the absence of the death penalty, had contributed to the rise in homicides.[13]

It is also noteworthy that the national homicide rate rose considerably during the economic depression in the 1930s, reaching almost as high a level as in the mid-1970s, despite the high number of executions in most areas during this period.[14] After the 1930s, when the use of the death penalty started to decline, the murder rate did not rise, but declined, remaining at a relatively stable level until the early 1960s.

Recent crime trends

Statistics from the US Justice Department reveal that, nationally, homicides dropped from 23,000 in 1980 to 19,000 in 1983 and declined by a further five per cent in 1984 to 18,050. There was a corresponding fall in most other crimes during this period. The general fall in crime is believed to be due partly to a fall in the number of men in the high crime age groups and partly to an increase in the length of prison terms imposed on convicted offenders. At the end of 1984 there were twice as many people in prison as in 1972, due largely to an increase in the length of sentences and time served.[15]

There is no evidence that the resumption of executions in some states contributed in any way to the fall in homicides (which appears

---

13. Klein, Forst and Filatov, "The Deterrent Effect of Capital Punishment", 1978 (*op. cit.*). Their study examined cross-state data over several periods.

14. Daniel Glaser, in an article in the *Toledo Law Review*, 1979 (*op. cit.*), cited US Public Health Service compilations showing the annual homicide rate in the early 1930s exceeded nine per 100,000. FBI records, based on police reports, show a rate of 7.1 per 100,000 in 1933 (the first year that such records were kept).

15. The *Washington Post* reported on 18 August 1985 that there were 463,000 people in prison at the end of 1984, compared with 196,000 12 years previously. The increase in the number of prisoners started in the mid-1970s. During this period several states introduced mandatory life terms for habitual offenders, and there is evidence that the length of other sentences and time served in prison in most states also increased.

to have levelled off or even decreased in the period 1984 to 1985). In fact, the two states which have carried out the most executions since 1979 — Florida and Georgia — had an increase in homicides in the period immediately following the resumption of executions.

Florida had carried out no executions for nearly 15 years when John Spenkelink was executed in May 1979. Although the murder rate had risen in the late 1960s and early 1970s, in line with the national trend, the three years 1976, 1977 and 1978 had the lowest murder rates on record in the state. However, the three years following the resumption of executions (1980, 1981 and 1982) had the highest murder rates in the state's recent history, with a 28 per cent increase in homicides in 1980 (see Appendix 7). Although the homicide rate fell in 1982 and 1983, it remained higher than in the period immediately before 1979, and rose again slightly in 1984.

In Georgia (where executions resumed in 1983), the homicide rate increased by 20 per cent in 1984, a year in which the national homicide rate fell by five per cent. Although these samples are too small to prove that the death penalty actually increases the rate of homicide, they at least do not show that the homicide rate falls when the death penalty is reintroduced.

Limiting capital crimes

Some government officials have expressed the belief that the death penalty, while having no special deterrent effect on homicides as a whole, should nevertheless be retained for certain categories of murder. The most commonly cited crimes were murders of police or prison officers and murders committed by prisoners already serving life sentences for homicide.

Yet there is no evidence that the death penalty has a special deterrent effect on this type of crime. Police and prison officers are not murdered more frequently in the states which have abolished the death penalty; in the United Kingdom and other countries, there was no increase in the rate of police killings after the abolition of the death penalty.[16] Murders of police officers are often "spontaneous", committed when the perpetrator is surprised in the course of

16. Thorsten Sellin compared US cities with populations of more than 10,000 in six abolitionist and 11 retentionist states between 1919 and 1954 and found that the rate of police homicides was slightly lower in abolitionist states. ("The Death Penalty and Police Safety", *Minutes of Proceedings and Evidence of the Joint Committee of the Senate and the House of Commons on Capital and Corporal Punishment*, No. 20, Ottawa Queen's Printer, Ottawa, 1955, pp. 718-728.) In a later comparison of police killings in 1975, Sellin found that risk rates were still generally lower in abolitionist states ("The Penalty of Death", *Sage Library of Social Research*, vol. 102, 1980, pp. 171-172).

committing another crime and is unlikely to be deterred by the thought of the death penalty. There is no evidence that the death penalty has deterred criminals from carrying potential murder weapons, and tighter gun laws and arms control would probably be far more effective in this regard.

FBI crime reports for 1970 to 1979 showed that killings of state and federal police officers amounted to a tiny fraction (0.006 per cent) of all murders reported for these years and that nearly one in seven of the killers were themselves killed by the police.[17]

A 1981 study of US prison murders committed by inmates serving life sentences showed that the murder rate differed little among states with and without death penalty laws.[18] The study also found that prison murders tended to be either spontaneous (and thus unlikely to be deterred by the punishment) or carefully planned against other inmates for retributive purposes, in circumstances in which the prisoner was unlikely to get caught (in about a third of the prison murders studied, the assailant was, in fact, unidentified).

Opinion polls show that many members of the public favour retaining the death penalty for especially heinous murders, such as those against children or "serial murders" (a series of apparently motiveless murders committed over a period of time). However, these types of killings are among the least likely to be deterred by any penalty. The most appalling and senseless killings are most likely to be committed by people who are seriously mentally disturbed and incapable of considering the consequences of their actions: some may even have "suicidal" tendencies and may actually wish to be executed.[19]

Recidivism

It has been argued that, even if the death penalty has no special effect in deterring others, the execution of the worst offenders is needed to protect society from the risk of their repeating their crimes.

However, the evidence suggests that, among offenders released on parole, convicted murderers present one of the lowest risks of

---

17. Figures cited in Bedau, *The Death Penalty in America*, taken from the *Uniform Crime Reports 1970-1979*.

18. Wendy Phillips Wolfson: *The Deterrent Effect of the Death Penalty upon Prison Murder*, reproduced in Bedau, *op. cit.*

19. Clinical studies by psychiatrists have revealed examples of suicidal murderers: people who are afraid to take their own lives and kill in the hope — subconsciously or otherwise — that their own lives will be taken by the state. See articles by Diamond, "Murder and the Death Penalty", and Solomon, "Capital Punishment as Suicide and Murder", both published in the *American Journal of Orthopsychiatry*, vol. 45, No. 44, July 1975, pp. 701-711, 712-722.

recidivism. In Michigan (a state without the death penalty), over 400 inmates serving life sentences for murder were released on parole between 1938 and 1972, after serving an average of 22 years in prison. Not one had committed another murder by 1976 (the year in which the figures were released). In California, a 10-year study of 342 first-degree murderers paroled after an average of 11 years in prison showed that 90 per cent completed parole successfully. Only one was subsequently convicted of criminal homicide.

The above figures are taken from research on recidivism by Hugo Adam Bedau, who found that, of 2,646 murderers released in 12 states during the years 1900 to 1976 inclusive, only 16 were returned for conviction of a subsequent criminal homicide. Commenting on his findings, Bedau stated:

". . . Both with regard to the commission of felonies generally and the crime of homicide, no other class of offender has such a low rate of recidivism. So we are left to choose among clear alternatives. If we cannot improve release and parole procedures so as to turn loose *no one* who will commit a further murder or other felony, we have three choices. Either we can undertake to *execute every* convicted murderer; or we can undertake to *release none* of them; or we can reconcile ourselves to the fact that release procedures, like all other human institutions, are not infallible, and continue to try to improve rehabilitation and prediction during incarceration."[20] (emphasis in original)

Other punishments may, in fact, be equally effective in protecting society from the small proportion of offenders convicted of capital crimes who are sentenced to death. The death penalty laws introduced in the 1970s included maximum alternative penalties for convicted capital offenders who did not receive the death penalty. Many of the statutes now provide mandatory minimum terms of 25 years' imprisonment before capital offenders serving life sentences may be even considered for parole, which is by no means automatic in such cases. Other states have introduced alternative penalties of life without parole.[21]

---

20. Bedau, *The Death Penalty in America*, pp. 175-176, 180.

21. It may be noted, however, that some countries without the death penalty do not impose sentences of life imprisonment without parole. For example, in the United Kingdom, which has effectively abolished the death penalty for peactime offences, procedures for executive review apply to all cases. In other countries, there is a maximum term of imprisonment, imprisonment for life having been abolished. In some US states sentences of life without parole may still be subject to executive review, although there is no minimum period after which the prisoner is to be considered for parole.

Although the death penalty has been supported by some people on the grounds that executions serve to "incapacitate" even a small proportion of offenders, it is doubtful whether this is the most effective means of doing so. It has been suggested that the death penalty may actually reduce the number of murderers serving maximum alternative penalties for their crimes, by encouraging guilty pleas to lesser charges. As noted earlier in this report, the cost and length of capital proceedings may discourage prosecutors from seeking first-degree murder indictments in many cases.

This latter argument is without regard to the possibility, mentioned above, that the death penalty may actually encourage murder by its brutalizing effect.

Costs of the death penalty

The death penalty in the USA is extremely costly. The US Supreme Court has recognized that — given the unique finality of the penalty — capital cases require greater procedural safeguards against possible error than other cases. The two-phased trial, automatic state review, post-conviction hearings and petitions to the Supreme Court which are routine in capital cases, mean that they cost far more than ordinary criminal proceedings in terms both of time and money. Jury selection and pre-trial motions also take longer in capital trials and issues such as insanity claims are also more likely to be raised at this stage in such cases, requiring experts to be retained to give psychiatric testimony for the state and defence. A 1982 study in New York calculated the cost of reinstating the death penalty there and concluded that the average capital trial and first stage of appeals would cost the tax-payer about $1.8 million, more than twice as much as it cost to keep a person in prison for life.[22] Added to this must be the cost of maintaining maximum security on death rows, clemency hearings and the execution itself.

A number of judges, prosecutors and other law officials oppose the death penalty on precisely these grounds, believing that the enormous concentration of judicial services on a relative handful of cases (many of which will, in any event, result in life imprisonment)

---

22. *Capital Losses: the Price of the Death Penalty for New York State*, a report from the New York State Defence Association to the Senate Finance Committee and other sections of the legislature, April 1982. The costs estimated in this study included provision for adequate defence services contained in New York's death penalty bill, which went beyond the services provided in many other states. Although this added to the cost of reinstating the death penalty in New York, most of the overall expenses would apply to other states as well. If other states provided better defence services for capital defendants, the costs of the death penalty nationally would escalate still further.

diverts valuable resources from other, more effective, areas of law enforcement.

'Just retribution'

Many of the government officials whom the mission met acknowledged doubts about the deterrent value of the death penalty, but said they believed that the death penalty was, nevertheless, the deserved punishment for the most heinous crimes.

Amnesty International rejects this argument on the grounds that no crime, however heinous, can justify the infliction of cruel and inhuman punishment. Contemporary standards of justice, moreover, have rejected the notion that "just retribution" may be achieved by repeating the acts which society condemns. Just as criminal codes do not sanction the raping of rapists or the burning of arsonists' homes, still less is the deliberate taking of a life by the state an appropriate punishment for murder.

Concern for the victims' relatives

It has been argued that the death penalty is the only way to acknowledge the suffering caused to the family and friends of the victims of murder and to ensure "just retribution" for their loss. An execution, however, cannot restore life or lessen the loss to the victim's family. In fact, far from relieving the pain, the lengthy procedures and uncertain outcome of capital cases may instead prolong the anguish and suffering caused to victims' families and hinder any healing process. Executions often also draw attention away from the victims, and focus it on the prisoner killed by the state, thereby increasing the feelings of rejection often experienced by victims' relatives.

While some families have said that the execution of the killer of a relative or friend brought a sense of relief, others have said that they believed no useful purpose was served by the death penalty in such cases. In either event, executions only add to the total amount of suffering by causing another innocent family — the prisoner's — to experience the pain and loss of having their relative killed by the state. In at least two cases where people have been executed since 1977, relatives of the victims actually appealed for clemency.

Laws authorizing the death penalty for certain crimes foster the belief that it is the appropriate penalty in such cases. The imposition of alternative penalties or the vacation of death sentences on appeal, albeit on valid legal grounds, may nevertheless cause families of the victims to feel that they have somehow been cheated of justice, creating unnecessary frustration and disillusionment with the law, and reinforcing their anguish.

There is no easy answer to the question of how best to respond to the deep and legitimate needs of the relations of murder victims, most of which are overlooked by the criminal justice system. However, execution is not an available remedy in the vast majority of murder cases. The diversion of resources into more effective law enforcement, ensuring swift and certain penalties, must surely be of greater benefit both to victims' relatives and to future potential victims of crime. Greater resources might also be spent on compensation and counselling.

Execution of the innocent

One of the strongest arguments against the death penalty is that it is irrevocable and, despite the most stringent safeguards, can be inflicted on the innocent.

A recent study has produced evidence of 349 US cases in which innocent people were wrongly convicted of offences punishable by death.[23] The cases — from 1900 to 1985 — concerned people who were either sentenced to death or to terms of imprisonment, usually for murder. In most cases, the convictions had been upheld on appeal but new evidence had come to light later which either established the prisoners' innocence or raised strong doubts about their guilt. In most cases this had led to acquittals, pardons, commutations of sentence or the dismissal of the charges, often years after the original conviction. Twenty-three prisoners, however, were executed.

Many other cases in which it was alleged that miscarriages of justice had occurred were excluded from the study's findings, through lack of adequate data.

Some of the errors described in the study were revealed through the efforts of defence attorneys in later appeals; others were discovered by chance or by investigations conducted by newspaper reporters or others not connected with the cases in a legal capacity. In 32 cases it was found that no crime had been committed, sometimes because the purported murder victim was found alive. In some cases other people had confessed to the crime, alibi evidence was found to be valid or witnesses had lied. The report listed some 50 cases

---

23. The study was conducted from 1983 to 1985 by Hugo Adam Bedau, Department of Philosophy, Tufts University, Massachussetts, and Michael L. Radelet, Department of Sociology, University of Florida, Gainsville. They compiled the cases from law journals, court records, newspapers, interviews with lawyers and other sources. Their findings are described in "Miscarriages of Justice in Potentially Capital Cases", prepublished draft dated 20 April 1986.

occurring after 1970, including several in which death sentences were imposed under the present death penalty laws.

Cases cited in the study included that of John Ross (black), convicted of raping a white woman in Louisiana in 1975. He was 16 at the time and confessed after being beaten by the police. He was sentenced to death after a trial lasting less than a day. His conviction was upheld on appeal, but because the death sentence had been imposed under a mandatory death penalty statute (which was later ruled unconstitutional by the US Supreme Court) his sentence was reduced to 20 years' imprisonment. After his conviction, Ross asserted his innocence in a letter to the Southern Poverty Law Center, which provides free legal services to poor defendants. It took up his case, paying for a private investigation. John Ross was released in 1981 after investigators discovered that a blood sample, alleged at the trial to be that of the rapist, did not match his blood group.

Another case cited in the study was that of Jerry Banks (black), convicted on two counts of murder and sentenced to death in Georgia in 1975. After having been tried twice and sentenced to death, he was granted a third trial in 1980 because of newly discovered evidence, including that of a witness who testified that the fatal shots could not have come from Jerry Banks' weapon. All charges against him were dismissed and he was released later that year — after five years on death row. When his wife asked for a divorce three months later, he killed her and himself. The Georgia county which had conducted the 1975 murder prosecution subsequently awarded damages to Jerry Banks' three children for its mishandling of the case.

The study also included the case of James Adams, sentenced to death in Florida in 1974 for murder and executed in 1984. According to the study, alleged exculpatory evidence in the case was discovered by an investigator one month before the scheduled execution. However, the Florida Governor declined to grant a stay of execution to enable the evaluation of this new evidence.

Although the legal appeals now available to US capital defendants may have reduced the risk of wholly innocent people being sentenced to death, no system can altogether exclude this possibility. Some evidence on which innocent people may be convicted, such as perjured testimony, may never come to light through the normal appeals process.

Apart from questions of guilt or innocence, there are many other ways in which death sentences may be unfair or wrongly imposed, such as through trial error or insufficient investigation of mitigating circumstances at the sentencing hearing. As is illustrated by several cases in this report, the criminal justice process cannot serve as a definitive safeguard against error, prejudice or injustice.

Public opinion

Governments often justify retention of the death penalty on the grounds of strong public support for it. Amnesty International's mission met several US government officials who expressed personal doubts about the death penalty but justified its retention on this basis.

Although opinion polls are not wholly accurate gauges of public attitudes, the numerous polls undertaken in the USA on this question have shown broad consistency in indicating general trends on the death penalty. They show that support for the death penalty declined after the 1930s to reach an all-time low in the mid-1960s, when 42 to 45 per cent of the population was found to favour the death penalty, while a small majority (42 to 47 per cent) opposed it. About 11 per cent of the population was uncertain.

Later polls indicate that public support for the death penalty has risen steadily since the 1960s, with a smaller percentage of those polled professing uncertainty as to their views. National polls conducted in 1984 and 1985 indicated that 75 to 84 per cent of the population supported the death penalty, the highest proportion recorded since 1936.

Public support for the death penalty has increased with, and apparently in response to, a rise in violent crime. Although the reasons for supporting the death penalty varied, the ones most commonly given by those polled were: that it was the deserved punishment for certain crimes; that it acted as a deterrent to violent crime, and that it protected society by the permanent incapacitation of the offender.

However, surveys have indicated that support for the death penalty is not unqualified. A Gallup poll published in January 1985 showed that while 72 per cent of the population supported the death penalty in general, this dropped to 56 per cent when those questioned were given the choice between executing murderers and sentencing them to life without parole. This finding was similar to a Harris poll taken in 1983, which showed a drop in support from more than 70 per cent to 52 per cent if it could be shown that long prison terms were as effective a deterrent as the death penalty. The January 1985 Gallup survey also indicated that a decline among supporters — from 71 per cent to 51 per cent — would occur if new evidence were to show conclusively that the death penalty was not a deterrent.

A recent poll carried out in Florida on behalf of the US Section of Amnesty International showed that, while 84 per cent of those polled in the state favoured the death penalty (62 per cent of this group "strongly favouring" and 22 per cent "somewhat favouring" it), 54 per cent said they would be less likely to support it if dangerous murderers were sentenced to life imprisonment without parole. Seventy per cent of those polled also said they would support an alternative to the death penalty that would sentence convicted murderers to life in prison with their earnings going directly to the victims' families or to a victims' relief fund. Only 37 per cent said they would still support the death penalty if it was shown that it had no deterrent effect (30 per cent said they would not support the death penalty in such circumstances and 33 per cent said they did not know).[24]

The Florida survey also revealed that there were certain types of cases where the death penalty had been imposed in which a large proportion of those polled said that they would oppose it. A majority said that they did not favour the imposition of death sentences on people who were mentally retarded, or who were mentally unbalanced at the time of the murder and had a history of mental illness.[25]

Respondents in the Florida survey also expressed opposition to the death penalty in four actual cases of prisoners who had been executed. An outright majority (57 per cent) said that they opposed the death penalty in two of the cases: those of James Terry Roach, a minor who also had a history of a debilitating disease (see Chapter 5), and Timothy Baldwin, a prisoner executed in Louisiana who, the respondents were informed, was inadequately represented at his trial and in whose case there was evidence suggesting possible doubt about his guilt. A third case was that of James Dupree Henry, a Florida prisoner who was sentenced to death and executed for an accidental killing during a robbery; in this case 47 per cent of those polled opposed the death penalty, while 40 per cent favoured it. In a fourth case, that of John Spenkelink, who was executed in Florida, 42 per cent of those polled said they opposed the death penalty.[26]

24. The poll was conducted for Amnesty International USA by Cambridge Survey Research. The first survey, of 500 registered voters, was conducted in February 1986 and a follow-up survey of 400 voters was conducted in April 1986. A series of detailed questions were put to those polled in telephone interviews.

25. In response to different hypothetical questions on how they would vote if they were jurors, 71 per cent of those polled said they would oppose the imposition of the death penalty if the convicted person was mentally retarded; 54 per cent said they would do so if the convicted offender was mentally unbalanced at the time of the crime and had a history of mental illness. In response to a different question, 85 per cent of those polled said that they would oppose the imposition of a death sentence on a mentally retarded offender who was an accomplice to a criminal homicide, where the actual killer received a life sentence in return for testifying for the state.

26. Without a complete record of the cases, those polled could not judge how they would have voted if they had been actual jurors at the trials. However, the

In an opinion poll conducted in Tennessee and Georgia in December 1985, more than two to one of those polled expressed opposition to the execution of offenders aged under 18 at the time of the crime.[27]

Opinion polls are not always reliable and results have differed according to how the questions were phrased. However, they indicate that public support for the death penalty is divided and is not unqualified.

Moreover, support for the death penalty is not always based on accurate information as regards its effectiveness or how it is applied in practice.

The generally high level of support for the death penalty is not shared by all sectors of the community. The churches, in particular, have expressed strong opposition. The General Board of the National Council of Churches of Christ adopted a statement on 13 September 1968, declaring its opposition to the death penalty. Its reasons for taking this position included "The belief in the worth of human life and the dignity of human personality as Gifts of God"; "The conviction that institutionalized disregard for the sanctity of human life contributes to the brutalization of society"; the possibility of error; doubts about its deterrent effect and the belief that "the protection of society is served as well by measures of restraint and rehabilitation, and that society may actually benefit from the contribution of the rehabilitated offender".

Since 1972, the leading bodies of at least 20 major religious denominations in the USA have passed resolutions expressing opposition to the death penalty on religious, moral, humanitarian and social grounds.[28]

---

respondents were given a summary of the crimes, who the victims were and other information relating to the circumstances of the cases: this information accorded with accounts of the cases given in court records and elsewhere.

27. The poll was commissioned by the Southern Coalition on Jails and Prisons and conducted by Information Associates of Washington, DC. Four hundred registered voters in each of the towns of Nashville (Tennessee), and Macon (Georgia) were polled.

28. Some of these statements and resolutions are published in the booklet "Capital Punishment: what the religious community says", published by the National Interreligious Task Force on Criminal Justice, New York. Churches whose statements against the death penalty are published in this booklet are: American Baptist Church in the USA, American Ethical Union, American Jewish Committee, American Lutheran Church, Christian Church (Disciples of Christ), Christian Reformed Church, Church of the Brethren, The Episcopal Church, American Friends Service Committee, Lutheran Church in America, The Mennonite Church, National Council of Churches of Christ in the USA, Presbyterian Church in the US, Reformed Church in America, Unitarian Universalist Association, United Church of Christ, United Methodist Church, United Presbyterian Church in the USA, United States Catholic Conference.

Some state governors have also successfully maintained their opposition to the death penalty, despite the majority of their constituents apparently favouring the death penalty. In November 1982 the majority of voters in Massachusetts voted in a referendum for the reintroduction of the death penalty. In the same month a state governor, Michael Dukakis, was elected who was an outspoken abolitionist and whose opponent was strongly in favour of the death penalty. In New York State in the 1970s, Governor Hugh Carey was elected for two successive terms, despite having used his power of veto to prevent legislation to reinstate the death penalty (passed by the state legislature) from becoming law. His successor, Mario Cuomo, was also elected despite being an outspoken abolitionist.

Amnesty International believes that public policy should lead public opinion in matters of human rights and criminological practice. In other countries the death penalty has been abolished even though a majority of the public appeared to favour its retention. Were the public to be fully informed about how the death penalty applies in practice, of its limited capacity, its high cost and lack of deterrent effect, and of alternative measures available to protect society, support for the death penalty in the USA would be likely to diminish.

International standards and the death penalty

The right to life and the right not to be subjected to cruel, inhuman or degrading treatment or punishment are enshrined in the Universal Declaration of Human Rights and other international human rights documents. There is growing international consensus that the death penalty is incompatible with these standards. In December 1971 the United Nations General Assembly adopted Resolution 2857 (XXVI), in which it affirmed that:

> ". . . in order fully to guarantee the right to life, as provided for in article 3 of the Universal Declaration of Human Rights, the main objective to be pursued is that of progressively restricting the number of offences for which capital punishment may be imposed, with a view to the desirability of abolishing this punishment in all countries."

This decision was reaffirmed by the General Assembly in Resolution 32/61 of 8 December 1977.

International and regional human rights treaties also impose restrictions on the application of the death penalty, while encouraging progress toward abolition.

Article 4(2) of the American Convention on Human Rights (ACHR) states that the "application of [capital punishment] shall not be extended to crimes to which it does not presently apply." Article 4(3) states: "The death penalty shall not be re-established in states that have abolished it."

Article 6 of the International Covenant on Civil and Political Rights (ICCPR) imposes restrictions on the use of the death penalty "In countries which have not abolished" it and states that "Nothing in this article shall be invoked to delay or to prevent the abolition of capital punishment by any State Party to the present Covenant".

The US Government has signed but not ratified the above treaties. However, as a signatory nation, it has an obligation under the Vienna Convention on the Laws of Treaties to do nothing to "defeat the object and purpose" of signed treaties.[1] A similar obligation would apply to all jurisdictions within the USA.

During its 63rd session, in 1984, the Inter-American Commission on Human Rights decided, in accordance with the spirit of Article 4 of the ACHR and the universal trend to eliminate the death penalty, to call on all countries in the Americas to abolish the death penalty. On 15 December 1980 the United Nations General Assembly adopted Resolution 35/172 urging all member states to "respect as a minimum standard the content of the provisions of articles 6, 14 and 15 of the International Covenant on Civil and Political Rights".[2]

The reintroduction of capital punishment into US state legislation and the increase in the number of executions in recent years is contrary to the spirit of Articles 4 and 6 of the above treaties and other international objectives on the death penalty. The proposals to reinstate capital punishment under federal law, including extension of the death penalty to crimes to which it did not previously apply, are also clearly contrary to Article 4(2) of the ACHR, as was the federal law passed in November 1985 extending the death penalty to military personnel convicted of peacetime espionage.

The laws allowing the execution of minors in some US states are in direct conflict with minimum recognized safeguards and standards of fairness applying to those countries which retain the death penalty. The above treaties and the 1949 Geneva Convention concerning the protection of civilians in time of war, provide for the exclusion from the death penalty in all circumstances of people under 18 at the time of the crime. The wide adherence to this standard in practice, together with the relevant treaties and guidelines, suggests that this provision is also part of customary international law.

A prohibition against the execution of minors is also contained in a series of safeguards guaranteeing protection of the rights of those facing the death penalty, adopted by the United Nations Economic and Social Council in May 1984 (ECOSOC Resolution 1984/50). Some US state practices would appear to be in conflict with some other safeguards contained in this document, which include guidelines on prisoners who have become insane and on the provision of legal assistance for condemned prisoners at all stages of the proceedings.

The ECOSOC safeguards were endorsed by the Seventh United

1. Article 18 of the Vienna Convention states that, during the period between signing and ratifying a treaty "a state is obliged to refrain from acts which would defeat the object and purpose" of the treaty.

2. UN Doc. A/35/48 (Articles 14 and 15 of the ICCPR relate to standards governing the trials of people charged with criminal offences.)

Nations Congress on the Prevention of Crime and the Treatment of Offenders (Milan, 26 August-6 September 1985) in a resolution in which it invited "all States retaining the death penalty and whose present standards fall short of the safeguards" to adopt them and to take the necessary steps to implement them by, among other things:

"(a) Incorporating or making provision for the safeguards in national legislation and regulations;

(b) Ensuring that judges, lawyers, police officers, prison officials and other persons, including military personnel, who may be concerned with the administration of criminal justice, are familiar with the safeguards, and any corresponding provisions in national legislation and regulations, by including them in courses of instruction and, by disseminating and publicizing them and by other appropriate means;"

ECOSOC, in a resolution adopted at its spring session on 21 May 1986,[3] urged "Member States that have not abolished the death penalty to adopt the safeguards . . . and the measures for the implementation of the safeguards approved by the Seventh United Nations Congress on the Prevention of Crime and the Treatment of Offenders . . ."

The involvement of physicians in some US executions has also appeared contrary to the ethical principles laid down by the World Medical Association in 1981 (see Chapter 10).

Amnesty International also believes that the involvement of doctors and other health professionals in executions is contrary to the Principles of Medical Ethics Relevant to the Role of Health Professionals, particularly Physicians, in the Protection of Prisoners and Detainees against Torture or Other Cruel, Inhuman or Degrading Treatment or Punishment, adopted by the United Nations General Assembly in December 1982.

Appendix 10 contains extracts of these treaties and standards.

Although the death penalty remains in force in most countries, there is an international trend towards abolition. Most West European countries have abolished the death penalty for all offences or for all but certain extraordinary offences such as wartime crimes; Turkey is the only country in the region to have carried out executions in recent years. Fifteen of the 21 member states of the Council of Europe have signed the Sixth Optional Protocol to the European Convention on Human Rights, outlawing the death penalty for peacetime offences and preventing its reinstatement in countries which have abolished it; it had been ratified by five member

---

3. Resolution 1986/10, 21 May 1986.

states by May 1986. Latin America has a long tradition of abolition: Nicaragua, Brazil, Argentina and El Salvador have all abolished the death penalty since 1979. In 1985 Australia became the 28th country to abolish the death penalty for all offences.

Appendix 12 contains a list of abolitionist and retentionist countries worldwide.

Summary of findings

1. The reintroduction of the death penalty in state legislation and the increase in executions in recent years are contrary to international human rights standards which encourage governments to restrict progressively the use of the death penalty, with a view to its ultimate abolition. Proposals to reinstate the death penalty in federal law and to extend it to crimes to which it did not previously apply are also in conflict with these standards.

2. Death penalty laws in some states, or their manner of application, contravene specific international standards applying to jurisdictions which have not yet abolished the penalty. Thirty states allow the imposition of death sentences on people aged under 18 at the time of the crime, in clear violation of international treaties and guidelines. Three such prisoners were executed between September 1985 and May 1986, the first executions of this kind in the USA for more than 20 years. These executions put the USA out of line with most other countries with the death penalty, which do not execute prisoners who were under 18 at the time of the crime: Amnesty International knows of only eight confirmed cases of such executions worldwide between 1980 and May 1986. As of May 1986 at least 32 other juvenile offenders were under sentence of death in 15 states (see Chapter 5).

Several prisoners have been executed who exhibited signs of mental illness, in contravention of guidelines set out by the UN Economic and Social Council in 1984 (ECOSOC Resolution 1984/50) which provide that executions shall not be carried out on "persons who have become insane" (see Chapter 6).

3. There are wide regional disparities in the rate at which death sentences are imposed. A Justice Department report showed that 63 per cent of those under sentence of death in 1984 were held by states in the South compared to only four per cent by states in the Northeast, a disparity which bears little relation to differences in the homicide rates between the two regions. Nearly all the executions carried out since 1976 have been in states in the South.

There are also marked disparities in the rate at which death sentences are imposed for similar crimes in different counties within those states most frequently applying the penalty. It was found, for example, that 85 per cent of death sentences in Georgia from 1973 to 1978 had been imposed in just 26 of Georgia's 159 counties, and that this was unrelated to differences in the homicide rates. Death sentences were, in fact, several times more likely to be imposed in rural areas, where homicides were less frequent, than in urban areas.

4. Although the present laws contain guidelines intended to eliminate arbitrary sentencing in capital trials, the possibility of a death sentence is largely determined by decisions taken by prosecutors at an early stage of the judicial process. Prosecutors have wide discretion in whether or not to seek the death penalty in criminal homicide cases, and, in practice, only a minority of crimes for which death is a possible penalty are tried as capital offences. Decisions to seek the death penalty may be largely determined by factors beyond the circumstances of the crime, including the financial resources available in a given district, local feeling about the death penalty and the level of publicity or community pressure in a particular case.

5. The evidence suggests that race — especially that of the victim — has an important bearing on the eventual likelihood of a death sentence. Fifty-three of the 58 prisoners executed between January 1977 and May 1986 had been convicted of killing whites, as had the large majority of those under sentence of death during this period — even though blacks and whites are victims of homicide in roughly equal numbers. Research in Florida, Georgia, Texas and other states has shown that homicides involving white victims are far more likely to be charged as capital offences and result in death sentences than those involving black victims. This disparity may partly be explained by the fact that more whites than blacks are liable to be the victims of "capital" homicides (such as felony-related murders). However, after taking this into account, researchers have found that racial disparities remain in otherwise similar cases.

The most detailed study of racial discrimination was conducted in Georgia, where researchers examined the outcome of all homicide arrests over a six-year period, taking into account more than 230 non-racial factors. They identified a mid-range of aggravated homicides where defendants in cases with white victims were significantly more likely to receive death sentences than those with black victims, at similar levels of aggravation. These were cases in which there was most room for discretion by prosecutors or juries in seeking or imposing death sentences. In cases involving white victims, black defendants were also found far more likely to be sentenced to death than white ones.

184

A federal appeals court dismissed an appeal which had cited the study's findings as evidence, on the grounds that the petitioner had failed to prove intentional discrimination by the state. Although the court did not dispute the study's findings, it concluded that they could not be said to cast doubt on the fairness of the system as a whole. An appeal against this decision was lodged with the US Supreme Court in October 1985. In July 1986 the Supreme Court said that it would hear the appeal. A ruling by the Court was not expected until the end of 1986 or early 1987.

6. In most US states, opponents of the death penalty are systematically excluded from serving as jurors in capital trials (partly because their presence may prevent the return of unanimous sentencing decisions). There is concern that this practice may produce juries not only more disposed to impose death sentences but also less impartial on the question of guilt or innocence than those selected under the normal procedures for criminal trials. Concern has been expressed also at the use of peremptory challenges to exclude blacks from sitting on capital trial juries, especially if the defendant is black.

After reviewing research studies into jury attitudes and the death penalty, a federal appeals court ruled in 1985 that opponents of the death penalty may be excluded only from the penalty phase of a capital trial. However, in May 1986 the US Supreme Court reversed this decision, ruling that it was constitutionally permissible to exclude opponents of the death penalty from serving as capital-trial jurors at both the trial and the sentencing hearing. The Court questioned the value of the studies into jury attitudes but said that its decision would still stand, even if the special selection procedures in capital trials did produce jurors who were "somewhat more conviction-prone" than ordinary trial juries.

A Supreme Court ruling in April 1986 (in a non-capital case) made it easier for black defendants to challenge the striking of members of their own race from their trial juries. However, the ruling did not apply retroactively to the cases of prisoners whose convictions had already been upheld on direct appeal. After the ruling at least one black prisoner was executed in a case in which the prosecutor had struck all black members from the trial jury.[1]

7. The separate trial and sentencing phases of capital cases, each requiring the investigation and presentation of separate evidence, and the special standards involved, have placed additional burdens on

1. Jerome Bowden, a mentally retarded black man who was executed in Georgia on 24 June 1986. He had been sentenced to death in December 1976 after pleading guilty to a murder committed during a robbery. The prosecutor had peremptorily excluded all blacks from the trial jury and as a result Jerome Bowden was tried by an

defence attorneys and created possibilities for error that do not arise in non-capital cases. However, there is evidence that many indigent offenders charged with capital crimes are assigned inexperienced counsel, ill-equipped to handle such cases and working with severely limited resources. Several prisoners have been executed whose trial lawyers were reported to have spent little time preparing the case, sometimes failing to present important mitigating evidence at the sentencing hearing. Appellate lawyers in capital cases have expressed concern that such deficiencies may have contributed to the imposition of death sentences in many cases.

Most states do not provide funds for defendants to be legally represented after their death sentences have been upheld on appeal to the state supreme court. They have to rely on volunteer lawyers when pursuing *habeas corpus* appeals on constitutional issues (a point at which many death sentences have been overturned). With the growing shortage of such lawyers, there is a risk that some prisoners may not be adequately represented at this important stage. Often, a lawyer is found only after an execution date has already been set, leaving little time to prepare appeals for consideration by the courts. The shortage of volunteer lawyers has caused particular concern in some southern states, where a large number of prisoners have exhausted state appeals and where execution warrants are issued with increasing frequency.

8. A relatively large number of capital defendants have had their death sentences overturned on state or federal appeal since 1976. However, there are procedural bars to appealing on issues that should have been raised at the time of trial and some trial errors may therefore not be remedied (see Chapter 3). The appeals courts are also limited in their ability to assess broader issues of arbitrariness or discrimination, especially where this occurs early in the judicial proceedings. Some state supreme courts try to ensure consistency in sentencing by comparing death sentences with penalties imposed in similar cases. However, many potentially capital crimes are not charged as such, because of decisions by prosecutors to accept guilty

---

all-white jury, even though the trial took place in a region of the state with a 34 per cent black population. Although his court-appointed lawyer had failed to preserve a claim on the race question, the (now unconstitutional) jury-selection procedures used in his case would not have been grounds for a stay of execution in any event, given the US Supreme Court ruling that the new standard would not apply retroactively to past cases.

As noted in Chapter 3, the Supreme Court left open the question of whether the April 1986 ruling on peremptory challenges would apply retroactively to cases still pending on direct appeal at the time of its decision. It granted *certiorari* in two cases raising this claim in early June and its decision was still pending as of October 1986.

pleas to lesser charges. This limits the range of "similar" cases available to the courts for comparative review. Some state courts do not conduct any form of proportionality review of death sentences by comparing them with other cases (see Chapter 7).

9. The federal courts have shown themselves increasingly unwilling to consider new constitutional questions in capital cases. Recent rulings by the US Supreme Court have tended to uphold state procedures, as is illustrated by its decision on juries (see 6 above).

Concerned about the long delays between the imposition of a death sentence and execution, the Supreme Court has also approved procedures that allow the lower federal courts to expedite their hearing of *habeas corpus* appeals in capital cases. Most capital defendants continue to spend several years awaiting the outcome of their automatic appeals to the state supreme courts; however, they may now have less time than non-capital defendants to have their final appeals on constitutional issues considered. The expedited proceedings leading up to execution in some cases have appeared contrary to the interests of justice (see Chapter 7).

10. Although the executive authorities retain the power to commute death sentences to life imprisonment as an act of mercy, clemency has rarely been granted in the cases considered by them so far. State governors and pardons boards appear to take a very narrow view of the role of clemency, believing that the decisions of the courts should stand unless there are doubts about the defendant's guilt or serious legal errors. Clemency has been denied, for example, in cases where there were strong mitigating circumstances in the offender's background which the defence lawyer had failed to raise during the trial and in cases where offenders were mentally retarded or mentally ill. International standards, such as those prohibiting the execution of juveniles or the mentally ill, have also not been considered grounds for granting clemency.

11. Both the experience of being under sentence of death, and the execution itself, may cause intense suffering. Several executed prisoners have not died instantly and prolonged suffering was manifestly inflicted. This has occurred both in executions by electrocution or gas and in those by lethal injection (see Chapter 9).

12. The participation by doctors in some executions appears in Amnesty International's view to have violated medical ethical standards enjoining doctors to practise for the good of their patients and never to harm them. Their actions have also contravened World Medical Association standards, which provide that a doctor's only role should be to certify death once an execution has been carried out. In Amnesty International's view, the role played by other health

professionals has also been contrary to recognized ethical standards (see Chapter 10).

13. Conditions on death rows in some states have improved in recent years, as a result of litigation in the federal courts. In many states, however, prisoners under sentence of death remain confined for prolonged periods to small, poorly equipped cells, with no opportunities for work, educational or rehabilitation programs and little association with other inmates. The prolonged isolation and lack of occupational facilities in such cases add to the inherent cruelty suffered by being under sentence of death (see Chapter 11).

14. Considerable research in the USA has provided no evidence that the death penalty deters crime more effectively than other punishments. These findings are consistent with what is known of the relationship between crime rates and the presence or absence of the death penalty in other countries. In some US states, the homicide rate has actually increased after the resumption of executions (see Chapter 13).

15. The cost and length of proceedings in capital cases have placed heavy burdens on the criminal justice system. Some judges and other law officials believe that the enormous concentration of judicial services on a relative handful of cases diverts resources from more effective areas of law enforcement (see Chapter 13).

16. The death penalty does not lessen the loss to the family and friends of murder victims. Far from relieving their pain, the lengthy procedures and uncertain outcome of capital cases may prolong the anguish and suffering caused to victims' families. Indeed, executions often draw attention away from the victims and focus it on the prisoners being killed by the state, thereby increasing the feelings of rejection that the relatives of victims often experience. More effective measures of law enforcement and swifter and more certain penalties would more greatly benefit victims' relatives and potential future victims of crime (see Chapter 13).

17. Many state governments justify retention of the death penalty on the grounds of strong public support for it. Although opinion polls show that a large majority of the US population favours the death penalty, this support may not be based on accurate information about the actual use of the death penalty and its effects on society. The polls also show that support for the death penalty is not unqualified. Were the public fully aware of the sound moral and practical reasons for not using the death penalty and of the alternative measures needed to protect society from violent crime, its support for the penalty would be likely to diminish.

18. The death penalty is irrevocable and can be inflicted on an innocent person despite the most stringent judicial standards. A recent study collected information on over 300 cases in the USA this century in which innocent people were wrongly convicted of offences punishable by death; some 50 of them occurred after 1970. Since 1900, 23 wrongly convicted prisoners have been executed. In many of the other cases information leading to acquittals, pardons or commutation of sentences came to light years after the original conviction. The study excluded, through lack of adequate data, many additional cases in which it was alleged that miscarriages of justice had occurred.

Conclusions and recommendations

The death penalty denies the right to life. It is a cruel and inhuman punishment, brutalizing to all who are involved in the process. It serves no useful penal purpose and denies the widely accepted principle of rehabilitating the offender. It serves neither to protect society nor to alleviate the suffering caused to the victims of crime. It is irreversible and, even with the most stringent judicial safeguards, may be inflicted on an innocent person.

No means of limiting the death penalty can prevent its being imposed arbitrarily or unfairly. This is borne out by the experience in the USA, where the introduction of elaborate judicial safeguards has failed to ensure that the death penalty is fairly and consistently applied.

On the basis of its findings, Amnesty International respectfully submits the following recommendations to the federal and state governments of the United States:

1. Amnesty International calls on all state governments in states whose laws provide for the death penalty to abolish the death penalty for all offences in law. All measures to abolish the death penalty or restrict its use should be applied retroactively to prisoners under sentence of death, in accordance with international standards.

2. Amnesty International urges that, until the death penalty has been abolished in law, no further executions be carried out; that steps be taken to commute the death sentences of all those currently on death row, and that no further death sentences be imposed.

3. International standards cited in this report hold that the death penalty should not be extended to crimes to which it does not at present apply nor should it be re-established in states that have abolished it. Amnesty International calls upon the federal government, in keeping with these standards, not to enact the death penalty under federal law. The death penalty should be abolished under the federal Uniform Code of Military Justice.

Pending the abolition of the death penalty in law, the following recommendations should be given immediate consideration:

4. State laws and practice should conform to minimum international standards that preclude the imposition of the death penalty on juvenile offenders and the mentally ill.

5. State governors and boards of pardons and paroles should broaden their criteria for granting clemency in capital cases, so that circumstances beyond the facts of the crime and the correctness of the legal proceedings are taken into account. Mitigating circumstances in the offender's background; the presence of mental illness or mental retardation; international standards and other factors cited in Chapter 8 of this report should constitute minimum grounds for commuting death sentences.

6. Amnesty International believes that the evidence of racial discrimination in the application of the death penalty is a matter for serious and urgent concern. Detailed studies, and statistics relating to the prisoners executed and those remaining on death row, suggest that disparities in death sentencing, based on racial factors, occur in states throughout the USA.

Should the findings of these studies be considered deficient, Amnesty International recommends that the executive or legislative branch of the federal government commission a serious inquiry into the question of racial discrimination and the death penalty. Amnesty International suggests that such an inquiry use impartial specialists to evaluate all relevant data concerning the arrest, charging and sentencing of criminal homicide offenders in given jurisdictions over a period of time. Information should be gathered from all those knowledgeable about the legal process, including judges, state prosecutors, defence attorneys, the police, boards of pardons and paroles, and state correctional departments.

The findings of a national inquiry into racial discrimination and the death penalty may have serious implications for the cases of many prisoners under sentence of death. In the absence of immediate measures to abolish the death penalty or commute the sentences of those on death row, a moratorium on executions should be imposed pending the outcome of the inquiry.

Any measures undertaken by the federal authorities to examine this question should not prevent individual state governments or legislatures from commissioning their own inquiries.

7. State governments should study the impact of the death penalty on the crime rate; the criminal justice system; the correctional services; the families of the victims of violent crime; and family members of condemned prisoners. They should also examine the adequacy of legal representation of poor defendants in capital proceedings, the

adequacy of state clemency procedures and the fairness of jury selection in death penalty cases.

Based on this and other information, they should take steps to inform the public about the penal and criminological effects of the death penalty, including its lack of proved special deterrent effect; its high cost and limited application to criminal homicide cases; and ways in which it may distort and impede the process of justice and result in unfairness. Amnesty International believes that, should the public be fully informed about the effects of the death penalty, there would be wider acceptance of moves to abolish it.

8. Pending the introduction of measures to suspend or commute the sentences of those currently under sentence of death, the appropriate state authorities should review arrangements for the treatment and custody of such prisoners, to ensure that they do not exacerbate the already cruel, inhuman and degrading experience of being under sentence of death.

Doctors and other health professionals

Amnesty International also calls on doctors and other health professionals not to participate in any way in executions or to use their professional expertise in any way which might lead to the imposition of death sentences. This would include being present at or monitoring executions while they are taking place; the treatment of insanity in order to render condemned prisoners mentally fit to be executed; and the giving of psychiatric testimony in trials which may lead to the imposition of death sentences.

Amnesty International believes that the above actions are contrary to the ethical principles relating to the role of health personnel in protecting all prisoners from torture or other cruel, inhuman or degrading treatment, adopted by the United Nations General Assembly in 1982. They are also contrary to principles adopted by the World Medical Association on doctors and the death penalty.

Appendices

Appendix 1
States with the death penalty (LDF Statistics as of 1 October 1986)

State	Method of execution	No. on death row	No. of executions from 1976 to 1 October 1986
Alabama	Electrocution	79	2
Arizona	Gas chamber	65	0
Arkansas	Lethal injection (or electrocution if sentenced before 3 April 1983)	29	0
California	Gas chamber	190	0
Colorado	Gas chamber	1	0
Connecticut	Electrocution	0	0
Delaware	Hanging	5	0
Florida	Electrocution	247	16
Georgia	Electrocution	105	7
Idaho	Lethal injection or firing-squad	14	0

State	Method of execution	No. on death row	No. of executions from 1976 to 1 October 1986
Illinois	Lethal injection	98	0
Indiana	Electrocution	38	2
Kentucky	Electrocution	29	0
Louisiana	Electrocution	49	7
Maryland	Gas chamber	19	0
Mississippi	Gas chamber or lethal injection	46	1
Missouri	Gas chamber	43	0
Montana	Hanging or lethal injection	5	0
Nebraska	Electrocution	13	0
Nevada	Lethal injection	36	2
New Hampshire	Hanging	0	0
New Jersey	Lethal injection	21	0
New Mexico	Lethal injection	5	0
North Carolina	Gas chamber or lethal injection	62	3
Ohio	Electrocution	67	0
Oklahoma	Lethal injection or firing-squad	63	0
Oregon	Lethal injection	1	0
Pennsylvania	Electrocution	87	0
South Carolina	Electrocution	44	2
South Dakota	Lethal injection	0	0
Tennessee	Electrocution	57	0
Texas	Lethal injection	218	18
Utah	Lethal injection or firing-squad	7	1
Vermont	Electrocution	0	0
Virginia	Electrocution	34	5
Washington	Hanging or lethal injection	8	0
Wyoming	Lethal injection	3	0

Appendix 2

Death row populations by race

State	White	Black	Hisp.*	Asian	Nat. Am.*	O/U*
Alabama	27	51	—	1	—	—
Arizona	48	6	9	—	2	—
Arkansas	18	10	1	—	—	—
California	81	75	28	3	3	—
Colorado	1	—	—	—	—	—
Delaware	1	4	—	—	—	—
Florida	145	87	13	—	1	1
Georgia	53	52	—	—	—	—
Idaho	13	—	1	—	—	—

State	White	Black	Hisp.*	Asian	Nat. Am.*	O/U*
Illinois	30	58	10	—	—	—
Indiana	20	16	2	—	—	—
Kentucky	21	8	—	—	—	—
Louisiana	25	24	—	—	—	—
Maryland	4	14	—	—	1	—
Mississippi	21	24	1	—	—	—
Missouri	24	18	—	—	1	—
Montana	4	1	—	—	—	—
Nebraska	9	2	—	—	2	—
Nevada	22	11	3	—	—	—
New Jersey	11	10	—	—	—	—
New Mexico	2	1	2	—	—	—
North Carolina	22	35	1	1	3	—
Ohio	33	32	2	—	—	—
Oklahoma	46	10	—	—	6	1
Oregon	1	—	—	—	—	—
Pennsylvania	35	47	3	—	—	2
South Carolina	22	22	—	—	—	—
Tennessee	38	18	—	—	1	—
Texas	96	85	31	—	6	—
Utah	3	4	—	—	—	—
Virginia	18	15	—	1	—	—
Washington	6	1	—	1	—	—
Wyoming	3	—	—	—	—	—

*Hisp. = Hispanic; Nat. Am. = Native American; O/U = Others or Unknown
Source: LDF, October 1986

Appendix 3

US states* without the death penalty

State*	Date of last execution (this century)
Alaska	
District of Columbia	1957
Hawaii	
Iowa	1963
Kansas	1965
Maine	
Massachusetts	1947
Michigan	
Minnesota	
New York	1963
North Dakota	1905
Rhode Island	
West Virginia	1959
Wisconsin	

* Plus District of Columbia

Appendix 4

Executions in the USA, July 1976 to May 1986

Date	Defendant	State	Race of defendant	Race of victim
17.01.77	Gary GILMORE	UT	W	W
25.05.79	John SPENKELINK	FL	W	W
22.10.79	Jesse BISHOP	NV	W	W
09.03.81	Steven JUDY	IN	W	W
10.08.82	Frank COPPOLA	VA	W	W
07.12.82	Charlie BROOKS	TX	B	W
22.04.83	John EVANS	AL	W	W
02.09.83	Jimmy Lee GRAY	MS	W	W
30.11.83	Robert SULLIVAN	FL	W	W
14.12.83	Robert Wayne WILLIAMS	LA	B	B
15.12.83	John Eldon SMITH	GA	W	W
26.01.84	Anthony ANTONE	FL	W	W
29.02.84	John TAYLOR	LA	W	W
14.03.84	James AUTRY	TX	W	W
16.03.84	James HUTCHINS	NC	W	W
31.03.84	Ronald O'BRYAN	TX	W	W
05.04.84	Arthur GOODE	FL	W	W
05.04.84	Elmo SONNIER	LA	W	W
10.05.84	James ADAMS	FL	B	W
20.06.84	Carl SHRINER	FL	W	W
12.07.84	Ivon STANLEY	GA	B	W
13.07.84	David WASHINGTON	FL	B	W, B
07.09.84	Ernest DOBBERT	FL	W	W
10.09.84	Timothy BALDWIN	LA	W	W
20.09.84	James Dupree HENRY	FL	B	B
12.10.84	Linwood BRILEY	VA	B	W
30.10.84	Thomas BAREFOOT	TX	W	W
30.10.84	Ernest KNIGHTON	LA	B	W
02.11.84	Velma BARFIELD	NC	W	W
08.11.84	Timothy PALMES	FL	W	W
12.12.84	Alpha Otis STEPHENS	GA	B	W
28.12.84	Robert Lee WILLIE	LA	W	W
04.01.85	David MARTIN	LA	W	W
09.01.85	Roosevelt GREEN	GA	B	W
11.01.85	Joseph Carl SHAW	SC	W	W
16.01.85	Doyle SKILLERN	TX	W	W
30.01.85	James RAULERSON	FL	W	W
20.02.85	Van Roosevelt SOLOMON	GA	B	W
06.03.85	Johnny Paul WITT	FL	W	W
13.03.85	Stephen MORIN	TX	W	W
20.03.85	John YOUNG	GA	B	W
18.04.85	James BRILEY	VA	B	B
15.05.85	Jesse DE LA ROSA	TX	H	W
29.05.85	Marvin FRANCOIS	FL	B	B
25.06.85	Charles MILTON	TX	B	B
25.06.85	Morris MASON	VA	B	W

Date	Defendant	State	Race of defendant	Race of victim
09.07.85	Henry MARTINEZ PORTER	TX	H	W
11.09.85	Charles RUMBAUGH	TX	W	W
16.10.85	William VANDIVER	IN	W	W
06.12.85	Carroll COLE	NV	W	U
10.01.86	James Terry ROACH	SC	W	W
12.03.86	Charles BASS	TX	W	W
21.03.86	Arthur Lee JONES	AL	B	W
15.04.86	Daniel Morris THOMAS	FL	B	W
16.04.86	Jeffrey Allan BARNEY	TX	W	W
22.04.86	David FUNCHESS	FL	B	W
15.05.86	Jay PINKERTON	TX	W	W
20.05.86	Ronald STRAIGHT	FL	W	W

States: UT = Utah; FL = Florida; NV = Nevada; IN = Indiana; VA = Virginia; TX = Texas; AL = Alabama; MS = Mississippi; LA = Louisiana; GA = Georgia; NC = North Carolina; SC = South Carolina

Race: B = black; H = Hispanic; W = white; U = unknown

Appendix 5

Executions state by state since July 1976

Name/Race/Age at time of crime	Date of execution	Year convicted	Race of victim	Crime	Other information
1. ALABAMA					
John EVANS W, 27	22.04.83	77	W	Murder/ robbery	Evans demanded death sentence at trial and twice dropped appeals. Execution required three charges of electricity before pronounced dead 14 minutes after execution began. During first electrical charge, electrode on leg burned through and had to be repaired.
Arthur JONES B, 43	21.03.86	81	W	2 murders/ robbery	
2. FLORIDA					
John SPENKELINK W,	25.05.79	73	W	Murder	Killed travelling companion who he alleged had raped and robbed him. Refused state offer of uncontested plea to second-degree murder.
Robert SULLIVAN W, 26	30.11.83	73	W	Murder/ robbery	Originally confessed to murder but later claimed had not been present. Stay granted two days before execution while US Supreme Court decided whether fresh evidence should be heard; Court voted against this. Co-defendant testified against him at trial for lighter sentence, and was paroled in 1981.

Name/Race/Age at time of crime	Date of execution	Year convicted	Race of victim	Crime	Other information
Anthony ANTONE W, 58	26.01.84	76	W	Contract-murder of police officer	Aged 66 at execution.
Arthur GOODE W, 22	05.04.84	77	W	Poisoned child	Mentally unstable; documented history of mental illness since age of three.
James ADAMS B, 37	10.05.84	74	W	Murder of farmer	Alleged new possibly exculpatory evidence presented to clemency hearing but execution went ahead as scheduled.
Carl SHRINER W, 21	20.06.84	76	W	Murder/robbery	
David WASHINGTON B, 26	13.07.84	76	W/B	3 murders/robbery	
Ernest DOBBERT W, 34	07.09.84	74	W	Murdered son and daughter	Reportedly suffering from extreme mental stress. Jury's recommendation of life sentence rejected by judge.
James D. HENRY B	20.09.84	74	B	Murder/robbery	Tied and gagged victim during robbery. Victim died after choking on gag. Lawyers claimed no intent to kill, but prisoner convicted under felony murder rule and jury voted by 7 to 5 for death penalty. Victim's relatives appealed for clemency.
Timothy PALMES W	08.11.84	77	W	Murder/robbery	Co-defendant executed 20 May 1986.
James RAULERSON W	30.01.85	75	W	Murder of police officer	Killing occurred in shoot-out with police in which Raulerson himself badly wounded. Said his injuries prevented him from preparing his defence. First death sentence vacated; reimposed August 1980.

Name/Race/Age at time of crime	Date of execution	Year convicted	Race of victim	Crime	Other information
Johnny P. WITT W, 29	06.03.85	74	W	Abduction/ murder of child	Accomplice given life sentence.
Marvin FRANCOIS B, 39	29.05.85	78	B	6 murders	The shooting murders reportedly occurred following a dispute between rival drug gangs.
Daniel M. THOMAS B, 26	15.04.86	77	W	Murder/ robbery/rape	
David FUNCHESS B, 27	22.04.86	79	W	Murder of two women during robbery	Vietnam war veteran. Received several commendations during tour of duty in South Vietnam, where badly wounded. Left army with heroin addiction. Several years after conviction was found to be suffering from post-traumatic stress, a psychological disorder not properly understood at time of his trial. Disorder medically recognized in 1980 as affecting many Vietnam war veterans.
Ronald STRAIGHT W, 32	20.05.86	77	W	Murder/ robbery	Co-defendant executed 8 November 1984.
3. GEORGIA					
John E. SMITH W, 44	15.12.83	74	W	2 murders	Murder of couple for insurance money. Victims were wife's ex-husband and his wife. Accomplice got life after testifying against Smith. Smith's wife also accused of planning and taking part in crime – got life sentence.

Name/Race/Age at time of crime	Date of execution	Year convicted	Race of victim	Crime	Other information
Ivon STANLEY B, 20	12.07.84	76	W	Murder/ robbery	His accomplice, who he alleged fired fatal shots, also sentenced to death.
Alpha O. STEPHENS B, 29	12.12.84	75	W	Murder/ robbery	Granted stay of execution by US Supreme Court in December 1983 pending ruling in a case on racial discrimination, a claim which Stephens had also raised. Stay abruptly lifted and execution date set, even though related case still pending decision by appeals court (in *Zant* v. *Spencer*). At his execution, first charge of electricity failed to kill him and he was reported to have "struggled for breath for eight minutes" before second fatal charge applied.
B. Roosevelt GREEN	09.01.85	76	W	Accomplice to rape/ murder	Judge acknowledged Green to be "only the accomplice" and absent when killer shot victim. Green maintained innocence to end. His application for an execution stay to US Supreme Court, pending outcome of *Zant* case (see above) denied by a tied 4-4 vote when one of Justices absent. Accomplice also sentenced to death.
Van Roosevelt SOLOMON B, 34	20.02.85	79	W	Murder/ robbery	Claimed he did not fire shots. Prosecutors asserted both he and accomplice shot victim. Accomplice also sentenced to death.

Name/Race/Age at time of crime	Date of execution	Year convicted	Race of victim	Crime	Other information
John YOUNG B, 18	20.03.85	76	W	3 murders/ robbery	His psychiatric trauma from witnessing mother's murder at age of three and subsequent neglected childhood not mentioned at sentencing hearing at his trial. His court-appointed trial lawyer, who was disbarred from legal practice on conviction of a drugs offence shortly after Young's trial, later submitted affidavit to appeals court stating he had been unable to conduct an adequate defence due to his own personal problems at time. This evidence rejected by court on grounds that submitted too late. Young alleged to have been under the influence of drugs at time of crime.
Jerome BOWDEN B, 33	24.06.86	76		Murder/ robbery	Diagnosed as mentally retarded, with IQ of 65. Convicted by all-white jury after prosecutor had struck all blacks from jury. Convicted partly on testimony of co-accused (a neighbour of victim), who received life sentence.
4. INDIANA					
Steven JUDY W, 20	09.03.81	79	W	4 murders/ rape	Voluntary execution (dropped legal appeals).
William VANDIVER W, 35	16.10.85	84	W	Murder	Voluntary execution. Given five jolts of electricity over 17 minutes.

Name/Race/Age at time of crime	Date of execution	Year convicted	Race of victim	Crime	Other information
5. LOUISIANA					
Robert WILLIAMS B, 27	14.12.83	79	B	Murder/ robbery	Claimed gun went off accidentally. Convicted by all-white jury. Court-appointed attorney reportedly spent only a few hours preparing for trial.
John TAYLOR B, 26	29.02.84	81	W	Murder	Claimed court-appointed attorney did not represent him adequately. Convicted by all-white jury.
Elmo SONNIER W, 28	05.04.84	78	W	Rape/murder of teenage couple	
Timothy BALDWIN W, 38	10.09.84	78	W	Murder/ robbery of elderly woman	Reportedly offered reduced charge in exchange for guilty plea but refused, claiming innocence. Victim, who knew Baldwin well, reportedly told police before she died she did not recognize her assailant. Some discrepancies in other witness testimony and some possible alibi evidence. Co-defendant serving life sentence.
Ernest KNIGHTON B	30.10.84	81	W	Murder/ robbery	Sentenced to death by all-white jury. Co-defendant plea-bargained and given life sentence.
Robert WILLIE W, 22	28.12.84	80	W	Rape/murder	Accomplice also convicted of murder but given life sentence.
David MARTIN W, 25	04.01.84	78	W	Murder of wife's lover and 3 others	History of drug/alcohol addiction. Reportedly suffered mental/physical abuse as child and emotional trauma following birth of his brain-damaged daughter.

Name/Race/Age at time of crime	Date of execution	Year convicted	Race of victim	Crime	Other information
6. MISSISSIPPI					
Jimmy Lee GRAY W , 28	02.09.83	76	W	Rape/murder of child	
7. NEVADA					
Jesse BISHOP W	22.10.79	78	W	Murder/robbery	Voluntary execution (dropped legal appeals).
Carroll COLE W, 46	06.12.85	84	U	Multiple murder	Voluntary execution (dropped legal appeals).
8. NORTH CAROLINA					
James HUTCHINS W, 49	16.03.84	79	W	Murder of three law enforcement officers	Killings occurred while Hutchins drunk; police had been called by his daughter during a domestic argument in which he had reportedly threatened her.
Velma BARFIELD	02.11.84	78	W	Poisoning murder of fiancé	Also reported to have confessed to three similar murders, including her mother's.
9. SOUTH CAROLINA					
Joseph SHAW W, 22	11.01.85	77	W	Rape/murder of two teenagers	Co-defendant of James Roach, executed 10.01.86.
James Terry ROACH W, 17	10.01.86	77	W	Rape/murder (as above)	Minor at time of crime. Trial record acknowledged Roach acting under domination of older man, and that he was mentally retarded. Later evidence that he was suffering from hereditary degenerative disease that could have affected mental state. Another co-defendant (also a minor at time of crime) got life sentence.

10. TEXAS

Name/Race/Age at time of crime	Date of execution	Year convicted	Race of victim	Crime	Other information
Charles BROOKS B, 34	07.12.82	76	W	Kidnap/ murder	First to die by lethal injection. Ex-heroin addict. Not known which of two men shot victim. Co-defendant had death sentence reversed on technicality.
James AUTRY W, 25	14.03.84	80	W	Murder of store clerk	Unclear whether he or co-defendant carried out shooting. In November 1983 Autry was granted stay 23 minutes before execution due to be carried out and needle already in arm. At his actual execution, he was reported to be moving and complaining of pain during injection of lethal drug.
Ronald O'BRYAN W, 29	31.03.84	75	W	Poisoned son aged 8	
Thomas BAREFOOT W, 32	30.10.84	78	W	Murder of police officer	
Doyle SKILLERN W, 38	16.01.85	74	W	Accomplice in shooting of police officer	Accomplice only; killer got life. Skillern got death sentence because of prior conviction in which he served five-year sentence for killing brother.
Stephen MORIN W, 37	13.03.85	82	W	3 murders	Former heroin addict. Technicians reported to have spent 40 minutes searching for vein in which to insert needle for lethal injection.
Jesse DE LA ROSA H, 18	15.05.85	81	W	Murder/ robbery	Co-defendant pleaded guilty to robbery only and received lesser sentence. De La Rosa had no previous criminal record.

Name/Race/Age at time of crime	Date of execution	Year convicted	Race of victim	Crime	Other information
Charles MILTON B, 26	25.06.85	78	B	Murder/ robbery	Claimed gun went off accidentally while store owner struggled to grab it. Gunshot hit and killed store owner's wife.
Henry MARTINEZ PORTER, H, 33	09.07.85	79	W	Murder	
Charles RUMBAUGH W, 17	11.09.85	80	W	Murder/ robbery	Minor at time of crime and had a history of mental disorder. Dropped his final appeals. His gun went off during struggle with jewellery store owner, killing latter.
Charles BASS W, 22	12.03.86	80	W	Murder of police officer during robbery	
Jeffrey BARNEY W, 23	16.04.86	82	W	Murder/rape	Dropped his final appeals.
Jay PINKERTON W, 17	15.05.86	81/82	W	Murder/rape	Minor at time of crime. Previous stay granted minutes before execution due to take place.
Rudy ESQUIVEL H	09.06.86	1978	W	Murder of undercover narcotics agent	Won stay of execution on 6 June by federal judge who gave his lawyers 20 days to present more evidence regarding his claim that members of own race improperly excluded from jury. The state appealed and stay lifted by appeals court.
Kenneth BROCK W	19.06.86	74		Murder of store manager during robbery	Killing may have been accidental. Brock shot victim as he was fleeing from police, using victim as shield. Victim's father appealed for clemency in letter to Texas Board of Pardons and Paroles.

Name/Race/Age at time of crime	Date of execution	Year convicted	Race of victim	Crime	Other information
11. UTAH					
Gary GILMORE W	17.01.77		W	Murder	Voluntary execution.
12. VIRGINIA					
Frank COPPOLA W, 34	10.08.82	78	W	Murder/ robbery	Voluntary execution.
Linwood BRILEY B, 25	12.10.84	80	W	Murder/ robbery/rape	Co-defendant brother James.
James BRILEY B, 23	18.04.85	80	W	Murder/ robbery/rape	Co-defendant brother Linwood.
Morris MASON B, 26	25.06.85	78	W	Rape/murder/ arson	Alcoholic, reported mental age of eight; had sought help and asked to be institutionalized the day before crime.

Appendix 6

Prisoners executed under civil authority in the USA, 1930 to 1986

	All offences		*All offences*
1930	155	1959	49
1931	153	1960	56
1932	140	1961	42
1933	160	1962	47
1934	168	1963	21
1935	199	1964	15
1936	195	1965	7
1937	147	1966	1
1938	190	1967	2
1939	160	1968	—
1940	124	1969	—
1941	123	1970	—
1942	147	1971	—
1943	131	1972	—
1944	120	1973	—
1945	117	1974	—
1946	131	1975	—
1947	153	1976	—
1948	119	1977	1
1949	119	1978	—
1950	82	1979	2
1951	105	1980	—
1952	83	1981	1
1953	62	1982	2
1954	81	1983	5
1955	76	1984	21
1956	65	1985	18
1957	65	1986*	16
1958	49		

* To end of October

Source: US National Prisoners Statistics, Capital Punishment 1978, Table 1, p. 16 (for all years except 1980 to 1986).

The death sentence and executions

Prisoners executed under civil authority in the USA — by region and state, 1930 to 1980

	Total	1980	1979	1978	1977	1976	1975	1970-1974	1965-1969	1960-1964	1955-1959	1950-1954	1945-1949	1940-1944	1935-1939	1930-1934
Total	3862	—	2	—	1	—	—	—	10	181	304	413	639	645	891	776
Federal	33	—	—	—	—	—	—	—	—	1	3	6	6	7	9	1
State	3829	—	2	—	1	—	—	—	10	180	301	407	633	638	882	775
Northeast	608	—	—	—	—	—	—	—	—	17	51	56	74	110	145	155
Maine	—	—	—	—	—	—	—	—	—	—	—	—	—	—	—	—
New Hampshire	1	—	—	—	—	—	—	—	—	—	—	—	—	—	1	—
Vermont	4	—	—	—	—	—	—	—	—	—	—	2	1	—	—	1
Massachusetts	27	—	—	—	—	—	—	—	—	—	—	—	3	6	11	7
Rhode Island	—	—	—	—	—	—	—	—	—	—	—	—	—	—	—	—
Connecticut	21	—	—	—	—	—	—	—	—	1	5	—	5	5	3	2
New York	329	—	—	—	—	—	—	—	—	10	25	27	36	78	73	80
New Jersey	74	—	—	—	—	—	—	—	—	3	9	8	8	6	16	24
Pennsylvania	152	—	—	—	—	—	—	—	—	3	12	19	21	15	41	41
North Central	403	—	—	—	—	—	—	—	5	16	16	42	64	42	113	105
Ohio	172	—	—	—	—	—	—	—	—	7	12	20	36	15	39	43
Indiana	41	—	—	—	—	—	—	—	—	1	—	2	5	2	20	11
Illinois	90	—	—	—	—	—	—	—	—	2	1	8	5	13	27	34
Michigan	—	—	—	—	—	—	—	—	—	—	—	—	—	—	—	—
Wisconsin	—	—	—	—	—	—	—	—	—	—	—	—	—	—	—	—
Minnesota	—	—	—	—	—	—	—	—	—	—	—	—	—	—	—	—
Iowa	18	—	—	—	—	—	—	—	—	2	—	1	4	3	7	1
Missouri	62	—	—	—	—	—	—	—	1	3	2	5	9	6	20	16
North Dakota	—	—	—	—	—	—	—	—	—	—	—	—	—	—	—	—
South Dakota	1	—	—	—	—	—	—	—	—	—	—	—	1	—	—	—
Nebraska	4	—	—	—	—	—	—	—	—	—	—	1	2	1	—	—
Kansas	15	—	—	—	—	—	—	—	4	1	1	5	2	2	—	—

	Total	1980	1979	1978	1977	1976	1975	1974	1969	1964	1959	1954	1949	1944	1939	1934
South	2307	—	—	—	—	—	—	—	2	102	183	244	419	413	524	419
Delaware	12	—	—	—	—	—	—	—	—	1	—	—	2	1	6	2
Maryland	68	—	—	—	—	—	—	—	—	1	4	2	19	26	10	6
District of Columbia	40	—	—	—	—	—	—	—	—	—	1	3	13	3	5	15
Virginia	92	—	—	—	—	—	—	—	—	6	8	15	22	13	20	8
West Virginia	40	—	—	—	—	—	—	—	—	—	4	5	9	2	10	10
North Carolina	263	—	—	—	—	—	—	—	—	1	5	14	62	50	80	51
South Carolina	162	—	—	—	—	—	—	—	—	8	10	16	29	32	30	37
Georgia	366	—	—	—	—	—	—	—	—	14	34	51	72	58	73	64
Florida	171	—	1	—	—	—	—	—	—	12	27	22	27	38	29	15
Kentucky	103	—	—	—	—	—	—	—	—	1	8	8	15	19	34	18
Tennessee	93	—	—	—	—	—	—	—	1	—	7	1	18	19	31	16
Alabama	135	—	—	—	—	—	—	—	—	4	6	14	21	29	41	19
Mississippi	154	—	—	—	—	—	—	—	—	10	21	15	26	34	22	26
Arkansas	118	—	—	—	—	—	—	—	—	9	7	11	18	20	33	20
Louisiana	133	—	—	—	—	—	—	—	—	1	13	14	23	24	19	39
Oklahoma	60	—	—	—	—	—	—	—	1	5	3	4	7	6	9	25
Texas	297	—	—	—	—	—	—	—	—	29	25	49	36	38	72	48
West	511	—	1	—	1	—	—	—	3	45	51	65	76	73	100	96
Montana	6	—	—	—	—	—	—	—	—	—	—	—	—	1	4	1
Idaho	3	—	—	—	—	—	—	—	—	—	1	2	—	—	—	—
Wyoming	7	—	—	—	—	—	—	—	1	—	—	—	—	2	1	3
Colorado	47	—	—	—	—	—	—	—	1	5	2	1	7	6	9	16
New Mexico	8	—	—	—	—	—	—	—	—	1	1	2	3	—	—	2
Arizona	38	—	—	—	1	—	—	—	—	4	6	2	1	6	10	7
Utah	14	—	—	—	—	—	—	—	—	1	4	2	—	3	2	—
Nevada	30	—	1	—	—	—	—	—	—	2	—	9	5	5	3	5
Washington	47	—	—	—	—	—	—	—	—	2	2	4	7	9	13	10
Oregon	19	—	—	—	—	—	—	—	—	1	—	4	6	6	1	1
California	292	—	—	—	—	—	—	—	1	29	35	39	45	35	57	51
Alaska*	—	—	—	—	—	—	—	—	—	—	—	—	—	—	—	—
Hawaii*	—	—	—	—	—	—	—	—	—	—	—	—	—	—	—	—

* As states, Alaska and Hawaii are included beginning 1 January 1960.

Source: US National Prisoner Statistics, Capital Punishment 1979, p. 17, reproduced in *The Death Penalty in America*, by Hugo Adam Bedau.

Appendix 7

National and state (Florida, Georgia, Texas)
violent crime statistics

US national crime statistics 1979 to 1985

Violent crime*

Year	Number	Rate per 100,000 inhabitants	% change over previous year	
			Number	*Rate per 100,000 inhabitants*
1979	1,208,030	548.9	—	—
1980	1,344,520	596.6	+11.30	+8.7
1981	1,361,820	594.3	+1.3	−0.39
1982	1,322,390	571.1	−2.9	−3.9
1983	1,258,090	537.7	−4.9	−5.8
1984	1,273,280	539.2	+1.2	+0.3
1985	1,327,440	556.0	+4.3	+3.1

Murder and non-negligent manslaughter

Year	Number	Rate per 100,000 inhabitants	% change over previous year	
			Number	*Rate per 100,000 inhabitants*
1979	21,456	9.7	+9.7	+7.8
1980	23,044	10.2	+7.4	+5.2
1981	22,516	9.8	−2.3	−3.9
1982	21,012	9.1	−6.7	−7.1
1983	19,308	8.3	−8.1	−8.8
1984	18,692	7.9	−3.2	−4.8
1985	18,976	7.9	+1.5	—

* murder, rape, robbery, aggravated assault.

Source: FBI Uniform Crime Reports

*Florida crime statistics 1971 to 1984 inclusive
(first execution since 1964 in May 1979)*

Violent crime*

Year	Number	Rate per 100,000 inhabitants	% change over previous year Number	% change over previous year Rate per 100,000 inhabitants
1971	38,571	547.8		
1972	40,268	541.1	+4.4	−1.2
1973	46,430	591.8	+15.3	+9.4
1974	54,852	665.0	+18.1	+12.4
1975	57,663	679.6	+5.1	+2.2
1976	54,543	637.8	−5.4	−6.2
1977	57,956	664.8	+6.3	+4.2
1978	65,784	733.6	+13.5	+10.3
1979	73,866	799.0	+12.3	+8.9
1980	94,088	982.2	+27.4	+22.9
1981	98,090	971.4	+4.3	−1.1
1982	93,406	900.3	−4.8	−7.3
1983	88,298	833.7	−5.5	−7.4
1984	95,368	872.5	+8.0	+4.7

Murder

Year	Number	Rate per 100,000 inhabitants	% change over previous year Number	% change over previous year Rate per 100,000 inhabitants
1971	932	13.2		
1972	944	12.7	+1.3	−3.8
1973	1,182	15.1	+25.2	+18.9
1974	1,190	14.4	+0.7	−4.6
1975	1,132	13.3	−4.9	−7.6
1976	902	10.5	−20.3	−21.1
1977	857	9.8	−5.0	−6.7
1978	949	10.6	+10.7	+8.2
1979	1,084	11.7	+14.2	+10.4
1980	1,387	14.5	+28.0	+23.9
1981	1,523	15.1	+9.8	+4.1
1982	1,410	13.6	−7.4	−9.9
1983	1,203	11.4	−14.7	−16.2
1984	1,264	11.6	+5.1	+1.8

* murder, rape, robbery, aggravated assault.
Source: Florida Crime Indexes 1971-1984

*Georgia crime statistics 1979 to 1984 inclusive
(first execution since 1964 in December 1983)*

Violent crime*

Year	Number	Rate per 100,000 inhabitants	% change over previous year	
			Number	Rate per 100,000 inhabitants
1979	28,594	558.7	+16.5	+15.7
1980	29,803	545.4	+4.2	−2.4
1981	29,598	532.1	−0.7	−2.4
1982	29,444	520.1	−0.5	−2.3
1983	26,442	459.2	−10.2	−11.7
1984	28,168	480.9	+6.5	+4.7

Murder

Year	Number	Rate per 100,000 inhabitants	% change over previous year	
			Number	Rate per 100,000 inhabitants
1979	877	17.1	+20.0	+18.8
1980	782	14.3	−10.8	−16.4
1981	836	15.0	+6.9	+4.9
1982	744	13.1	−11.0	−12.7
1983	460	8.0	−38.2	−38.9
1984	562	9.6	+22.2	+20.0

* murder, rape, robbery, aggravated assault.

Source: Georgia Criminal Justice Data, 1983 and 1984, prepared by The Georgia Crime Information Center and The Georgia Criminal Justice Coordinating Council.

Texas crime statistics 1979 to June 1985 inclusive
(first execution since 1964 in December 1982)

Violent crime*

Year	Number	Rate per 100,000 inhabitants	% change over previous year	
			Number	Rate per 100,000 inhabitants
1979	67,799	506.5		
1980	77,866	549.5	+14.8	+8.4
1981	78,443	531.7	+0.7	−3.2
1982	88,101	576.6	+12.0	+8.4
1983	80,536	512.1	−8.5	−11.1
1984	80,732	505.0	+0.2	−1.3
Jan-June 1985	41,124		+7.7	

Murder

Year	Number	Rate per 100,000 inhabitants	% change over previous year	
			Number	Rate per 100,000 inhabitants
1979	2,226	16.6		
1980	2,389	16.9	+7.3	+1.8
1981	2,438	16.5	+2.0	−2.3
1982	2,463	16.1	+1.0	−2.4
1983	2,238	14.2	−9.1	−11.8
1984	2,091	13.1	−6.5	−7.7
Jan-June 1985	1,060		+8.7	

* murder, rape, robbery, aggravated assault.

Source: Crime in Texas, Calendar Year 1984 and January through June 1985, Uniform Crime Reporting Bureau, Crime Records Division, Texas Department of Public Safety.

Appendix 8

Summary of important Supreme Court rulings on the death penalty

Furman v. *Georgia* 408 U.S. 238 (1972)

The Court ruled by five to four that the death penalty, as it was then applied, constituted "cruel and unusual punishment" in violation of the Eighth and Fourteenth Amendments to the US Constitution. The ruling was based on what the judges found to be the death penalty's arbitrary and capricious application, arising from the unlimited discretion afforded to the sentencing authority (judge or jury) in capital trials. The ruling concerned two cases in Georgia and one in Texas, but it had the effect of invalidating most existing state and federal death penalty laws, which contained similar sentencing procedures to these statutes. Only two of the judges found that the death penalty would be "cruel and unusual punishment" in all circumstances. The others left open the question of whether the death penalty could ever be constitutionally imposed.

Gregg v. *Georgia* 428 U.S. 153 (1976) and companion cases: *Proffit* v. *Florida* 428 U.S. 242 (1976) *Jurek* v. *Texas* 428 U.S. 262 (1976)

The Court ruled by seven votes to two that the death penalty for murder was constitutional as imposed under the revised capital punishment statutes enacted in Georgia, Florida and Texas. Each of the statutes provided that judges or juries must weigh aggravating and mitigating circumstances at a separate sentencing hearing before imposing a sentence of death or life imprisonment on offenders convicted of capital crimes. The ruling thus sanctioned the reintroduction of the death penalty under a form of "guided discretion" in sentencing.

Although the procedures varied somewhat in each state, the statutes upheld in the ruling provided that the sentence of death may be imposed only in cases of murder with aggravating circumstances. The statutes also provided for the automatic review of death sentences by the state supreme courts.

Woodson v. *North Carolina* 428 U.S. 280 (1976) and companion case: *Roberts* v. *Louisiana* 248 U.S. 325 (1976)

The Court ruled by five votes to four that mandatory death sentences were unconstitutional. The North Carolina and Louisiana statutes invalidated by these decisions had each provided mandatory death sentences for convicted first-degree murderers. In *Roberts* v.

Louisiana 431 U.S. 633 (1977), the Court ruled that mandatory death sentences were unconstitutional even when imposed for a restricted category of crime (murder of a police officer acting in the course of his duty) on the grounds that the sentencing authority must still consider mitigating or aggravating circumstances in such cases.

Coker v. *Georgia* 433 U.S. 485 (1977)

The Court ruled that the death penalty was "grossly disproportionate and excessive" and therefore unconstitutional when imposed for the (non-homicide) rape of an adult woman.

Eberheart v. *Georgia* 433 U.S. 917 (1977)

Citing the *Coker* ruling in a summary opinion, the Court held that sentence of death for the non-homicidal crime of kidnapping would be "cruel and unusual".

Lockett v. *Ohio* 438 U.S. 586 (1978)

The Court ruled by seven votes to one* that the Eighth and Fourteenth Amendments required the sentencing authority to consider any circumstances presented in mitigation at the sentencing stage of a capital trial. The ruling invalidated an Ohio statute which had limited the consideration of mitigating circumstances in such cases.

Enmund v. *Florida* 458 U.S. 782 (1982)

The Court ruled by five votes to four that the Eighth Amendment prohibits the imposition of death sentences upon accomplices to felony-murder (killings which occur, even if only accidentally, during the commission of a serious contemporaneous offence) unless the accomplice actually did the killing or attempted to kill, or intended that the killing should occur or that lethal force should be employed.

Witherspoon v. *Illinois* 391 U.S. 510 (1968)

The ruling held that prospective jurors who are unequivocally opposed to the death penalty may be excluded from serving as jurors in capital trials (a practice known as "challenging for cause"). A footnote to the main opinion stated that prosecutors could exclude only those jurors who had made it "unmistakeably clear (1) that they would *automatically* vote against the imposition of capital punishment without regard to any evidence that might be developed at the trial of the case before them, or (2) that their attitude toward the death penalty would prevent them from making an impartial decision as to the defendant's *guilt*."

The decision established that states were entitled to remove jurors

---

* One judge did not participate.

who would never vote for the death penalty, but not those who merely had some qualms about its imposition.

Wainwright* v. *Witt 83 L. Ed. 841 (1985)

The Court revised the standard given in *Witherspoon* for deciding when opponents of the death penalty may be excluded from serving as jurors in capital trials. It ruled by seven votes to two that prosecutors may exclude any prospective juror whose views would "prevent or substantially impair the performance of his duties . . . in accordance with his instructions and oath" but that it was no longer necessary to show that the juror had made it "unmistakeably clear" that he would "automatically" vote against a death sentence in all circumstances. The Court also emphasized that the lower federal courts, if faced with appeals on this issue, should generally defer to the state trial judge, "who sees and hears prospective jurors and makes the final decision on whether they should be seated."

Lockhart* v. *McCree No. 84-1865 (1986)

The Court ruled by six votes to three that the Constitution did not prohibit the exclusion of committed opponents of the death penalty from serving as jurors at both the trial of guilt and innocence and the sentencing stage of capital trials.

The decision reversed a ruling by a federal appeals court, which had held that the exclusion of opponents of the death penalty from serving as jurors in capital trials violated a defendant's constitutional right to be tried by a fair cross section of the community: it had ruled that such people may be excluded only from the *sentencing* stage of a capital trial. The appeals court's decision was based in part on studies into jury attitudes, which suggested that juries from which opponents of the death penalty were systematically excluded tended to be less impartial on the question of guilt or innocence than those chosen under the normal procedures for criminal trials.

In the *Lockhart* decision, the Supreme Court expressed doubts about the value of the studies into jury attitudes. The Court stated, however, that, even assuming that these were adequate to establish that "death-qualified" juries (those from whom opponents of the death penalty are excluded) were "somewhat more 'conviction-prone' than 'non-death-qualified' juries", this would not violate a defendant's right to a fair trial.

The Court held that the constitutional requirement of a fair cross-section of the community applied only to the larger jury panel and not to the actual trial jury chosen. While the "wholesale exclusion" of groups distinguished solely by their race or sex would not be permissible, this did not apply to groups defined only by their "shared attitudes", such as toward a particular penalty.

Spaziano v. *Florida* 468 U.S. 82 L. Ed. 2d 340 (1984)

Among several issues addressed in this opinion, the Court ruled by six votes to three that the Florida statute, allowing the trial judge to impose the death penalty by overruling a jury's recommendation of life imprisonment, did not violate the Constitution. The opinion stated that "there is no constitutional imperative that a jury should have the responsibility of deciding whether the death penalty should be imposed".

Strickland v. *Washington* 466 U.S. 80 L. Ed. 674 (1984)

The Court set a new standard for reversing a conviction or sentence on grounds of "ineffective assistance of counsel". It ruled by seven votes to two that errors by trial counsel would not merit a retrial unless the defendant could prove that they had actually prejudiced the outcome of the case. The ruling reversed a lower appeals court's granting of *habeas corpus* relief to a capital trial defendant on the grounds that his trial counsel had erred in failing to seek out character witnesses or request a psychiatric examination. In upholding the death sentence imposed in this case, the Supreme Court ruled that the omitted evidence would not have changed the trial court's decision to impose the death penalty, since it would not have altered its finding that the aggravating circumstances outweighed the mitigating circumstances.

Pulley v. *Harris* 104 S. Ct. 871: 79 L. Ed. 2d 99 (1984)

The Court ruled by seven votes to two that there was no constitutional requirement for the state supreme courts to conduct a "proportionality" review of death sentences by comparing them with sentences imposed in similar capital cases. The Court said that, although most state supreme courts did conduct a comparative review of death sentences, this practice was not indispensible in safeguarding against arbitrary or inconsistent sentencing. The decision overturned a ruling by a federal appeals court in a California case, which had held that the California Supreme Court should have conducted such a review.

Barefoot v. *Estelle* 463 U.S. 880 (1983)

In a six to three decision given in a Texas case, the Court ruled that the federal appeals courts may promulgate their own rules for expediting their handling of *habeas corpus* appeals in capital cases. The ruling held that in cases where a federal district court has denied a petition for *habeas corpus* but has granted leave to appeal, the appeals courts may summarily consider the merits of the appeal at the same time as an application to stay an execution. (Before this ruling, many appeals courts had automatically issued stays of execution, pending a separate hearing on the merits of an appeal.) The Court ruled that the appeals courts must consider the merits of an appeal, even if doing so summarily, and inform the defence counsel that the merits may be decided upon the motion for a stay. The Court held also that the federal district courts should grant leave to appeal only upon a "substantial showing of a denial of a federal right".

The Court also denied the merits of Thomas Barefoot's appeal, ruling that the use of psychiatric testimony to predict "future dangerousness" (one of the factors that had led to the imposition of the death penalty in this case) was constitutionally permissible, and that such testimony "need not be based on personal examination of the defendant and may be given in response to hypothetical questions".

Ake v. *Oklahoma* No. 84 L. Ed. 53 (1985)

The Court ruled by eight votes to one that states must provide indigent criminal defendants with free psychiatric assistance in preparing an insanity defence if the defendant "demonstrates to the trial judge that his sanity at the time of the offense is to be a significant factor at trial". The ruling overturned a death sentence imposed by an Oklahoma court on a man convicted of murder whose trial lawyer had pleaded that the defendant was suffering from paranoid schizophrenia: the state had refused to provide a psychiatrist to assist him in presenting his insanity plea.

Batson v. *Kentucky* No. 84 L. Ed. 6263 (1986) (a non-capital case)

The Court ruled by seven votes to two that prosecutors may not use their peremptory challenges to exclude members of a defendant's own race from his or her trial jury solely on account of their race. The Court further held that defendants objecting to the use of such challenges could make a *prima facie* case of discrimination solely on the facts relating to their own case. The onus then fell to the state to provide a "neutral explanation" for challenging the potential jurors.

The ruling established a new evidentiary standard for defendants objecting to the striking of members of their own race from their trial juries. In the past, the courts had held that the use of peremptory challenges was racially discriminatory only if a defendant could prove that members of his or her own race were being systematically excluded by prosecutors from trial juries in a given jurisdiction.

Ford v. *Wainwright* 1986 (26 June)

The Court ruled by five votes to four that the Eighth Amendment prohibits the state from carrying out a sentence of death upon a prisoner who is insane. The ruling also held that Florida's statutory procedure for determining the mental competency of a condemned prisoner (which gave the final decision to the state governor and failed to provide the prisoner with sufficient opportunity to be heard) was inadequate. The opinion did not specify the exact methods to be used, but noted that the procedures for determining a prisoner's competence to stand trial could provide guidance.

Appendix 9

Sixth, Eighth and Fourteenth Amendments (extract) to US Constitution

ARTICLE [VI]

In all criminal prosecutions the accused shall enjoy the right to a speedy and public trial, by an impartial jury of the State and district wherein the crime shall have been committed, which district shall have been previously ascertained by law, and to be informed of the nature and cause of the accusation; to be confronted with the witnesses against him; to have compulsory process for obtaining witnesses in his favor, and to have the assistance of counsel for his defence.

ARTICLE [VIII]

Excessive bail shall not be required, nor excessive fines imposed, nor cruel and unusual punishments inflicted.

ARTICLE [XIV] (extract)

Section I. . . . No State shall make or enforce any law which shall abridge the privileges or immunities of citizens of the United States; nor shall any State deprive any person of life, liberty, or property, without due process of law; nor deny to any person within its jurisdiction the equal protection of the laws.

Appendix 10

International standards relevant to the death penalty

Articles of the International Covenant on Civil and Political Rights (signed by the US Government on 5 October 1977).

Article 6

1. Every human being has the inherent right to life. This right shall be protected by law. No one shall be arbitrarily deprived of his life.

2. In countries which have not abolished the death penalty, sentence of death may be imposed only for the most serious crimes in accordance with the law in force at the time of the commission of the crime and not contrary to the provisions of the present Covenant and to the Convention on the Prevention and Punishment of the Crime of Genocide. This penalty can only be carried out pursuant to a final judgement rendered by a competent court.

3. When deprivation of life constitutes the crime of genocide, it is understood that nothing in this article shall authorize any State Party to the present Covenant to derogate in any way from any obligation assumed under the provisions of the Convention on the Prevention and Punishment of the Crime of Genocide.

4. Anyone sentenced to death shall have the right to seek pardon or commutation of the sentence. Amnesty, pardon or commutation of the sentence of death may be granted in all cases.

5. Sentence of death shall not be imposed for crimes committed by persons below eighteen years of age and shall not be carried out on pregnant women.

6. Nothing in this article shall be invoked to delay or to prevent the abolition of capital punishment by any State Party to the present Covenant.

General comment on Article 6 of the International Covenant on Civil and Political Rights, adopted at its 378th meeting (16th session); on 27 July 1982 by the Human Rights Committee set up under the International Covenant on Civil and Political Rights

1. The right to life enunciated in article 6 of the Covenant has been dealt with in all State reports. It is the supreme right from which no derogation is permitted even in time of public emergency which threatens the life of the nation (article 4). However, the Committee has noted that quite often the information given concerning article 6

was limited to only one or other aspect of this right. It is a right which should not be interpreted narrowly.

*Articles of the American Convention on Human Rights
(signed by the US Government on 1 June 1977)*

Article 4. Right to Life

1. Every person has the right to have his life respected. This right shall be protected by law, and, in general, from the moment of conception. No one shall be arbitrarily deprived of his life.

2. In countries that have not abolished the death penalty, this may be imposed only for the most serious crimes and pursuant to a final judgment rendered by a competent court and in accordance with a law establishing such punishment, enacted prior to the commission of the crime. Its application shall not be extended to crimes to which it does not presently apply.

3. The death penalty shall not be re-established in states that have abolished it.

4. In no case shall capital punishment be inflicted for political offences or related common crimes.

5. Capital punishment shall not be imposed upon persons who, at the time the crime was committed, were under 18 years of age or over 70 years of age; nor shall it be applied to pregnant women.

6. Every person condemned to death shall have the right to apply for amnesty, pardon, or commutation of sentence, which may be granted in all cases. Capital punishment shall not be imposed while such petition is pending a decision by the competent authority.

Resolution 1984/50 on safeguards guaranteeing protection of the rights of those facing the death penalty, adopted by the United Nations Economic and Social Council at its 1984 spring session on 25 May 1984

1. In countries which have not abolished the death penalty, capital punishment may be imposed only for the most serious crimes, it being understood that their scope should not go beyond intentional crimes, with lethal or other extremely grave consequences.

2. Capital punishment may be imposed only for a crime for which the death penalty is prescribed by law at the time of its commission, it being understood that if, subsequent to the commission of the crime, provision is made by law for the imposition of a lighter penalty, the offender shall benefit thereby.

3. Persons below 18 years of age at the time of the commission of the crime shall not be sentenced to death, nor shall the death sentence be carried out on pregnant women, or on new mothers or on persons who have become insane.

4. Capital punishment may be imposed only when the guilt of the person charged is based upon clear and convincing evidence leaving no room for an alternative explanation of the facts.

5. Capital punishment may only be carried out pursuant to a final judgement rendered by a competent court after legal process which gives all possible safeguards to ensure a fair trial, at least equal to those contained in article 14 of the International Covenant on Civil and Political Rights, including the right of anyone suspected of or charged with a crime for which capital punishment may be imposed to adequate legal assistance at all stages of the proceedings.

6. Anyone sentenced to death shall have the right to appeal to a court of higher jurisdiction, and steps should be taken to ensure that such appeals shall become mandatory.

7. Anyone sentenced to death shall have the right to seek pardon, or commutation of sentence; pardon or commutation of sentence may be granted in all cases of capital punishment.

8. Capital punishment shall not be carried out pending any appeal or other recourse procedure or other proceeding relating to pardon or commutation of the sentence.

9. Where capital punishment occurs, it shall be carried out so as to inflict the minimum possible suffering.

Resolution on safeguards guaranteeing the rights of those facing the death penalty, adopted by the Seventh United Nations Congress on the Prevention of Crime and the Treatment of Offenders (Milan, 26 August-6 September 1985) (extract)

"*The Seventh United Nations Congress on the Prevention of Crime and the Treatment of Offenders . . .*

1. *Endorses* the safeguards approved by the Economic and Social Council in its resolution 1984/50;

2. *Invites* all States retaining the death penalty and whose present standards fall short of the safeguards to adopt the safeguards and to take the necessary steps to implement them by:

(a) Incorporating or making provision for the safeguards in national legislation and regulations;

(b) Ensuring that judges, lawyers, police officers, prison officials and other persons, including military personnel who may be concerned with the administration of criminal justice, are familiar with the safeguards, and any corresponding provisions in national legislation and regulations, by including them in courses of instruction, by disseminating and publicizing them and by other appropriate means;

(c) Drawing the attention of persons facing the death penalty, and their representatives, to the safeguards and to any corresponding provisions in national legislation and regulations, and disseminating to the public those safeguards by all appropriate means . . ."

Resolution 1986/10 on implementation of the conclusions and recommendations of the Seventh United Nations Congress on the Prevention of Crime and the Treatment of Offenders, adopted by the United Nations Economic and Social Council at its 1986 spring session on 21 May 1986 (extract)

"*The Economic and Social Council,* . . .

X. Safeguards guaranteeing protection of the rights of those facing the death penalty

1. *Urges* Member States that have not abolished the death penalty to adopt the safeguards guaranteeing protection of the rights of those facing the death penalty approved by the Economic and Social Council in its resolution 1984/50 of 25 May 1984 and the measures for the implementation of the safeguards approved by the Seventh United Nations Congress on the Prevention of Crime and the Treatment of Offenders . . ."

United Nations General Assembly resolution 32/61 of 8 December 1977 on capital punishment

"The General Assembly, . . .

i. Reaffirms that, as established by the General Assembly in resolution 2857 (XXVI) and by the Economic and Social Council in resolutions 1574 (L), 1745 (LIV) and 1930 (LVIII), the main objective to be pursued in the field of capital punishment is that of progressively restricting the number of offences for which the death penalty may be imposed with a view to the desirability of abolishing this punishment."

World Medical Association resolution and news release

Resolution on physician participation in capital punishment (WMA, 1981)

Following concern about the introduction of an execution method (lethal injection) which threatened to involve doctors directly in the process of execution, the WMA Secretary-General issued a press statement opposing any involvement of doctors in capital punishment. The 34th Assembly of the WMA, meeting in Lisbon some weeks after the issuing of the press statement, endorsed the Secretary-General's statement in the following terms:

Resolution on physician participation in capital punishment

RESOLVED, that the Assembly of the World Medical Association endorses the action of the Secretary General in issuing the attached press release on behalf of the World Medical Association condemning physician participation in capital punishment.

FURTHER RESOLVED, that it is unethical for physicians to participate in capital punishment, although this does not preclude physicians certifying death.

FURTHER RESOLVED, that the Medical Ethics Committee keep this matter under active consideration.

Secretary General's press release

The first capital punishment by intravenous injection of lethal dose of drugs was decided to be carried out next week by the court of the State of Oklahoma, USA.

Regardless of the method of capital punishment a State imposes, no physician should be required to be an active participant. Physicians are dedicated to preserving life.

Acting as an executioner is not the practice of medicine and physician services are not required to carry out capital punishment even if the methodology utilizes pharmacological agents or equipment that might otherwise be used in the practice of medicine.

A physician's only role would be to certify death once the State had carried out the capital punishment.

September 11, 1981

Principles of Medical Ethics Relevant to the Role of Health Personnel, Particularly Physicians, in the Protection of Prisoners and Detainees against Torture and Other Cruel, Inhuman or Degrading Treatment or Punishment

Adopted by the General Assembly of the United Nations on 18 December 1982 (resolution 37/194)

Principle 1

Health personnel, particularly physicians, charged with the medical care of prisoners and detainees have a duty to provide them with protection of their physical and mental health and treatment of disease of the same quality and standard as is afforded to those who are not imprisoned or detained.

Principle 2

It is a gross contravention of medical ethics, as well as an offence under applicable international instruments, for health personnel, particularly physicians, to engage, actively or passively, in acts which constitute participation in, complicity in, incitement to or attempts to commit torture or other cruel, inhuman or degrading treatment or punishment.

Principle 3

It is a contravention of medical ethics for health personnel, particularly physicians, to be involved in any professional relationship with prisoners or detainees the purpose of which is not solely to evaluate, protect or improve their physical and mental health.

Appendix 11

Amnesty International Declaration on the Participation of Doctors in the Death Penalty

Amnesty International,

RECALLING

that the spirit of the Hippocratic Oath enjoins doctors to practise for the good of their patients and never to do harm,

CONSIDERING

that the Declaration of Tokyo of the World Medical Association provides that "the utmost respect for human life is to be maintained even under threat, and no use made of any medical knowledge contrary to the laws of humanity",

FURTHER CONSIDERING THAT

the same declaration forbids the participation of doctors in torture or other cruel, inhuman or degrading procedures,

NOTING

that the United Nations Secretariat has stated that the death penalty violates the right to life and that it constitutes cruel, inhuman or degrading punishment,

MINDFUL

that doctors can be called on to participate in executions by, *inter alia*,

— determining mental and physical fitness for execution,

— giving technical advice,

— prescribing, preparing, administering and supervising doses of poison in jurisdictions where this method is used,

— making medical examinations during executions, so that an execution can continue if the prisoner is not yet dead,

DECLARES

that the participation of doctors in executions is a violation of medical ethics;

CALLS UPON

medical doctors not to participate in executions;

FURTHER CALLS UPON

medical organizations to protect doctors who refuse to participate in executions, and to adopt resolutions to these ends.

This declaration was formulated by the Medical Advisory Board of Amnesty International and was adopted by Amnesty International's International Executive Committee on 12 March 1981.

228

Appendix 12

Abolitionist and retentionist countries (as of May 1986)

Abolitionist by law for all crimes
(Countries whose laws do not provide for the death penalty for any crime)

Australia	Kiribati
Austria	Luxembourg
Bolivia	Netherlands
Cape Verde	Nicaragua
Colombia	Norway
Costa Rica	Panama
Denmark	Portugal
Dominican Republic	Solomon Islands
Ecuador	Sweden
Finland	Tuvalu
Federal Republic of Germany	Uruguay
France	Vanuatu
Holy See	Venezuela
Honduras	Total: 28 countries
Iceland	

Abolitionist by law for ordinary crimes only
(Countries whose laws provide for the death penalty only for exceptional crimes such as crimes under military law or crimes committed in exceptional circumstances such as wartime)

Argentina	Monaco
Brazil	New Zealand
Canada	Papua New Guinea
Cyprus	Peru
El Salvador	San Marino
Fiji	Spain
Israel	Switzerland
Italy	United Kingdom
Malta	Total: 18 countries
Mexico	

Retentionist

(Countries and territories whose laws provide for the death penalty for ordinary crimes. However, some of these countries have not in practice carried out executions in recent years.)

Afghanistan
Albania
Algeria
Angola
Anguilla
Antigua and Barbuda
Bahamas
Bahrain
Bangladesh
Barbados
Belgium
Belize
Benin
Bermuda
Bhutan
Botswana
British Virgin Islands
Brunei Darussalam
Bulgaria
Burkina Faso
Burma
Burundi
Cameroon
Cayman Islands
Central African Republic
Chad
Chile
China (People's Republic)
Comoros
Congo
Cuba
Czechoslovakia
Djibouti
Dominica
Egypt
Equatorial Guinea
Ethiopia
Gabon
Gambia

Lesotho
Liberia
Libya
Liechtenstein
Madagascar
Malawi
Malaysia
Maldives
Mali
Mauritania
Mauritius
Mongolia
Monserrat
Morocco
Mozambique
Namibia
Nepal
Niger
Nigeria
Oman
Pakistan
Paraguay
Philippines
Poland
Qatar
Romania
Rwanda
Saint Christopher and Nevis
Saint Lucia
Saint Vincent and The Grenadines
Samoa
Sao Tome and Principe
Saudi Arabia
Senegal
Seychelles
Sierra Leone
Singapore
Somalia
South Africa

German Democratic Republic
Ghana
Greece
Grenada
Guatemala
Guinea
Guinea-Bissau
Guyana
Haiti
Hong Kong
Hungary
India
Indonesia
Iran
Iraq
Ireland
Ivory Coast
Jamaica
Japan
Jordan
Kampuchea
Kenya
Korea (Democratic People's
  Republic) [North Korea]
Korea (Republic) [South Korea]
Kuwait
Laos
Lebanon

Sri Lanka
Sudan
Suriname
Swaziland
Syria
Taiwan (Republic of China)
Tanzania
Thailand
Togo
Tonga
Trinidad and Tobago
Tunisia
Turkey
Turks and Caicos Islands
Uganda
Union of Soviet Socialist
  Republics
United Arab Emirates
Viet Nam
Yemen (Arab Republic) [North
  Yemen]
Yemen (People's Democratic
  Republic) [South Yemen]
Yugoslavia
Zaire
Zambia
Zimbabwe
Total: 129 countries and territories

Countries which have abolished the death penalty since 1975

In recent years, at least one country a year has abolished the death penalty in law or, having done so for ordinary offences, has gone on to abolish it for all offences.

1975: Mexico abolished the death penalty for ordinary offences.
1976: Canada abolished the death penalty for ordinary offences.
1977: Portugal abolished the death penalty for all offences.
1978: Spain abolished the death penalty for ordinary offences.
1979: Luxembourg, Nicaragua and Norway abolished the death penalty for all offences.

Brazil[1] and Fiji abolished the death penalty for ordinary offences.

1980: Peru abolished the death penalty for ordinary offences.

1981: France abolished the death penalty for all offences.

1982: The Netherlands abolished the death penalty for all offences.

1983: Cyprus and El Salvador abolished the death penalty for ordinary offences.

1984: Argentina[2] and Australia abolished the death penalty for ordinary offences.

1985: Australia abolished the death penalty for all offences.

Moves to reintroduce the death penalty have been defeated in a number of countries in recent years.

---

1. Brazil had abolished the death penalty in 1882 but reintroduced it in 1969 while under military rule.

2. Argentina had abolished the death penalty for all offences in 1921 and again in 1972 but reintroduced it in 1976 following a military coup.

Appendix 13

*Execution of James Terry Roach (extract from an affidavit by David I.
Bruck, a lawyer who helped with his defence)*

I assisted with Terry Roach's defense during the last month before his
execution, and I spent the last four hours with Terry Roach in his cell
when he was electrocuted on January 10, 1986.

Although I have known Terry slightly for several years, meeting
him in the course of visits to see other inmates on South Carolina's
death row, my first long conversation with Terry occurred less than a
month before his death. An execution date had already been set, and
he seemed frightened and very nervous. I was struck at that time by
how obviously mentally retarded Terry was. . . I had known from
following his case through the courts that he had been diagnosed as
mildly mentally retarded, but I was still surprised at his slack-jawed
and slow way of speaking, and at the evident lack of understanding of
much of what we were telling him about the efforts that were
underway to persuade Governor Riley to grant clemency.

The next time that I would see Terry Roach was on the night of his
execution. The lawyers who had worked on his case for the past eight
years were at the Supreme Court in Washington, so I had decided to
look in on with Terry that night after his family had had to leave for
the last time, to see if I could help him with anything or just keep him
company. When I arrived, he had decided to ask me to stay with him
through the night and to accompany him when he was taken to the
chair. So along with Marie Deans, a paralegal and counselor who
works with condemned prisoners in Virginia, I stayed.

Although Terry was twenty-five years old by the time of his death,
he seemed very childlike. In general, his demeanor and his reactions
to the people around him appeared to me to comport with the
finding, made at his last psychological evaluation, that his IQ was 70
— a score which placed his intellectual functioning at about the level
of a twelve-year-old child. When his family minister showed him
some prayers from the Bible that they would read together, Terry
asked him which ones he thought would be especially likely to help
him into heaven: his questions about this seemed based on the
childish assumption that one prayer was likely to "work" better than
another, and that he just needed some advice about which ones
would work best. Later in the night, he asked me to read him a long
letter about reincarnation that a man from California had sent him
just that day: he listened to the letter with wonder, like a small child
at bedtime, trusting and uncritical. Both Marie and I were struck by

how calmed Terry seemed by the sound of a voice reading to him in the resonant cell, and we spent much of the remaining time reading to him while he listened, gazing at the reader with rapt attention.

He had a final statement which his girlfriend had helped him write. When I arrived that night, the statement was on three small scraps of paper, in his girlfriend's handwriting. I copied it out for him, and I got him to read it out loud a few times. No matter how many times he tried, the word "enemies" came out "emenies". He kept practicing it, but pronouncing the written word just seemed beyond his capabilities. Still, he seemed to like the rehearsal: like everything we did that night, it filled up the time and acknowledged that he was doing something very difficult.

Terry was a very passive young man, and that showed all through the night. Although he was obviously frightened, he was as cooperative as possible with the guards, and he tried to pretend that all of the ritual preparation — the shaving of his head and right leg, the prolonged rubbing in of electrical conducting gel — was all a normal sort of thing to have happen. He wanted the approval of those around him, and he seemed well aware that this night he could gain everyone's approval by being brave and by keeping his fear at bay.

Still, when the warden appeared in the cell door at 5.00 a.m. and read the death warrant, while Terry stood, each wrist immobilized in a manacle known as a "claw", his left leg began to shake in large, involuntary movements. After that, everything happened quickly. I walked to the chair with him, and talked to him as much as I could. He wanted me to read his statement for him, but I told him that he ought to try and I'd read it if he couldn't. His voice was only a little shaky, and he managed quite well, except for "emenies". After he had read the statement we had a couple of last words: he repeated the name of a friend of mine who had recently died, and whom he had offered to look up for me when he got to heaven. I left him and walked to the witness area, where I gave him a "thumbs-up" sign. He signalled back with his fingers, as much as the straps permitted. We signalled to each other once more just before the mask was pulled down over his face.

A few seconds later the current hit. Terry's body snapped back and held frozen for the whole time that the current ran through his body. After a few seconds, steam began to rise from his body, and the skin on his thigh just above the electrode began to distend and blister. His fists were clenched and very white. His body slumped when the current was turned off, and jerked erect again when it was resumed. When he was declared dead, several guards wrestled his body out of the chair and onto a stretcher, while taking care to conceal his face (no longer covered by the mask) from the view of the witnesses and me by covering it with a sheet. I left the death house at about this time in the company of the warden. As we stepped out of the building, I heard the whoops of a crowd of about 150 or 200 demonstrators who had apparently come to celebrate the execution, and were yelling and cheering outside the prison gates.

Appendix 14

'Execution guidelines during active death warrant'
(As issued to prison personnel by the Superintendent of Florida State Prison) (extract)
Effective May 1, 1979 Revised November 1, 1983

1. Execution Guidelines for Week of Active Death Warrant

Execution day — minus five (5)
1. Execution squad identified
2. Media & official witnesses escort identified
3. Support personnel for entrance and other check points identified
4. Medical support staff for execution identified
5. Electrician tests all execution equipment to include emergency generator and telephone.
6. Superintendent briefs all CO 111 and above regarding execution activities.

Execution day — minus four (4)
1. Security Coordinator notified
2. Assign Death Watch Supv. & Cell Front Monitor
3. Inmate personally re-inventory all property and seal property for storage.
4. Institution Chaplain notified to visit daily
5. All visiting changed to non-contact
6. Telephone check of outside line by ASO
7. Establish communications with DOC Attorney for consultation as required.
8. Establish notification list and contact staff in event of significant legal change (G. Georgieff)
9. Schedule meeting for crowd strategy pursuant to FSP 10P no. 65 by Security Coordinator
10. Designated electrician tests all execution equipment to include emergency generator
11. Measure inmate(s) for clothing
12. Inmate specifies in writing funeral arrangements
13. Specifies recipient of personal property in writing
14. Execution squad drill

Execution day — minus three (3)
No activities — Monitor

Execution day — minus two (2)

1. Execution squad drill
2. Asst. Supt. Operations tests telephone
3. Electrician tests equipment

Execution day — minus one (1)

1. Execution squad drill
2. Asst. Supt. Operations tests telephone
3. Electrician tests equipment to include emergency generator
4. Waiting area for execution set up by Asst. Supt. Operations
5. Electrician makes up ammonium chloride solution and soaks sponges
6. Condemned inmate orders last meal
7. Chief Medical Officer prepares certificate of death = cause "legal execution by electrocution"
8. Official witness list finalized by Central Office (12 + 4 alt)
9. Executioner contacted and liaison set up for execution day
10. Asst. Supt. Programs confirms funeral arrangements with family
11. Information office arrives to handle media inquiry
12. Security Meeting held
13. External Death Watch Observer identified
14. Designated media pool observer identified by Information Office (twelve)

Execution day

4.30 am: The Food Service Director will personally prepare and serve the last meal. Eating utensils allowed will be a plate and spoon.

5.00 am: The Administrative Assistant or designate will pick up executioner, proceed to the institution, enter through Sally Port and leave the executioner in the Waiting Room of the Death Chamber at 5:00 am. A security staff member will be posted in the chamber area.

6.00 am: A. Beginning at 5:30 am, the only staff authorized on Q-1-E are:
   1. Observer, designated by the Secretary
   2. Superintendent
   3. Assistant Superintendent for Operations
   4. Chief Correctional Officer IV
   5. Death Watch Supervisor
   6. Second Shift Lieutenant
   7. Chaplain

8. Grille Gate Monitor
9. Cell Front Monitor
Any exception to the above designated staff must be approved by the Superintendent.
B. The Assistant Superintendent for Operations will supervise the shaving of the condemned inmate's head and right leg.
C. Official witnesses will report to Florida State Prison's Main Gate no later than 5.30 am, be greeted by two designated Department of Corrections escort staff, security cleared and moved to the staff dining room where they will remain until later escorted to the witness room of the execution chamber.

5.50 am: Authorized Media Witnesses will be picked up at the media onlooker area by two designated Department of Corrections staff escorts. They will be transported to the Main Entrance of Florida State Prison, as a group, be security cleared and then escorted to the Classification Department where they will remain until later escorted to the witness room of the execution chamber.

6.00 am: A. The Assistant Superintendent for Operations will supervise the showering of the condemned inmate. Immediately thereafter he will be returned to his cell and given a pair of shorts, a pair of trousers, a dress shirt, and socks. The Correctional Officer Chief IV will be responsible for the delivery of the clothes.
B. Switchboard operator will be instructed by Superintendent to wire all calls to Execution Chamber from Governor's Office through switchboard.
C. The Administrative Assistant, or designate, three designated electricians, a physician, and a physician's assist. will report to the execution chamber for preparation. The Administrative Assistant or designate will check the phones in the chamber. The electrician will ready the equipment and the Physician and Medical Technician or Physician's Assistant will stand by.

6.30 am: The Administrative Assistant or designate will establish phone communication with those officials designated by the Superintendent.

6.50 am: A. The Asst. Superintendent for Operations will supervise the application of conducting gel to the right calf and crown of the condemned inmate's head.
B. The Superintendent will read the Death Warrant to the condemned inmate.

C. Official witnesses will be secured in the witness room by two designated Dept. of Corrections staff no later than 6.50 am.

D. Authorized media witnesses will be secured in the witness room by two designated Dept. of Corrections staff no later than 6.50 am.

E. Beginning at 6.55 am, the only persons authorized in the witness room are:

12 official witnesses
4 alternate witnesses
1 physician
1 medical technician
12 authorized media representatives
4 designated Dept. of Corrections staff escorts

Any exception to the above designated persons must be approved by the Superintendent.

6.56 am: A. Beginning at 6:56 am, the only staff authorized in the execution chamber are:

Observer, designated by the Secretary
Superintendent
Asst. Superintendent for Operations
Correctional Officer Chief IV
Administrative Assistant or Supt. Designate
Chaplain (Optional)
Two (2) Electricians
One (1) executioner
One (1) physician
One (1) Physician's Assistant

Any exception to the above designated staff must be approved by the Superintendent.

B. The Superintendent, Asst. Superintendent for Operations, and Correctional Officer Chief IV, will escort the condemned inmate to the execution chamber. The Adm. Asst. or designate will record the time the inmate entered the chamber.

C. The Asst. Superintendent for Operations and Correctional Officer Chief IV will place the condemned inmate in the chair.

D. The Superintendent and Asst. Superintendent for Operations will secure back and arm straps and then forearm straps.

E. When the inmate is secured, the Asst. Superintendent for Operations and Correctional Officer Chief IV will remove the restraint apparatus and then secure lap, chest, and ankle straps. The anklet will then be laced and the electrode attached.

7.00 am: A. The Superintendent will permit the condemned inmate to make a last statement. The Supt. will then proceed to the outside open telephone line to inquire of possible stays.
B. The electrician will place the sponges on the condemned inmate's head, secure the head set and attach electrode.
C. The Assistant Superintendent for Operations engages the circuit breaker.
D. The electrician in the booth will activate the Executioner Control Panel.
E. The Superintendent will give the signal to the Executioner to turn the switch and the automatic cycle will begin. The Adm. Asst. or designate will record the time the switch is thrown.
F. Once the cycle runs its course the electrician indicates the current is off. The Adm. Asst. or designate will record the time the current is disengaged.
G. The Assistant Superintendent for Operations then disengages the manual circuit behind the chair.
H. The Superintendent invites the Doctor to conduct the examination.
I. The man is pronounced dead. The Adm. Asst. or designate records the time death is pronounced.
J. The Administrative Assistant or designate announces that the sentence has been carried out, and invites witnesses and media to exit.
"The sentence of ------- has been carried out. Please exit to the rear at this time."
K. The official witnesses and media pool will then be escorted from the witness room by the designated Department of Correction's staff escorts.

7.20 am   A. O/S Lieutenant notified by ASP to bring in ambulance
to   attendants.
7:30am   B. The inmate will be removed from the chair by ambulance attendants under the supervision of the Assistant Superintendent for Programs.
C. The ambulance will be cleared through Sally Port by escorting officer.
D. Admin. Asst. or designate will return the executioner and compensate him.

POST EXECUTION

    A. The physician must sign the Death Certificate

    B. The Superintendent will return the Death Warrant to the Governor indicating execution has been carried out.

    C. Superintendent will file a copy with the Circuit Court of Conviction.

    D. Classification Supervisor will advise Central Office Records by teletype.

Amnesty International — a worldwide campaign

In recent years, people throughout the world have become more and more aware of the urgent need to protect human rights effectively in every part of the world.

● Countless men and women are in prison for their beliefs. They are being held as prisoners of conscience in scores of countries—in crowded jails, in labour camps and in remote prisons.

● Thousands of political prisoners are being held under administrative detention orders and denied any possibility of a trial or an appeal.

● Others are forcibly confined in psychiatric hospitals or secret detention camps.

● Many are forced to endure relentless, systematic torture.

● More than a hundred countries retain the death penalty.

● Political leaders and ordinary citizens are becoming the victims of abductions, "disappearances" and killings, carried out both by government forces and opposition groups.

An international effort

To end secret arrests, torture and killing requires organized and worldwide effort. Amnesty International is part of that effort.

Launched as an independent organization over 20 years ago, Amnesty International is open to anyone prepared to work universally for the release of prisoners of conscience, for fair trials for political prisoners and for an end to torture and executions.

The movement now has members and supporters in more than 160 countries. It is independent of any government, political group, ideology, economic interest or religious creed.

It began with a newspaper article, "The Forgotten Prisoners", published on 28 May 1961 in *The Observer* (London) and reported in *Le Monde* (Paris).

Announcing an impartial campaign to help victims of political persecution, the British lawyer Peter Benenson wrote:

242

Open your newspaper any day of the week and you will
find a report from somewhere in the world of someone
being imprisoned, tortured or executed because his opinions
or religion are unacceptable to his government. . . . The
newspaper reader feels a sickening sense of impotence. Yet
if these feelings of disgust all over the world could be
united into common action, something effective could be
done.

Within a week he had received more than a thousand offers of
support—to collect information, publicize it and approach governments. The groundwork was laid for a permanent human rights
organization that eventually became known as Amnesty International. The first chairperson of its International Executive Committee (from 1963 to 1974) was Sean MacBride, who received the
Nobel Peace Prize in 1974 and the Lenin Prize in 1975.

The mandate

Amnesty International is playing a specific role in the international
protection of human rights.

It seeks the *release* of men and women detained anywhere
because of their beliefs, colour, sex, ethnic origin, language
or religious creed, provided they have not used or advocated
violence. These are termed *prisoners of conscience.*

It works for *fair and prompt trials* for *all political prisoners*
and works on behalf of such people detained without charge
or trial.

It opposes the *death penalty* and *torture* or other cruel,
inhuman or degrading treatment or punishment of *all prisoners*
without reservation.

Amnesty International acts on the basis of the Universal Declaration of Human Rights and other international convenants. Amnesty
International is convinced of the indivisibility and mutual depend-
ence of all human rights. Through the practical work for prisoners
within its mandate, Amnesty International participates in the wider
promotion and protection of human rights in the civil, political,
economic, social and cultural spheres.

Amnesty International does not oppose or support any government or political system. Its members around the world include
supporters of differing systems who agree on the defence of all
people in all countries against imprisonment for their beliefs, and
against torture and execution.

Amnesty International at work

The working methods of Amnesty International are based on the principle of international responsibility for the protection of human rights. The movement tries to take action wherever and whenever there are violations of those human rights falling within its mandate. Since it was founded, Amnesty International groups have intervened on behalf of more than 25,000 prisoners in over a hundred countries with widely differing ideologies.

A unique aspect of the work of Amnesty International groups—placing the emphasis on the need for *international* human rights work—is the fact that each group works on behalf of prisoners held in countries other than its own. At least two prisoner cases are assigned to each group; the cases are balanced geographically and politically to ensure impartiality.

There are now 3,341 local Amnesty International groups throughout the world. There are sections in 43 countries (in Africa, Asia, the Americas, Europe and the Middle East) and individual members, subscribers and supporters in more than 120 other countries. Members do not work on cases in their own countries. No section, group or member is expected to provide information on their own country and no section, group or member has any responsibility for action taken or statements issued by the international organization concerning their own country.

Continuous research

The movement attaches the highest importance to balanced and accurate reporting of facts. All its activities depend on meticulous research into allegations of human rights violations. The International Secretariat in London (with a staff of 175, comprising 30 nationalities) has a Research Department which collects and analyses information from a wide variety of sources. These include hundreds of newspapers and journals, government bulletins, transcriptions of radio broadcasts, reports from lawyers and humanitarian organizations, as well as letters from prisoners and their families. Amnesty International also sends fact-finding missions for on-the-spot investigations and to observe trials, meet prisoners and interview government officials. Amnesty International takes full responsibility for its published reports and if proved wrong on any point is prepared to issue a correction.

Once the relevant facts are established, information is sent to sections and groups for action. The members then start the work of trying to protect the individuals whose human rights are reported to have been violated. They send letters to government ministers and

244

embassies. They organize public meetings, arrange special publicity events, such as vigils at appropriate government offices or embassies, and try to interest newspapers in the cases they have taken up. They ask their friends and colleagues to help in the effort. They collect signatures for international petitions and raise money to send relief, such as medicine, food and clothing, to the prisoners and their families.

A permanent campaign

In addition to case work on behalf of individual prisoners, Amnesty International members campaign for the abolition of torture and the death penalty. This includes trying to prevent torture and executions when people have been taken to known torture centres or sentenced to death. Volunteers in dozens of countries can be alerted in such cases, and within hours hundreds of telegrams and other appeals can be on their way to the government, prison or detention centre.

Symbol of
Amnesty International

Amnesty International condemns as a matter of principle the torture and execution of prisoners by *anyone*, including opposition groups. Governments have the responsibility of dealing with such abuses, acting in conformity with international standards for the protection of human rights.

In its efforts to mobilize world public opinion, Amnesty International neither supports nor opposes economic or cultural boycotts. It *does* take a stand against the international transfer of military, police or security equipment and expertise likely to be used by recipient governments to detain prisoners of conscience and to inflict torture and carry out executions.

Amnesty International does not grade governments or countries according to their record on human rights. Not only does repression in various countries prevent the free flow of information about human rights abuses, but the techniques of repression and their impact vary widely. Instead of attempting comparisons, Amnesty International concentrates on trying to end the specific violations of human rights in each case.

Policy and funds

Amnesty International is a democratically run movement. Every two years major policy decisions are taken by an International Council comprising representatives from all the sections. They elect an International Executive Committee to carry out their decisions and supervise the day-to-day running of the International Secretariat.

The organization is financed by its members throughout the world, by individual subscriptions and donations. Members pay fees and conduct fund-raising campaigns—they organize concerts and art auctions and are often to be seen on fund-raising drives at street corners in their neighbourhoods.

Its rules about accepting donations are strict and ensure that any funds received by any part of the organization do not compromise it in any way, affect its integrity, make it dependent on any donor, or limit its freedom of activity.

The organization's accounts are audited annually and are published with its annual report.

Amnesty International has formal relations with the United Nations (ECOSOC), UNESCO, the Council of Europe, the Organization of African Unity and the Organization of American States.